REG

Regulation

Written By:

Roger Philipp, CPA, CGMA

UWorld
9111 Cypress Waters Blvd
Suite 300
Dallas, TX 75019
accounting.uworld.com/cpa-review

Permissions

The following items are utilized in this program, and are copyright property of the American Institute of Certified Public Accountants, Inc. (AICPA), all rights reserved:

- Uniform CPA Examination and Questions and Unofficial Answers, Copyright © 1991 – 2021
- Audit and Accounting Guides, Auditing Procedure Studies, Risk Alerts, Statements of Position, and Code of Professional Conduct
- Statements on Auditing Standards
- Statements on Standards for Accounting and Review Services
- Statements on Quality Control Standards
- Statements on Standards for Attestation Engagements
- Accounting Research Bulletins, APB Opinions
- Uniform CPA Examination Blueprints
- Independence Standards Board (ISB) Standards

Portions of various FASB and GASB documents, copyright property of the Financial Accounting Foundation, 401 Merritt 7, PO Box 5116, Norwalk, CT 06856-5116, are utilized with permission. Complete copies of these documents are available from the Financial Accounting Foundation. These selections include the following:

Financial Accounting Standards Board (FASB)

- The FASB Accounting Standards Codification™
- Statements of Financial Accounting Concepts
- FASB Statements, Interpretations, and Technical Bulletins

Governmental Accounting Standards Board (GASB)

- GASB Codification of Governmental Accounting and Financial Reporting Standards and GASB Statements
- GASB Concepts Statements
- GASB Interpretations and Technical Bulletins

© 2023 UWorld, LLC. All rights reserved.

Reproduction or translation of any part of this work beyond that permitted by sections 107 and 108 of the United States Copyright Act without the permission of the copyright owner is unlawful.

Printed in English, in the United States of America.

About the Author

Roger S. Philipp, CPA, CGMA

Founder and Instructor, UWorld Roger CPA Review

Roger Philipp, CPA, CGMA, is one of the most celebrated motivators and instructors in the accounting profession. Roger believes you should enjoy what you do—in life, business, and learning. Guided by this philosophy, he strives to create dynamic and engaging instruction that makes learning concepts enjoyable. This focus has helped aspiring accountants across the globe reach career success for almost 30 years.

Roger launched Roger CPA Review in 2001 with the goal to create a CPA review course that would alter the landscape of accounting education. With the program now part of UWorld, Roger continues to act as a key inspiration and spark for company innovation. The success of the program is fueled by his unique approach to teaching, in which he breaks down and simplifies complex topics, with support from memory aids and mnemonic devices, to help students understand and retain information.

Roger's early career began in public accounting at Deloitte & Touche, where he earned his CPA designation, before transitioning to educational instruction. He was a lead instructor at Mark Dauberman CPA Review, before starting Roger CPA Review. Roger attributes his entrepreneurial success to the many doors his CPA license opened, as well as his passion for making professional education engaging and relevant for optimum effectiveness. In recent years, Roger was featured as one of Accounting Today's Top 100 Most Influential People in Public Accounting.

Today, Roger is a member of the AICPA, CalCPA, and has served on the Board of Directors for the American Professional Accounting Certification Providers Association (APACPA). He resides in San Francisco with his wife and co-founder of the company, Louisa, and their three children. He enjoys traveling with his family, enjoying the arts, and volunteering at his local food bank.

Acknowledgements

Keeping the course materials updated and accurate would not be possible without the contribution of our team of content experts. The team continues to be the driving force behind the updates and improvements for this year's textbooks.

Financial Accounting & Reporting

Table of Contents

Introduction   Intro-1

Taxation (55% - 80%)

REG 1	Individual Taxation	1-1
REG 2	Corporate Taxation	2-1
REG 3	S Corporations	3-1
REG 4	Partnership Taxation	4-1
REG 5	Trusts, Gift Taxes & Tax-Exempt Organizations	5-1
REG 6	Depreciation	6-1
REG 7	Property Tax Transactions	7-1

Ethics, Responsibilities & Federal Tax Procedures (10% - 20%)

REG 8	Ethics & Responsibilities in Tax Practice	8-1
REG 9	Accountant Liability	9-1

Business Law (10% - 20%)

REG 10	Contracts	10-1
REG 11	Sales Contracts	11-1
REG 12	Business Structures	12-1
REG 13	Property & Regulation of Business	13-1
REG 14	Agency	14-1
REG 15	Debtor-Creditor Relationships	15-1
REG 16	Research Appendix	16-1
REG 17	Final Review	17-1

Introduction

Introduction

0.01 Course Introduction — 1
    How to Best Use Your Course — 1
    CPA Exam Blueprints — 3

0.02 REG Introduction — 8
    Plan Your Time! — 8

0.01 Course Introduction

How to Best Use Your Course

Welcome to the UWorld Roger CPA Review course! Our expert team is passionate about helping you succeed and have developed an award-winning program that is proven to yield results. Before you get started, please read through this helpful guide on how to best use your course so that you can master all of the topics laid out for you in the AICPA Blueprints and ultimately pass the CPA Exam.

Plan your Studies

> **Tip!**
> Download the app! This gives you access to everything your course offers while on-the-go.

When preparing for the CPA Exam, half the battle is setting yourself up for success with a solid plan from the get-go. This includes establishing short and long-term goals to ensure you're staying on track to pass within the 18-month window.

To get started, use the provided Study Planners in your course (located under "Study Resources"). Select either the 3-, 6-, 9- or 12- month planner and customize to meet your unique needs and schedule. It is important to follow your planner steadily so that you can ensure you hit your goals. If you miss a day, make it up!

Master the Concepts Through Active Learning

With this program, you will build your foundational knowledge and mastery of core exam topics through **active learning**. This evidence-based learning methodology centers around the principle that students *learn by doing* to maximize retention and improve learning outcomes. When preparing for the CPA Exam, the "doing" is working through exam-like questions.

- **Start with the QBank** – The QBank is where you work through multiple choice questions and simulations that align with the **AICPA Blueprints**. Start by creating a quiz, which can be customized down to the topic level. Begin with the first topic and work your way down the list. This granular level of filtering allows you to focus your energy around each concept, providing clarity as you run through groups of questions in the same area.

> **Tip!**
> Keep the quizzes to under 30 questions. This will help keep you focused and avoid burnout.

- **It's Okay to be Wrong** – You will be surprised at how much of the material you remember from school or in the field. However, if you answer questions incorrectly, don't worry! That's why you're here—to learn! And it's here in the questions that you are participating in active learning.

- **Learn Through the Answers** – Whether you've answered a question correctly or not, it's important that you know *why*. For this reason, questions are paired with clear and concise, expert-written answer explanations. Pay close attention to these because **this is where much of the learning happens!** Answer explanations include vivid imagery to summarize the concepts, plus a full breakdown of why each answer option is correct or incorrect.

Ultimately, explanations are designed to build your body of knowledge while teaching you the *what*, *why*, and *how* behind each concept.

Track Your Progress and Performance

As you complete each chapter, track your progress and performance using our signature **SmartPath Predictive Technology™**. SmartPath is a data-driven platform that provides recommended targets based on previous students who have passed the CPA Exam. This is an important tool to help you study efficiently and gauge whether you are *exam-ready*. Your goal is to hit both your progress target (Questions Attempted) and performance target (Score) for each chapter.

> **Tip!**
> Don't over-study. SmartPath™ helps determine when you can move on to the next topic.

As you work through the material, don't worry about hitting your "Score" target right away and focus your efforts on hitting the "Questions Attempted" target first. This approach may feel uncomfortable, but trust that you are building your knowledge as you absorb the answer explanations.

Once you've completed all the topics in a chapter, you can go back and focus your efforts on hitting the "Score" target. If you are falling short, drill down in the Performance tab to see which topics need extra attention.

Solidify the Concepts

Need extra help mastering the concept? Take advantage of the additional learning tools that are integrated into your course. For example, you could be working through a difficult question and find you need further explanation. No problem! There's a link to the supporting lecture right there in the question. Want to remember something for later review? Easily transfer content directly from the question to a digital flashcard. These are just a few ways we make it easy to navigate to and access the right tools you need at the right time.

These additional tools are designed to enhance your studies—**you do not necessarily need to read or watch all of this material!** Rather, use these tools as a means to improve on weak areas:

- **Video Lectures** – From the Lectures tab or directly integrated in the link at the bottom of each practice question, you have access to the profession's most motivating and effective lecturers, including lead instructor Roger Philipp, CPA, CGMA. Lectures break down difficult topics into simplified concepts and provide helpful memory aids. These are especially recommended for visual and auditory learners.

- **Textbooks** – Digital eTextbooks are accessible side-by-side with the video lectures or in a printed format with some of our course packages. These can be used as a reference if you need further explanation of a concept. Many students also find it beneficial to follow along in the textbook while watching the lectures and either take notes directly in the physical books or by using the Notes feature and highlighting tool in the platform.

- **Digital Flashcards –** Create custom flashcards directly from your practice questions by clicking on the lightning bolt symbol. Depending on your program package, your course may also be pre-loaded with an "Expert Deck" of flashcards covering the most heavily tested topics. You can review all your cards in Study Mode or using our **Spaced Repetition**

Technology. This is an evidence-based learning method that presents cards you've marked as *difficult* more frequently, and cards you've marked as *easy* less frequently. The spacing of how and when the flashcards are introduced has been proven to increase retention and strengthen memory recall.

Get Exam-Ready

The final days leading up to the exam are a critical time in which you're going to want to review your SmartPath data and ask, "Am I *exam-ready*?" If you have hit all the targets, you are in a really good spot. However, if any areas are still marked "Needs Improvement," now is the time to focus your efforts on meeting those targets.

Finally, we recommend you **take at least one full practice exam before exam day** (click on the "Exam Sim" tab in the QBank). This allows you to hone your test-taking skills in an exam-like environment that follows the same 5-testlet, 4-hour structure as the exam.

We hope you found some helpful information in this guide and that you can start the study process with confidence! As Roger always says, "You do not have to be a genius to pass the CPA Exam. If you study, you will pass!" You've got this. Happy Studying!

CPA Exam Blueprints

This course is based on the CPA Exam Blueprints, which are created by the American Institute of Certified Public Accountants (AICPA) to help candidates know what skills and content topics will be tested on the CPA Exam.

Not only are the CPA Exam Blueprints intended to assist candidates in preparing for the exam, but they also take into account the minimum level of knowledge and skills necessary for initial licensure once candidates become CPAs.

We have already used the blueprints to guide our course materials, so you are already on the right path. However, if you'd like to reference the blueprints to better understand what's required on the exam, we've provided a helpful guide below.

Overview of the CPA Exam

The blueprints provide an overview of how much time candidates have for each section and how many questions by question type each section contains. Question types include Multiple Choice Questions (MCQ), Task-based Simulations (TBS), and Written Communication (WC).

Section	Time	MCQs	TBSs	WC
AUD	4 hrs	72	8	-
BEC	4 hrs	62	4	3
FAR	4 hrs	66	8	-
REG	4 hrs	76	8	-

Scoring Weight for All Question Types

Here candidates can see how the question types for each section are weighted and account for their overall score.

Section	MCQs	TBSs	WC
AUD	50%	50%	-
BEC	50%	35%	15%
FAR	50%	50%	-
REG	50%	50%	-

Skill Levels to be Assessed

Each exam section has a Skill Allocation framework based on the revised Bloom's Taxonomy of Educational Objectives. These are the skills that CPA candidates need to learn and successfully demonstrate on the CPA Exam.

Evaluation	The examination or assessment of problems and use of judgment to draw conclusions.
Analysis	The examination and study of the interrelationships of separate areas in order to identify causes and find evidence to support inferences.
Application	The use or demonstration of knowledge, concepts, or techniques.
Remembering & Understanding	The perception and comprehension of the significance of an area utilizing knowledge gained.

Skill Allocations

To break it down even further, here's how each of the skills above will be assessed on each section of the exam.

Introduction

Section	Remembering & Understanding	Application	Analysis	Evaluation
AUD	25-35%	30-40%	20-30%	5-15%
BEC	15-25%	50-60%	20-30%	-
FAR	10-20%	50-60%	25-35%	-
REG	25-35%	35-45%	25-35%	-

Content Allocations

Below is an overview of the content allocation for each section of the exam.

AUD Content Area Allocation	Weight
I. Ethics, Professional Responsibilities & General Principles	15-25%
II. Assessing Risk and Developing a Planned Response	25-35%
III. Performing Further Procedures & Obtaining Evidence	30-40%
IV. Forming Conclusions and Reporting	10-20%

BEC Content Area Allocation	Weight
I. Enterprise Risk Management, Internal Controls & Business Processes	20-30%
II. Economics	15-25%
III. Financial Management	10-20%
IV. Information Technology	15-25%
V. Operations Management	15-25%

FAR Content Area Allocation	Weight
I. Conceptual Framework, Standard-Setting, & Financial Reporting	25-35%
II. Select Financial Statement Accounts	30-40%
III. Select Transactions	20-30%
IV. State and Local Governments	5-15%

REG Content Area Allocation	Weight
I. Ethics, Professional Responsibilities & Federal Tax Procedures	10-20%
II. Business Law	10-20%
III. Federal Taxation of Property Transactions	12-22%
IV. Federal Taxation of Individuals	15-25%
V. Federal Taxation of Entities	28-38%

How Skills are Applied to Exam Tasks (A Sample)

Each blueprint area is broken down further by content topic, skill, and representative task. This helps candidates identify the topics and subtopics they will be tested on in each section and which skill they will be required to demonstrate as they answer questions regarding those topics. Lastly, the representative task gives detailed, specific information on what they will be expected to perform on the exam related to those topics. As the AICPA points out though, the representative tasks are *not* an all-inclusive list of items that will appear on the exam.

Introduction

To see how the content topic, skill, and representative tasks are presented in the blueprints, here is an excerpt from the AUD section:

Content group/topic	Remembering and Understanding	Application	Analysis	Evaluation	Representative task
A. Nature and scope					
1. Nature and scope: audit engagements	✓				Identify the nature, scope and objectives of the different types of audit engagements, including issuer and nonissuer audits.
2. Nature and scope: engagements conducted under Government Accountability Office Government Auditing Standards	✓				Identify the nature, scope and objectives of engagements performed in accordance with Government Accountability Office Government Auditing Standards.
3. Nature and scope: other engagements	✓				Identify the nature, scope and objectives of attestation engagements and accounting and review service engagements.
B. Ethics, Independence and professional conduct					
1. AICPA Code of Professional Conduct	✓				Understand the principles, rules and interpretations included in the AICPA Code of Professional Conduct.
	✓				Recognize situations that present threats to compliance with the AICPA Code of Professional Conduct, including threats to independence.
		✓			Apply the principles, rules and interpretations included in the AICPA Code of Professional Conduct to given situations.
		✓			Apply the Conceptual Framework for Members in Public Practice included in the AICPA Code of Professional Conduct to situations that could present threats to compliance with the rules included in the Code.
		✓			Apply the Conceptual Framework for Members in Business included in the AICPA Code of Professional Conduct to situations that could present threats to compliance with the rules included in the Code.
		✓			Apply the Conceptual Framework for Independence included in the AICPA Code of Professional Conduct to situations that could present threats to compliance with the rules included in the Code.

Conclusion

We hope you found this guide on how to read and understand the blueprints helpful. As we mentioned before, the UWorld Roger CPA Review course curriculum is directly mapped to and guided by these blueprints, so there is no need for you to spend considerable time studying the blueprints, as your course will guide you through the material. Rest assured that the practice questions in this course are designed to challenge critical thinking skills, ensuring you are thoroughly prepared to pass the CPA Exam.

To see the full AICPA Blueprints, visit
https://www.aicpa.org/becomeacpa/cpaexam/examinationcontent.

0.02 REG Introduction

Plan Your Time!

Ensure success on the exam by following our recommended time allocations per testlet and per question.

REG Exam	
Testlet 1 *38 MCQ*	48 min
Testlet 2 *38 MCQ*	48 min
Testlet 3 *2 TBS*	30 min
Testlet 4 *3 TBS*	57 min
Testlet 5 *3 TBS*	57 min
Total Time:	4 hours

Things to consider:

- Allocate 75 seconds per multiple choice question
- Allocate 15-20 minutes per simulation, depending on complexity
- Plan to use no more than 10 minutes per research question
- Take the standard 15-minute break after the 3rd testlet – it doesn't count against your time

REG 1
Individual Taxation

REG 1: Individual Taxation

1.01 Individual Taxation — 1
OVERVIEW — 1

1.02 Filing Requirements — 3
KIDDIE TAX — 3
METHODS OF ACCOUNTING FOR TAX PURPOSES — 5

1.03 Gross Income — 7
CONSTRUCTIVE RECEIPT — 9
EARNED INCOME — 9
SCHOLARSHIPS — 10
INTEREST (SCHEDULE B) — 10
DIVIDENDS (SCHEDULE B) — 11
STOCK OPTIONS — 12
INJURY AWARDS — 12
PRIZES & AWARDS — 12

1.04 Gross Income (Continued) — 13
SOCIAL SECURITY BENEFITS — 13
DEBT FORGIVENESS — 13
PENSIONS & ANNUITIES — 13
FOREIGN EARNED INCOME EXCLUSION — 14
TAX REFUNDS — 14
INHERITANCES, GIFTS & LIFE INSURANCE PROCEEDS — 14
CAPITAL ASSETS (SCHEDULE D) — 14
GAINS FROM THE SALES OF PERSONAL ASSETS ARE TAXED AS CAPITAL GAINS. — 15
NET OPERATING LOSSES (NOL) — 15

1.05 Tax Schedules — 17
1.06 Adjustments for (to) AGI — 18
I-EMBRACED HEALTH, FARMERS & CHARITY — 18

1.07 Adjustments for (to) AGI (Continued) — 22
CONTRIBUTIONS TO RETIREMENT PLANS — 22
CONTRIBUTIONS TO EDUCATION SAVINGS ACCOUNTS — 23
OTHER CONTRIBUTIONS — 24
EARLY WITHDRAWAL PENALTY — 25
JURY DUTY — 25
HEALTH SAVINGS ACCOUNTS (HSAs) — 25
FARM INCOME — 26
CHARITY — 26

1.08 Standard & Itemized Deductions — 27
STANDARD DEDUCTION — 27
ITEMIZED DEDUCTIONS (SCHEDULE A) (COmMITT) — 27

1.09 Dependents & Filing Status — 34
PERSONAL EXEMPTIONS — 34
DEPENDENTS — 34
FILING STATUS — 35

1.10 Tax Credits & Other Taxes 37
    TAX CREDITS 37
    OTHER TAXES 40

1.01 Individual Taxation

Overview

The Internal Revenue Code (IRC) is the foundation of federal tax laws and represents a codification of the federal tax laws of the United States.

 The AICPA has historically only tested amounts applicable to the calendar year previous to the year of the exam (eg, 2021 tax numbers for the first half of 2022 and then 2022 numbers for the second half of 2022 and the first half of 2023); however, the examiners tend not to focus on inflation-adjusted numbers in exam questions.

Form 1040

"For/To AGI"
- Gross Income
- ± Adjustments → Schedule B, C, D, E, F (I EMBRACED)

= AGI
(Deductions)
- Itemized (Sch. A)
- Standard deduction[3] ($25,900/$12,950-2022)
- 20% §199A QBI Deduction[5]

(Net Exemptions) ($0[4])

"From AGI"
= Taxable Income
× Tax Rate

= Tax Liability
  (Credits)
+ SE tax
+ AMT
  (Withholdings)
  (Prepayments)

= Tax Due

"For AGI" Adjustments (I-EMBRACED)
Interest on student loans ($2,500)
Employment tax-50%, med. premiums-100%
Moving expenses (military only)[1]
Business expense (Sch. C)
Rent/Royalty & flow-through entities (Sch. E)
Alimony (grandfathered only)[2]
Contributions to retirement (KEOGH/IRA)
Early withdrawal penalty
Jury Duty pay
Health savings accounts (HSA)
Farm income (Sch. F)

Itemized (Sch. A)
Charitable contributions[6]
Other miscellaneous[7]
Medical expenses
Interest[8]
Taxes[9]
Theft or Casualty (disasters only)[10]

Tax Cuts and Jobs Act of 2017 (TCJA) & Other Changes

1. The deduction for **moving** expenses has been suspended for 2018 – 2025 for most individuals; however, there is an exception for members of the U.S. armed forces on active duty.

2. **Alimony** is not deductible for divorces/separations executed after 2018. Alimony payments attributable to divorce/separation agreements finalized prior to 2019 remain deductible by the payer and includible in the recipient's income.

3. **Standard deductions** have essentially been doubled for 2018 – 2025 and will continue to be adjusted for inflation.

4. **Personal exemptions** (including dependency exemptions) have been eliminated for 2018 – 2025.

5. For 2018 – 2025, we now have a **20% deduction for qualified business income** (Section 199A) from certain flow-through entities. This will be discussed in another section.

6. TCJA increased the limitation for **cash contributions** donated to public charities to 60% of AGI through 2025 (however, this limitation was temporarily increased to **100% of AGI** for 2021).

7. **Miscellaneous** itemized deductions *subject to the 2-percent of AGI limitation* have been suspended for 2018 – 2025.

8. No longer includes **home equity** indebtedness that is not considered acquisition indebtedness for 2018 – 2025.

9. The deduction for **state and local income and property taxes** paid is now limited to a total of $10,000 ($5,000 MFS) for 2018 – 2025. Also, deductions for foreign real property taxes will not be allowed during this time.

10. The deduction for **personal casualty losses** is now generally limited to losses attributable to federally declared disasters for 2018 – 2025. This limitation does not apply to the extent the taxpayer has personal casualty gains; that is, any personal casualty loss may be deducted to the extent of the personal casualty gain.

1.02 Filing Requirements

An Individual **must file** a tax return if their income is greater than their standard deduction ($12,950 single / $19,400 HOH / $25,900 MFJ – 2022), or if they:

- Have net self-employment earnings of $400 or more
- Are claimed as a dependent on another taxpayer's return, and have gross income greater than the dependent's standard deduction—
    - $1,150 (2022) or,
    - If larger, earned income plus $400 (not to exceed individual standard deduction)

> For example, Suzie, who is claimed on her parents' return, has no unearned income but works at the corner store and makes $1,300 in 2022. She does not have to file a return because her standard deduction as a dependent is $1,300 plus $400, or $1,700. If Suzie had unearned income from dividends of $500 on top of her $1,300 earned income, she would have to file a return because her gross income would be $1,800 and her filing threshold is $1,700.

- Are receiving advanced payments of the Earned Income Credit (EIC)
- Are subject to the Kiddie Tax

Kiddie Tax

The Kiddie tax was established to prevent the "wealthy" from avoiding taxes on their investment income by transferring the investments into the names of their children, who might not be subject to tax or, if so, would be taxed at lower rates. Thus, a child's unearned income above the following thresholds in 2022 is subject to tax at the parent's tax rate*:

- $2,300, or
- If greater, $1,150 plus itemized deductions related to the production of the unearned income.

The Kiddie Tax applies to children meeting the following conditions:

- The child has unearned income in excess of the threshold for the year ($2,300 - 2022);
- Either parent is alive as of the end of the taxable year;
- The child does not file a joint tax return for the year; and
- The child is:
    1. Under 18 years old as of the end of the tax year, or
    2. 18 years old with earned income that does not exceed 50% of the child's support, or

3. A student between the ages of 19 and 24 with earned income that does not exceed 50% of the child's support.

In calculating the Kiddie Tax, the child's unearned income can generally be broken down into three tiers as follows:

Tier	Child's Income	Amount of Unearned Income	Applicable Tax Rate
1	Unearned income up to dependent's standard deduction • If the child also has *earned* income, the $1,150 standard deduction will be applied to it first. (Remember, if larger, standard deduction = earned income + $400, not to exceed standard deduction for single individuals.)	$0 to $1,150	Not taxed
2	Unearned income above standard deduction up to $2,300 threshold • If the child also has *earned* income, up to $2,200 of unearned income is still shielded from higher tax rates.	$1,150 - $2,300	Child's regular rate
3	Unearned income above $2,300 threshold	>$2,300	Parent's tax rate

For example, Richie, age 16, has $25,000 in unearned income and no earned income. The amount of Richie's unearned income subject to the Kiddie tax is $25,000 total income – $2,300 threshold = $22,700.

1. $1,150 will not be taxed;
2. $1,150 will be subject to Richie's tax rate; and
3. $22,700 will be subject to his parent's tax rate (ie, the Kiddie Tax).

If, however, Richie has $25,000 in unearned income and $500 earned income, the amount of Richie's unearned income subject to the Kiddie Tax is still $22,700: $25,500 total income – $500 earned income – $2,300 threshold = $22,700.

1. $1,150 (ie, $500 earned + $650 unearned) will not be taxed;
2. $1,650 (all unearned) will be subject to Richie's tax rate; and
3. $22,700 will be subject to his parent's tax rate.

$650 + 1,650 = $2,300 unearned

If Richie has $25,000 in unearned income and $2,000 earned income, the amount of Richie's unearned income subject to the Kiddie Tax is still $22,700: $27,000 − $2,000 earned income − $2,300 threshold = $22,700.

1. $2,450 (ie, $2,000 earned + $450 unearned) will not be taxed;
2. $1,850 (all unearned) will be subject to Richie's tax rate; and

$450 + 1,850 = $2,300 unearned

3. $22,700 will be subject to his parent's tax rate.

Methods of Accounting for Tax Purposes

Section 446 of the tax code generally requires taxpayers to use the basis of accounting that is used in keeping their books; however, the overarching principle is that the method of accounting chosen should *clearly reflect income*. This means that the vast majority of individuals use the cash basis of accounting while entities are more likely to use the accrual basis of accounting. There are some other circumstances that further dictate which method must be used though:

- If the taxpayer's annual gross receipts exceed $27 million (for 2022) on average for the most recent 3 tax years (ie, the gross receipts test), the accrual method may be required if purchases and sales of inventory are necessary for the determination of income.
- Some entities are **prohibited from using the cash basis** under Section 448:
  - C corporations unless they fall below the $27M gross receipts test
  - Partnerships that have a C corporation as a partner unless they meet the $27M gross receipts test
  - Tax shelters

Other Exceptions: This limitation generally does not apply to farming businesses and qualified personal service corporations (PSCs), where 95% of stock is owned by owner-employees (ie, ownership test) and 95% of activities are in certain fields, such as health, law, accounting, etc. (ie, function test).

Cash Basis

- Recognize income when:
  - Cash or property is received, at fair market value (FMV).
    - Even if "unearned" (ie, advance payments) – still income when received (eg, prepaid rent).
  - Actually or constructively received, whichever is earlier.
    - Income is constructively received when payment has been *made available* to the taxpayer and the taxpayer has an *unrestricted right to it*.
- Report deductions when:
  - Cash or check is disbursed.
  - Expenses are charged to a credit card.

Note: Prepaid interest is generally not deductible; it must be amortized over the period to which it applies.

Accrual Basis

- **Recognize income** generally when "earned."
    - This means that (1) all events have occurred that fix the taxpayer's right to the income and (2) the amount can be reasonably determined (ie, all events test).
    - The all events test is considered to be met no later than when the income is included in revenue in the financial statements (F/S) of the taxpayer. F/S for these purposes generally include only those certified as being prepared in accordance with GAAP/IFRS or those that are otherwise prepared for filing with certain regulatory or governmental agencies.
    - Advance payments (ie, unearned income) generally must be recognized in the year received, unless the taxpayer makes an election to include only the part of the payment required to be recognized in the year of receipt (ie, the part included in revenue for F/S purposes) and the remainder in the following year. Such election may be made for any category of advance payment and will remain in effect until consent to revoke the election is obtained from the IRS.

    Note: Advance payments for these purposes do not include rent and insurance premiums received. Rents and royalties received in advance must be included in taxable income in the period received.

- **Book expenses** as "incurred."
    - This means that (1) a liability exists, (2) the amount can be *reasonably determined*, and (3) *economic performance* has occurred (ie, property and/or services have been provided).

1.03 Gross Income

Generally Income	Not Income
Compensation for services including: - Wages and salaries (W-2) - Tips - Fees for jury duty service - Bonuses and commissions - Unemployment compensation - Most fringe benefits, such as the rental value of using a company car on weekends for personal purposes - Bargain purchases of employer merchandise/services	- Health insurance coverage - Group term life insurance coverage, up to a $50,000 policy - Fringe benefits that primarily are incurred for the employer's benefit, such as free housing given to an on-site hotel manager - Immaterial fringe benefits, such as free photocopies made on the company machine - Employer-provided educational assistance - Up to $5,000* of benefits under an employer dependent care assistance plan - Up to employer's gross profit percentage of regular merchandise price - Up to 20% of FMV of employer services obtained at discount
- Prizes and awards - Gambling winnings - Illegal drug income (net of COGS) - Treasure trove (ie, if you find money or something of value and you keep it; it's taxable)	A prize or award that is both: - Tangible personal property up to certain dollar values - Received by an employee for his years of company employment or safety achievement OR a prize or award where: - No services required of recipient; - Selected without action on recipient's part; *and* - Payment assigned by recipient to a governmental unit or charitable organization.
- Scholarships and fellowships	A scholarship or fellowship that is both: - Not compensation for required services - Spent by a degree candidate for tuition
- Interest accrued each year on a zero-coupon bond or bond purchased at a discount - Interest on U.S. Treasury obligations - Interest on Series HH U.S. savings bonds (paid semi-annually)	- Interest on state or municipal bonds - Interest earned on qualified higher education bonds - Interest on a Series EE U.S. savings bond is not reported as income until the time that the bond is redeemed.

Generally Income	Not Income
• Dividends	• Stock dividends • Dividends received from an S corporation • Dividends received on a life insurance policy • Dividends received from a mutual fund that invests in tax-exempt bonds
Rents and royalties, including: • Rent collected in advance by a landlord • Nonrefundable deposits collected from tenants	Refundable security deposits
The **bargain discount** from exercising a stock option to buy an employer's stock for a price below market value	A special type of stock option, called an incentive stock option (ISO)
Proceeds withdrawn from a traditional IRA or pension plan if the original contributions to the plan were excluded or deducted from income	The portion, if any, of a traditional IRA pension withdrawal that represents the recovery of prior nondeductible contributions and all Roth IRA withdrawals.
Injury awards, if they are for: • Punitive damages • Lost business profits • Nonphysical injuries, such as age or race discrimination • Emotional distress (in excess of associated medical bills)	• Damages for bodily injury, pain and suffering, and lost wages • Emotional distress attributable to physical injury or sickness • Workers' compensation benefits
Up to 85% of Social Security benefits if the taxpayer has substantial income in addition to the benefits	Up to 100% of Social Security benefits, if the taxpayer does not have much income in addition to benefits
State tax refunds, if the state taxes paid were originally claimed as a deduction in an earlier year	• Federal tax refunds • State tax refunds in excess of the amount deducted in an earlier year
• The interest component of an annuity. For example, assume that a person spends $400 to buy an annuity of $100 for each of 5 years, or $500 proceeds in total. Since a $100 interest profit is part of the $500 proceeds, the portion of each payment that is reported as income is: Profit/Total Proceeds=$100/$500=20% • Income generated by gifts and inheritances (eg, rent received on inherited rental property)	• Gifts • Inheritances • Life insurance proceeds paid upon the death of the insured • Child Support • Property Settlement • Alimony (no longer considered income for divorces/separations executed *after 2018*).

Individual Taxation REG 1

Generally Income	Not Income
Cancellation of Debt	• Debt forgiven as gift, bequest, or inheritance • Discharge of qualified student loans (2021–2025 under ARPA) • Debt that would have provided a tax deduction • Debt cancelled in Title 11 bankruptcy • Debt cancelled when debtor is insolvent • Qualified farm indebtedness • Qualified real property business indebtedness • Qualified principal residence indebtedness
Capital gains	• Up to $250,000 gain on personal residence ($500,000 MFJ)

Note: This is not meant to be an all-inclusive list. IRC Section 61 provides that all income from whatever source derived is includible in gross income unless specifically excluded by law.

Constructive Receipt

An item must be included in the gross income of an individual in the year it is **constructively received.** This refers to when the cash becomes available to the taxpayer. Thus, a dividend that is credited to the shareholder's brokerage account but automatically reinvested in the purchase of additional shares is considered received by the taxpayer. The receipt of property or services is treated as the receipt of the cash that normally would have been required to pay for them.

Earned Income

- *Salaries and wages* (**W-2**) are reported when cash or other consideration is received. **For example**, an expensive watch or stock in the corporation that is given to an employee is treated as compensation at the FMV of the property.
- *Tips* are normally reported by the employee to their employer and are included in the reported wages of that employee. Tips not reported to the employer must be directly reported on the tax return by the employee based on when the tips are **received**.
- Jury duty fees
- Unemployment compensation
- Payment in nonmoney form reported at FMV when received (stock, property)
- Premiums on group term life insurance over $50,000 are taxable (fringe benefits), but the death benefits received are tax free.
- Life insurance proceeds are generally tax free, unless purchased from a person other than the insurance co (as an investment) or if paid out in installments; then a pro rata part of the receipts is taxable as interest.

- A qualified cafeteria plan (menu of benefits) is an employer-sponsored benefit plan where the employee can choose either cash (taxable) or benefits (accident insurance, life insurance, legal services – not taxable). With the exception of 401(k) plans, deferred compensation plans are excluded from qualifying cafeteria plans.
- Gambling winnings – Gross winnings must be included in gross income. Gambling losses may be claimed as itemized deductions to the extent of winnings.
- Prizes and awards are taxable, unless received for years of service or safety achievement and such prizes and awards do not exceed $400 (reported at FMV).
- Health and medical insurance coverage is not taxable.
- Immaterial fringe benefits are not taxable (eg, Xeroxing resume).
- Illegal drug income, net of COGS (not any other expenses), is taxable.

Scholarships

Taxable unless both (no strings):

- Not compensation for services, *and*
- Money spent for tuition, books, or class supplies for degree-seeking student.

Interest (Schedule B)

- State and local municipal bond interest is not taxable.
- All other government interest is taxable (eg, Federal bonds, T-bills).
- Accrual basis taxpayers are taxed on interest on U.S. savings bonds in the period it accrues, regardless of when received.
- **Series HH** bonds, the last of which mature in 2024, were issued at face value.
  - Interest is payable twice per year.
  - Cash basis taxpayers are taxed on interest in the period received.
- **Series EE** savings bonds
  - Taxable interest is equal to the difference between the redemption value and the purchase price.
  - May be paper or electronic
    - Paper issued at discount and redeemed at face value
    - Electronic issued at face and redeemed at face plus accrued interest
  - Exempt if used for *higher education* for self, spouse, or dependent
    - Bought by taxpayer (or spouse)
    - Buyer at least 24 years of age
    - Redeem directly – need not transfer to school
    - Tuition and fees qualify, but room and board do not qualify.

Individual Taxation · REG 1

- **Series E** savings bonds, which were issued prior to Series EE savings bonds, were issued at a discount and redeemed at face value.
- **Series I** savings bonds, which are inflation-indexed bonds, are issued at face value and redeemed at maturity at face value plus accrued interest.
- A **cash basis** taxpayer can choose either of the following methods for reporting interest income on Series E, EE, or I bonds:
    - Report all interest when bonds are redeemed or sold
    - Report interest as the increase in the redemption value of the bond each year

Dividends (Schedule B)

- Taxable when received *unless:*
    - Life insurance dividend - return of premium
        - But interest on the dividend is taxable
    - Received from an S corporation
    - Stock dividends or stock splits on common stock
        - Stock dividends from Preferred stock are taxable at FMV.
        - Cash and property dividends from common stock are taxable.
    - Liquidating dividend - return of capital
- Qualified dividends are taxed at special 0%, 15% or 20%, *similar to long-term capital gains*. For 2018 – 2025, the applicable rate is determined based on income levels (adjusted for inflation after 2018), rather than tax brackets (see text box below for prior law). For 2022:
    - **0%** tax rate if income is below $41,675 for single individuals, $83,350 for married filing jointly (MFJ) and surviving spouses (SS), and $55,800 for head of households (HOH)
    - **15%** tax rate if income is between the applicable 0% rate amount and below $459,750 for single individuals, $517,200 for MFJ and SS, and $488,500 for HOH
    - **20%** tax rate for all other **"high-income"** individuals above these thresholds
    - Applies to *qualified dividends* from a domestic corporation and certain qualified foreign corporations. Must hold 60+ days during 121-day period beginning 60 days prior to ex-dividend date (ie, the date on which the dividend payee is determined, usually 2 days prior to the record date).

    Note: Special rates do not apply to dividends from nontaxable entities, such as REITs or dividends that are deductible by the payer organization. Treatment of mutual fund distributions is based on the source of income being distributed (eg, dividends representing distribution of interest earned by a bond-oriented mutual fund don't qualify).

Prior Law
• 0% tax rate if in the first two tax brackets—10%, 15%
• 15% tax rate if in the middle four tax brackets— 25%, 28%, 33%, 35%
• 20% tax rate if in the highest tax bracket—39.6%

Stock Options

- *Nonqualified* – taxed when **exercised**; excess of FMV over exercise price treated as compensation.
- *Qualified* (incentive stock option – **ISO**) – taxed when **sell** stock; difference between sales price and exercise price treated as capital gain or loss.
    - ISO must be held 2 years from grant date and 1 year from exercise date.

Injury Awards

- Nonphysical – **Taxable**
    - Age, race discrimination
    - Punitive damages
    - Lost business profits
- Bodily injury – **tax free (blood)**
    - Pain & suffering for physical injury
    - Workers' compensation
    - Reimbursement of medical expenses paid and not itemized on Schedule A

Prizes & Awards

Taxable at FMV unless *all* conditions satisfied:

- No services required of recipient.
- Selected without any action on recipient's part.
- Payment assigned by recipient to a governmental unit or charitable organization so that recipient *never actually receives* the prize or award.

1.04 Gross Income (Continued)

Social Security Benefits

Social security benefits may or may not be taxable based on a complicated calculation using **provisional income** (adjusted gross income before social security + tax-exempt income + one-half of social security benefits). As a result of the calculation, anywhere from 0 to 85% of benefits may be taxable.

In general, a person collecting social security who has **less than $25,000** of provisional income can *exclude all* social security benefits, while taxpayers with provisional income **exceeding $60,000** usually are subject to the maximum **85%** inclusion.

Debt Forgiveness

In general, when a debtor's debts are cancelled, forgiven, or discharged, such as through relief in bankruptcy, the amount forgiven is *taxable to the debtor*. However, there are certain debts that are *not taxable* when forgiven:

- Amounts excludable from income such as gifts, bequests, or inheritances
- Cancellation of qualified student loans (2021– 2025)
- Debt that, upon payment, would provide a tax deduction to the taxpayer
- Debt that is cancelled in a Title 11 bankruptcy case
- Debt that is cancelled when the debtor is insolvent, which is when debts exceed the market value of the debtor's assets
- Qualified farm indebtedness
- Qualified real property business indebtedness
- Qualified principal residence indebtedness (through 2025)

Pensions & Annuities

Pension benefits and annuities (other than excluded recovery of capital), including distributions from IRAs (other than Roth IRA accounts), may be taxable. The amount considered a return of capital will NOT be taxable. If the taxpayer did not pay any portion of the cost of the pension plan, such as one in which all costs were incurred by an employer, all benefits are taxable.

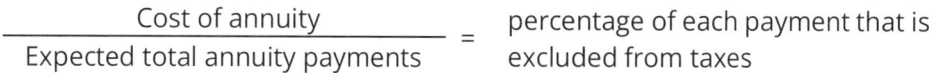

$$\frac{\text{Cost of annuity}}{\text{Expected total annuity payments}} = \text{percentage of each payment that is excluded from taxes}$$

Lump-sum distributions from qualified pension, profit-sharing, stock bonus, and Keogh plans (but not IRAs) may be eligible for special tax treatment. Certain distributions may be rolled-over tax-free (within 60 days) to a traditional IRA account.

Foreign Earned Income Exclusion

An individual meeting either a *bona fide residence test* or a *physical presence test* may elect to exclude up to $112,000 (2022) of income earned in a foreign country. Qualifying taxpayers also may elect to exclude additional amounts based on foreign housing costs.

To qualify, an individual must be a (1) U.S. citizen who is a foreign resident for an uninterrupted period that includes an entire taxable year (bona fide residence test), or (2) U.S. citizen or resident present in a foreign country for at least 330 full days in any 12-month period (physical presence test).

Tax Refunds

- Federal
  - **Interest** – YES, taxable
  - **Refund** – Not taxable (a return of YOUR money)
- State
  - **Interest** – YES, taxable
  - **Refund** – Generally, if the taxpayer itemized and took a deduction on Schedule A in the prior year, a refund is taxable in the current year (Form 1099G). A refund is taxable to the extent the taxpayer received a *tax benefit* in the prior year. Thus, if the taxpayer didn't itemize in the prior year, a refund is not taxable in current year.

> For example, if the taxpayer itemizes their deductions because $500 in state taxes allowed their deductions to exceed the standard deduction by $100, then only the $100 tax benefit is taxable in the current year since the taxpayer would have otherwise claimed the standard deduction.

Inheritances, Gifts & Life Insurance Proceeds

Inheritances, gifts and life Insurance proceeds are **not taxable** to the recipient; however, any income received from the property is taxable. This is discussed in more detail in a later chapter.

Capital Assets (Schedule D)

Individuals receive special tax rates for **long-term capital gains** (ie, held over 1 year). For 2018 – 2025, the applicable rate is determined based on income levels (adjusted for inflation after 2018), rather than tax brackets, as previously discussed. For 2022:

- **0%** tax rate if income is below $41,675 for single individuals, $83,350 for MFJ/SS, and $55,800 for HOH
- **15%** tax rate if income is between the applicable 0% rate amount and below $458,750 for single individuals, $517,200 for MFJ/SS, and $488,500 for HOH
- **20%** tax rate for all other **"high-income"** individuals above these thresholds

Individual Taxation

- Short-term capital gains (ie, held 1 year or less) are taxed at ordinary tax rates.

Net **capital loss** up to **$3,000** is allowable against an individual's ordinary income ($1,500 for MFS). Any unused amount can be **carried forward indefinitely**.

Note that corporations cannot deduct a net capital loss, and no special tax rates apply; however, they can carry them back 3 years and forward 5 years to offset capital gains.

- In most cases, one must report capital gains and losses on Form 8949 and then report the totals on Schedule D.
- Personal assets, such as the family home or automobile, are also considered capital assets.

   Gains from the sales of personal assets are taxed as capital gains.

   Exception: Gain on personal residence excludable up to $250,000, or $500,000 if MFJ.

- Losses, however, on the sale or abandonment of personal use assets are not deductible.

   Note: IRC §165(c) generally limits the deduction of losses by an individual to (1) losses incurred in a trade or business; (2) losses incurred in a transaction entered into for profit; and (3) losses of property arising by casualty or theft (discussed in more detail in the Property Tax section).

Net Operating Losses (NOL)

NOLs may no longer be carried back 2 years unless the taxpayer is a farmer. NOLs may be **carried forward indefinitely** until they are used up. For any tax year to which an NOL deduction is carried forward, such deduction is now **limited** to **80% of taxable income** for the year before the NOL.

- Generally, an NOL results from a business loss, but it could also result from a personal casualty loss. (Note that personal casualty losses are no longer deductible unless they are incurred as a result of a Federally Declared Disaster.)
- Include in calculation all taxable income and all deductions except the following:
    - Capital losses in excess of capital gains
    - Nonbusiness deductions (eg, standard deduction) in excess of nonbusiness income
        - Wages and rental income are considered business income for NOL purposes.
    - NOL carryforwards
    - The Section 199A Qualified Business Income deduction
    - Personal exemption ($0 for 2018 – 2025 anyway)

Sammy is in the comic book business. He is single and has the following income and deductions on his Form 1040 for year 1 (2023):

Income

Wages from part-time job	$1,500	
Interest on savings	500	
Net long-term capital gain on sale of real estate used in business	2,500	
Sammy's total income		**$4,500**

Deductions

Net loss from business ($42,000 income – $50,000 expenses)	$8,000	
Net short-term capital loss—sale of stock	1,000	
Standard deduction*	12,000	
Sammy's total deductions		$21,000

Sammy's deductions exceed his income by $16,500 ($21,000 – $4,500). However, to figure whether he has an NOL, the following deductions are **not** allowed:

Nonbusiness net short-term capital loss	$1,000	
Nonbusiness deductions (standard deduction, $12,000)		
– *nonbusiness* income (interest, $500)	11,500	
Total deductions **not** allowed in NOL calculation		$12,500
Total deductions allowed		**$8,500**
Sammy's NOL ($4,500 total income – $8,500 deductions allowed)		**$4,000**

Carryforward

Sammy may carry the $4,000 NOL forward to the following year, but the amount he can take will be limited to 80% of taxable income. So, if Sammy's taxable income is $4,200 in year 2 (2022), then he may offset only $3,360 ($4,200 × 0.80), with the NOL deduction in year 2 and carry the remainder to the following year.

*Note: An unadjusted standard deduction of $12,000 is used in this example for simplification purposes.

 The 2020 CARES Act provides that for taxable years beginning after 2020, the 80% limitation equals 80% of taxable income in *excess* of any pre-2018 NOL carryover. Therefore, any pre-2018 NOL carried forward to a tax year after 2020 is fully deductible, and any NOL created after 2017 and carried forward to a tax year after 2020 is subject to the 80% limitation.

 The exam generally uses vague years in questions, such as "year 1," and the candidate is to assume that the current rules apply. However, when exam questions have different tax treatments based on timing, like NOLs, the question will indicate the actual year so that the appropriate tax treatment can be determined.

1.05 Tax Schedules

A. Itemized Deductions (personal expenses)

B. Interest and dividend income

C. Profit and loss from a business (Employer expenses / 1099 Income)

D. Capital gains and losses (S/T and L/T investments)

E. Supplementary income or loss (RRF-COP)
- **R**ental Income
- **R**oyalties
    - **C**opyrights
    - **O**il/Gas leases
    - **P**atents
- **F**low-through entities (Schedule K-1 income)
    - S corps, Partnerships, Estates & Trusts

F. Profit and Loss from Farming

Form 1040X – Amended return (3 years)

Form 1116 – Foreign Tax Credit

Form 4562 – Depreciation and Amortization

Form 4797 – Sale of L/T business property (not inventory or receivables – Schedule C)

See the IRS website for the most recent versions of the forms.

1.06 Adjustments for (to) AGI

I-EMBRACED Health, Farmers & Charity

*I*nterest on Student Loans for Higher Education

- $2,500, phase out applies
- Applies to entire repayment period

Self-*E*mployment Tax

- Pays for both employer and employee's share (15.3%)
- 50% of SE tax (7.65%) is deductible on return
  - 6.2% Social Security - on wages up to $147,000 – 2022
  - 1.45% Medicare – unlimited
- 100% of medical insurance premiums paid by a self-employed taxpayer for self and family are deductible (no member of the family may have coverage through an employer).

*M*oving Expenses for Military

The deduction for moving expenses has been suspended for 2018 – 2025 for most individuals. There is an exception for members of the U.S. armed forces on active duty, but this exception is less likely to be tested.

*B*usiness Expenses (Schedule C – Sole Proprietorship/1099 Income)

- All costs of running a business
- All taxes paid by the business
- Bad debts recognized under direct write-off method
- The Uniform Capitalization Rules (UNiCAP – Section 263A), if applicable, requires that certain costs be capitalized to inventory produced or held for sale ($27 million gross-receipts test applies).
- Interest paid in advance is not deductible when paid, even by a cash basis taxpayer.
- Rent paid in advance is *generally* not deductible when paid, even by a cash basis taxpayer. Only the amount that applies to use of rented property during the tax year can be deducted. The rest can be deducted over the period to which it applies.
  - Exception: Prepaid amounts are deductible if such amounts do not extend a right or benefit to the taxpayer beyond the earlier of:
    - 12 months after date the taxpayer first realizes the right or benefit, or
    - The end of the following tax year.

- Gifts to customers up to $25 per recipient per year
- $4 per promotional item
- 50% meals (Entertainment expenses are generally no longer deductible after 2017.)
- 100% travel
- Similar to a small corporation
- **Hobby Losses** – If no profit in 3 of 5 years, loss generally not deductible.
    - Expenses are not currently deductible as Misc. 2% deductions have been suspended until 2026.

Rental, Royalty, & Flow-Through Entities (Schedule E)

- Generally, income is taxable when earned by an accrual basis taxpayer and when received by a cash-basis taxpayer. When rents or royalties are received in advance, however, even an accrual basis taxpayer will include them in taxable income in the period received.
- **Passive Activity** – Any business venture in which the taxpayer does NOT *materially participate*.
    - Includes, but is not limited to:
        - All limited partnership interests
        - All rental activities (unless taxpayer is "real estate professional")
    - **Seven Tests for Material Participation**—Taxpayer must meet at least one of the following tests on an annual basis (Note: the first three are the most important to know):
        - Taxpayer participates in the activity *more than 500 hours*.
        - Taxpayer's participation is *substantially all* of participation by all owners/nonowners (ie, Taxpayer does most of the work).
        - Taxpayer participates *more than 100 hours* and not less than any other owner/nonowner.
        - Activity is a "significant participation activity" (ie, more than 100 hours participation) and taxpayer participated in all significant participation activities for more than 500 hours.
        - Materially participated in activity for 5 of last 10 years.
        - Materially participated in activity for any 3 prior years for personal service activities.
        - Depending on facts and circumstances, participation occurs on a *regular, continuous, and substantial* basis.
- **Passive Activity Losses** (PALs) are generally deductible only to the extent of passive gains. Note: These rules apply to individuals, estates, trusts (other than grantor trusts), closely held or nonpublicly traded C corporations, and personal service corporations. There is no limit on PALs that may be deducted by grantor trusts, partnerships, and S corporations, since they are flow-through entities and these items are passed through to the individual shareholders and partners.
    - Unused losses carried forward until disposal of activity

- **Real Estate Professional Exception** – If taxpayer is considered a "real estate professional," then losses from real estate rental activities may be treated as ordinary business losses and, thus, deducted against ordinary income. A taxpayer is a real estate professional if:
  - *More than half* of the taxpayer's personal services performed in trades/businesses during the year were performed in real property trades/businesses, and
  - They materially participated in such activities for *more than 750 hours* during the year.
- **Active Participation Exception** – If taxpayer only *actively participates* in the rental activity and has at least a *10% interest* in the activity, they may deduct **up to $25,000** of losses against ordinary income each year.
  - Reduced by 50% of modified AGI over $100,000.
  - No deduction if modified AGI exceeds $150,000.

> If the taxpayer meets the active participation requirements and has modified AGI of $110,000, the maximum amount of net losses from rental activities that can be deducted is $25,000 – 50% × ($110,000 MAGI – $100,000 threshold) = $20,000.

- Allocation is required when various passive activities involve both gains and losses.
  - Excess loss allocated among activities involving losses
  - Allocation in proportion of activity's loss to total of losses

> For example, assume an entity has 3 passive activities with losses totaling $100,000 and 1 passive activity with a gain of $25,000:
> - Activity 1 = $20,000 loss
> - Activity 2 = $30,000 loss
> - Activity 3 = $50,000 loss
> - Activity 4 = $25,000 gain
>
> The excess loss of $75,000 will be allocated as follows:
> - Activity 1: $20,000/$100,000 x $75,000 = $15,000
> - Activity 2: $30,000/$100,000 x $75,000 = $22,500
> - Activity 3: $50,000/$100,000 x $75,000 = $37,500

- The treatment of rental income and expenses for a dwelling unit that is also used for personal purposes (**Vacation home**) depends on whether the taxpayer uses it as a *home*. A dwelling unit is used as a home if **personal use exceeds** the greater of **14 days or 10%** of the number of **days rented**.
  - If a dwelling unit is used as a home and it is *rented for less than 15 days* during the tax year, rental income is *excluded* from gross income and expenses are not deductible as rental expenses. Can deduct on Schedule A.

- If it is rented for more than 14 days:
  - And *personal use is more than* the greater of 14 days or 10% of the number of days rented (considered a *home*), rental income is *included* and deductions are limited to gross rental income. Unused deductions may be *carried forward* to future years.
  - And *personal use is not more than* the greater of 14 days or 10% of the number of day's rented (considered a *real rental*), rental income is *included* and all expenses allocated to the rental portion are allowed. Expenses in excess of income are subject to *passive activity loss limits.*

- Depreciation is discussed in detail in another section.
- Income from flow-through entities (eg, partnerships, S corporations – discussed in another section) is taxable to the individual in the period in which it is reported (Schedule K-1) by the flow-through entity.

Alimony Paid

TCJA has repealed the deduction of alimony (and the corresponding inclusion in income for the payee) for divorces/separations executed after 2018. Alimony payments attributable to **divorce/separation agreements** finalized **prior to 2019** will remain **deductible** by the payer and **includible** in the recipient's income. To be considered alimony, payment must satisfy all the following conditions:

- **C**ash only or its equivalent (not property)
- **A**part when payments made (do not live together)
- **N**ot child support (Child support must be fully paid; thus, payments are applied to child support first.)
- **N**ot designated as property settlement (not taxable/not deductible)
- **O**wn return for payer and payee
- **T**erminates on death of recipient

Tax treatment of alimony payments

Divorce decree is issued or modified:	
In 2018 or earlier	In 2019 or later
• Income to Payee	• Not income to Payee
• Deductible by Payer	• Not deductible by Payer

Child Support and Property Settlements

Payments for child support and property settlements are **exempt from taxation** and are thus **not deductible** by the payer. Because divorce settlements are not taxable, the recipient spouse assumes the payer spouse's carryover basis and holding period for the property.

1.07 Adjustments for (to) AGI (Continued)

Contributions to Retirement Plans

Any taxpayer with earned income is generally entitled to establish and make contributions to an **Individual Retirement Account** (IRA). They can do so even if they are actively participating in other pension or profit-sharing plans. For purposes of eligibility for the IRA, earned income includes:

- Salaries and wages
- Net self-employment income

Contributions are limited for 2022 to $6,000 ($12,000 MFJ) per year, per individual (+$1,000 for individuals 50+). A married couple filing a joint return can establish and contribute $6,000 ($7,000 50+) each to separate IRAs as long as the earned income of the couple is at least $12,000 ($14,000 if both 50+). IRAs come in **two basic varieties:**

- Traditional
- Roth

Traditional IRAs

Contributions to a traditional IRA are **deductible** in arriving at AGI *unless both* of the following conditions apply:

- The individual is actively participating in another pension or profit-sharing plan, and
- AGI exceeds a threshold amount ($78,000 single, $129,000 MFJ for 2022).

For a married couple, if the individual is not actively participating in another plan but the individual's spouse *is* a participant, contributions for the nonparticipating spouse cannot be deducted if the joint AGI exceeds $214,000 for 2022.

Withdrawals from a traditional IRA are fully taxable (except to recover nondeductible contributions made earlier).

Roth IRAs

Contributions to a *Roth IRA* are **not deductible**. The benefit of a Roth IRA is that all withdrawals after the age of 59 ½ are exempt from taxation (as long as the Roth IRA has been in effect for at least 5 years), including both contributions and earnings. Withdrawals of contributions are exempt from taxation in all cases.

The full contribution limit for Roth IRAs applies to taxpayers with modified AGI below $129,000 ($204,000 MFJ) for 2022. The allowed contribution amount is reduced above these thresholds. Roth IRAs are not available if the taxpayer's modified AGI exceeds, for 2022, $144,000 ($214,000 MFJ).

Individual Taxation

Early Withdrawal Penalties

Withdrawals from either type of IRA prior to the **age of 59½** may result in a tax **penalty of 10%** of the amount withdrawn (in addition to the inclusion in gross income). The **penalty** does **not** apply (but amounts withdrawn from a traditional IRA are still included in gross income) when the withdrawal is the result of:

- Payment of deductible **medical expenses**
- Payment of qualified higher **education** costs
- **Death** or disability of the participant
- First time purchase of a **home** (up to $10,000 withdrawal)
- The **birth** or adoption of a child (up to $5,000 withdrawal)

	Traditional IRA	Roth IRA
Contribution Limit?	$6,000 (+$1,000 catch-up contribution for > age 50) Limited to taxable compensation	
Contributions Deductible?	Yes	No
Contribution Deadline?	Filing deadline (no extensions) – eg, April 15	
Income Limit?	No	< $144,000 ($214,000 MFJ) - 2022
Withdrawals Generally Taxable?	Yes	No
	10% penalty for distributions prior to age 59 ½	
Required Minimum Distributions (RMDs)?	Yes, at age 72	No

Contributions to Education Savings Accounts

Contributions of up to **$2,000 per year** can be made on behalf of any beneficiary (even someone unrelated to the contributor) under the age of 18 to **Coverdell Education Savings Accounts (ESA)** (formerly known as *education IRAs*).

- Contributions are *not deductible*, but amounts may be withdrawn free of taxation to pay elementary, middle, high school and college expenses (including tuition, fees, books, room and board) of the beneficiary.
- Amounts not spent by the time the beneficiary reaches the age of 30 are distributed to the beneficiary and subject to taxation and penalties. However, unspent amounts may be transferred to the ESA of another family member of the same generation without taxation or penalties.

- Contributions can be made up to the due date of the return (not including extensions).

Qualified Tuition Programs (QTP – 529 plans) were set up to allow a taxpayer to make *nondeductible* contributions to be used for qualified higher education* (undergraduate and graduate level).

- Earnings accumulate tax free as long as the money stays in the plan and is used for educational purposes.
- Educational purposes include tuition, room and board, books, supplies, fees, computer hardware, software, peripherals and internet access.
- There is a federal *penalty of 10%* if the funds are withdrawn for noneducational purposes.
- Two types of plans include either a *Prepaid program* (paid to the school) or a *Savings account plan*.
- Can contribute up to annual gift tax exclusion ($16,000 for 2022) or file an election that allows contributions larger than the exclusion amount to be taken into account ratably over 5 years (eg, $75,000, as long as no further gifts to the same person for the next 5 years - $16,000 per year).
- No AGI phase-out limitation exists, and taxpayers can contribute to a Coverdell ESA and a QTP for the same beneficiary during the same year.
- Up to $10,000 of distributions from a 529 plan may be used, per student, for elementary or secondary school tuition expenses.

Other Contributions

An **ABLE account** is a tax-advantaged savings account available to the disabled.

- Similar to a 529 plan, *nondeductible* contributions may be made to an ABLE account on behalf of a disabled beneficiary, and the earnings in the account accumulate tax free as long as the money is spent on qualifying expenses for the beneficiary.
- Qualifying expenses include education, housing, transportation, and assistive technology.
- Funds held in an ABLE account do not count for the purposes of means testing for the receipt of various government disability benefits.
- Contributions are limited to the annual gift tax exclusion ($16,000 for 2022), plus (through 2025) contributions from the designated beneficiary up to the lesser of their compensation for the year or the amount equal to the poverty line for a one-person household. The designated beneficiary may claim the saver's credit with respect to the contributions they make.
- Through 2025, rollovers from 529 plans may be made to ABLE accounts (within annual contribution limits) for the same designated beneficiary or a family member of the designated beneficiary.

Other retirement contributions that may be deducted from gross income include:

- **Keogh plans** (ie, qualified plans, which include defined contribution plans and defined benefit plans, but most are defined contribution plans)
- **Simplified employee pensions (SEPs)**

- Up to lesser of 25% of compensation or $61,000 (2022)
- SIMPLE plans

These plans are established by business owners. On an individual return, contributions on behalf of the owner are deducted from gross income in arriving at AGI, while contributions on behalf of employees of the owner are claimed as ordinary business deductions in the computation of net business profit or loss.

The deduction for contributions to a defined-contribution **Keogh** plan for the self-employed individual is limited to **25% of net** self-employment income after the Keogh deduction and the self-employment tax deduction (this works out to 20% of self-employment income before the Keogh deduction). For instance, if the client has $100,000 self-employment income before making a Keogh contribution, the maximum allowable deduction is $20,000, and net self-employment income is $80,000. The maximum contribution allowed (as opposed to the deduction allowed for tax purposes) to a Keogh plan is the lesser of $61,000 (2022), or 100% of earned income. Contributions in excess of the deduction allowed for the year may be carried forward.

SIMPLE plans (**S**avings **I**ncentive **M**atch **Pl**an for **E**mployees) allow voluntary contributions up to $14,000 (2022) per year by each employee and by the individual employer, up to 100% of income. Withdrawals within 2 years are subject to a 25% tax penalty instead of the usual 10%.

*E*arly Withdrawal penalty

A premature interest withdrawal penalty (eg, from a CD) is deductible.

Jury *D*uty

The fee received for jury duty is always included in gross income, but the amount is deductible for AGI if the payment is remitted to the taxpayer's employer.

Health Savings Accounts (HSAs)

Contributions to Health Savings Account (HSA) may be deducted by a self-employed taxpayer or employee (Form 8889 must be filed).

- Taxpayer must have high-deductible health plan (HDHP). Deductible must be at least $1,400 (2022) for self-only coverage and $2,800 (2022) for family coverage.
- Contribution is limited to lesser of deductible or limit of $3,650 in 2022 for self-only and $7,300 in 2022 for family.
- Taxpayers 55 or older may increase limit by $1,000.
- Amounts contributed by employer are excluded from W-2 gross income but reduce amount that employee can contribute.
- Distributions from HSA tax free if used for qualified medical expenses (those that would have normally been deductible on Schedule A for itemizers, excluding premiums on the HDHP itself).
- Schedule A deduction cannot be claimed for expenses paid from the HSA.

- Distributions that are not used for medical expenses are subject to taxation and 20% penalty. No penalty if distributions are made after the account beneficiary dies, becomes disabled, or turns 65.
- Unused amounts at year end may be rolled over (ie, from 2020 to 2021 and 2021 to 2022).

Farm Income

- Schedule F – similar to Schedule C
- Accounting methods include:
  - Cash, Accrual, Crop method (Cost of producing the crop is deducted in the year the crop income is realized) or the Hybrid/combination method may be used if show income and is used consistently.
    - If cash method is used for figuring income, must be used for reporting expenses.
    - If accrual method is used for reporting expenses, must be used for figuring income.
- Income Items (farmers may elect to average farm income over 3 years)
  - Schedule F Income (subject to SE tax):
    - Raised livestock, produce, and grains held for sale
    - Livestock and other items bought for resale
  - Form 4797 Income (Not subject to SE tax):
    - Animals not held primarily for sale
    - Livestock held for draft, breeding, dairy or sporting purposes
    - Gains from sales of farmland or depreciable farm equipment
- Expense Items
  - Car and truck expense, chemicals and pesticides, depreciation and Section 179 deductions, feed purchased, fertilizers, mortgage interest, seeds and plants. Reasonable wages paid to children, meals to feed workers.
- Depreciation (discussed in another section)
  - Section 179 deduction allows farmers to immediately expense new and used machinery and equipment, milk tanks, livestock (eg, horses, cattle, hogs, sheep, goats, mink and other fur-bearing animals), single-purpose agricultural structures (constructed to house, raise and feed livestock) and horticultural structures (greenhouse), as well as bulk-storage facilities.

Charity

 There is a temporary **$300 ($600 MFJ) above-the-line** (ie, for AGI) charitable deduction for those who do not itemize through 2022.

1.08 Standard & Itemized Deductions

Standard Deduction

The IRS gives every taxpayer a standard deduction based on filing status ($12,950 single /$25,900 MFJ/ $19,400 HOH).

- If being *claimed as a dependent* of another, the standard deduction is the greater of $1,150 (2022) or earned income plus $400, never to exceed the regular standard deduction.

- If elderly *65 or older* and/or blind, additional deductions of $1,400 to $1,750 (2022).

- A taxpayer may claim a standard deduction where the amount depends on filing status. This is an **alternative** to claiming itemized deductions. The amount of the standard deduction based on filing status may be increased if the taxpayer (and/or spouse if MFJ) reached their 65th birthday during the tax year, and it may be increased further if the taxpayer (and/or spouse) is legally blind. The highest standard deduction would result from a married couple filing jointly if both taxpayer and spouse are at least 65 and both are legally blind.

> The dollar amounts of the standard deductions are indexed for inflation and change on an annual basis. The CPA exam consistently avoids testing amounts that change each year.

Itemized Deductions (Schedule A) (COmMITT)

Charitable contributions

- **Charitable contributions to qualified organizations** are generally deductible to the extent the taxpayer has provided cash or property that exceeds any value received from the charity. For example, if the taxpayer makes a contribution to their local public television station for $240 and receives books and videos worth $60 as thanks, the actual charitable contribution is only $180.

  Note: Amounts paid in exchange for the rights to purchase seats at a college athletic event are no longer deductible.

    o If donations of *$250 or more* are given, written substantiation from the donee organization is required.

    o Donations are deductible in the year the charity receives the funds. (Contributions made by credit card are deductible when they are charged.)

    o Ordinary payments to charitable organizations for services rendered (eg, school tuition paid to a parochial school) are not contributions.

    o Donations to qualified organizations only (ie, donations to needy individuals are not deductible.)

- *Volunteer services* to a charitable organization may not be deducted except for out-of-pocket costs incurred in the performance of the volunteer work (such as *transportation expenses* between home and the site of the work – (**Mileage, Parking & Tolls**).

- Contributions of **property** are normally subject to **two rules**:
  - **Ordinary Income Rule** – Property is ordinary income property if its sale at FMV on the date it was contributed would have resulted in ordinary income or in short-term capital gain. This includes inventory, self-created works of art, and capital assets held for ≤ 1 year. The amount you can deduct is its FMV minus the amount that would be ordinary income or short-term capital gain if you sold the property for its FMV. Generally, this rule limits the deduction to the **lower** of the **tax basis** in the property or the **FMV** on the date of the contribution.
  - **Long-Term Capital Gain Rule** – Property is capital gain property if its sale at FMV on the date of the contribution would have resulted in a long-term capital gain. Long-term capital gain property includes nonbusiness capital assets held more than 1 year and inherited assets (considered long-term regardless of holding period) that have increased in value, such as stocks, bonds, personal items (clothes, furniture, autos). This allows the taxpayer to claim the **higher FMV** of long-term capital gains property. The deduction of such property is limited to **30% of AGI** in a tax year.

Assume a taxpayer with AGI of $100,000 donates stock to a qualified charity. The stock was purchased 10 years ago for $10,000 and was worth $40,000 on the date of the contribution. Since it qualifies as long-term capital gain property, the taxpayer may claim the FMV of $40,000, except that this exceeds 30% of AGI, so the deduction in the tax year is limited to $30,000 (ie, $100,000 AGI × 30% limitation). The remaining $10,000 can be carried forward.

- Overall contributions are generally limited to **50% of AGI**.

TCJA increased the limitation for **cash contributions** donated to public charities to 60% of AGI through 2025 (however, this limitation was temporarily increased to 100% of AGI for 2021).

- Contributions exceeding any of the AGI limitations may be **carried forward up to five years**.

Other Miscellaneous Expenses

- Gambling losses are deductible as an itemized deduction to the extent of winnings. Note: Gambling winnings are reported in income separately on Form 1040.
- Excess losses may not be carried over.
- Professional gamblers can deduct nonwagering business expenses on Schedule C.
  - For 2018 – 2025, gambling losses include any expense incurred in connection with a gambling activity for *any individual taxpayer* (not just professionals) if such expense would otherwise be allowed as a deduction. This means other related expenses incurred (eg, the individual's travel expense to and from a casino), in addition to the cost of wagers, are also deductible, *up to gambling winnings*.

- Estate taxes on income in respect of a decedent (IRD).
- Miscellaneous itemized deductions subject to 2-percent of AGI limitation have been suspended for 2018 – 2025 (ie, they will not be deductible again until 2026). See the "Prior Law" box below for a list of items no longer currently deductible.

Prior Law

Miscellaneous Expenses (**BIT**) Subject to 2% of AGI Limitation

- *B*usiness expenses of an *Employee* (eg, mileage, travel, AICPA and Union dues, CPE/Job education, Uniforms, home office expense, etc.)
- *I*nvestment expenses (eg, Safety deposit box; investment advisory fees and newsletters; and IRA custodial fees if paid separately and contributions do not cover the fees)
- *T*ax preparation and Attorney fees (with respect to *taxable* income)

Medical expenses – paid and not reimbursed

 A 7.5% of AGI limitation applies.

- Deductible expenses include:
  - Most medical services (eg, hospitals, doctors, dentists, nurses, labs, eye exams, x-rays, etc.)
    - Generally, nothing cosmetic, unless for **specific injury, illness, or birth defect**
  - Most medical goods/devices (eg, hearing aid and batteries, prescription glasses and contacts, crutches, wheelchair, etc.)
  - Health insurance premiums (except to the extent they've already been claimed for self-employed taxpayers in arriving at AGI or were paid out of HSAs with tax-free funds)
  - Long-term care insurance premiums on qualified policies
  - **Transportation costs** for medical and dental care (ie, actual expenses for cab, bus, ambulance, personal vehicle, etc. or mileage, tolls and parking)
  - Prescription drugs and insulin
    - Minus insurance reimbursement in year received
  - Costs to install **medically prescribed facilities** in a home, such as a swimming pool for physical therapy to treat a specific medical condition or an elevator, to the extent the costs exceed the increase in the value of the home resulting from the addition
- Examples of **nondeductible expenses** tested on previous exams include:
  - Nonprescription drugs and medicines
  - Costs for general health improvement that are not treatments for specific medical conditions

- Premiums on life insurance and policies to cover loss of earnings from injuries and illnesses
- Plastic surgery, except to cure disfiguring illnesses, injuries, or birth defects
- Medicare portion of social security and self-employment taxes

- Costs must be paid by the taxpayer (or spouse) during the tax year, but may be payments on behalf of the taxpayer, spouse, a dependent, or **other people for whom the taxpayer provides over 50% of support**, even if they do not qualify as dependents because the *income or joint return* tests are not satisfied.
- Medical expenses paid for a deceased spouse or dependent are deductible as medical expenses in the year paid, regardless of whether they were paid before or after the decedent's death, provided the individual qualified as the taxpayer's spouse or dependent either at the time the expenses were incurred or at the time payment was made.
- Reimbursements by insurance must be subtracted from deductible expenses.
- Payments made by credit card are considered to have been made in the period they are charged to the credit card, not in the period in which the taxpayer pays the credit card balance.

*I*nterest paid

Interest on investments or personal residences may be claimed as itemized deductions. Note: Interest related to a business is claimed as a business deduction in arriving at net business profit or loss on Schedule C and is part of the reported gross income.

- **Investment interest expense**—refers to interest paid on borrowings that are used to make personal investments, such as margin loans in the purchase of stock.
    - Deductible to extent of net investment income (*Schedule B*)
    - Unused carried forward indefinitely
    - Interest paid in advance is not deductible in the period paid, even by a cash basis taxpayer; it is required to be allocated over the tax years to which it applies.
- Mortgage loan interest
    - The deduction for home mortgage interest has been limited to interest incurred on **acquisition indebtedness up to $750,000** for 2018 to 2025. The new limitation only applies to debt incurred after December 15, 2017. Refinancing a mortgage that was incurred prior to this date will be treated as if incurred on the original date of indebtedness and, thus, will be grandfathered in under the old rules as well.

> Home Mortgage = $750,000
> (2 homes)
> Equity = $0, unless "acquisition indebtedness"

- *Acquisition indebtedness* means debt used to *buy, build*, or *substantially improve* the home that secures the loan. Includes loans that replace previous acquisition indebtedness.

Individual Taxation REG 1

- Interest on home equity indebtedness that is not considered acquisition indebtedness has been eliminated for 2018 – 2025.
- May be claimed on both a primary and secondary residence.
- Includes **"points"** paid on a loan to acquire the residence (deductible immediately) or points paid on other qualified personal residence loans (deductible by amortization over the life of the loan).
- Home equity loan interest is not deductible unless the loan is considered acquisition indebtedness.

Prior Law
Home Mortgage = $1,000,000 (2 homes)
Equity = $100,000 regardless of use

For example, in January year 1, a taxpayer takes out a $500,000 mortgage to purchase a main home with a FMV of $800,000. In February year 1, the taxpayer takes out a $250,000 home equity loan to put an addition on the main home. Both loans are secured by the main home, and the total does not exceed the cost of the home, so all the interest is deductible since the total of both loans ($500,000 + $250,000) does not exceed the $750,000 limitation.

Now assume that the taxpayer uses the $250,000 home equity loan to purchase a vacation home instead. Since the loan is secured by the main home and not the vacation home, the interest on the home equity loan would not be deductible. However, if the taxpayer takes out a separate loan that is secured by the vacation home, then the interest on that loan would be deductible as acquisition indebtedness.

Taxes paid

If a taxpayer itemizes, certain taxes may be deducted on Schedule A (subject to limits for 2018–2025):

- State and local **personal property taxes** (eg, registration on a car—a tax based on the value of the vehicle would be deductible, but not standard fees.)
- State and local **real estate property taxes** (must be the owner of the property—joint tenancy is okay)
  - Taxes due in a year in which the property is sold are apportioned between the buyer and seller on a daily basis within the real property tax year.
  - Assessments for improvements (eg, streets, sewers) are not deductible but are added to the basis of the property.
- State, local, or foreign **income taxes**
  - Foreign income taxes paid may be claimed as a credit or deduction, but not both.
  - For people who live in one of nine states with no state taxes, state and local **sales taxes** (based on actual amount paid or an IRS table) may be deducted INSTEAD of state and local income taxes.
- Fees, Fines, Federal, FICA, **FORGET IT!!**

- There is no deduction for taxes paid to the federal government or for gas or excise taxes.
- Fees charged by state and local governments may not be deducted unless they are based specifically on income or property values.

- The deduction for state and local income and property taxes paid is limited to a total of $10,000 ($5,000 MFS) for 2018 through 2025. Also, deductions for foreign real property taxes will not be allowed during this time. These limitations do not apply to taxes paid in connection with a trade or business.

Theft & Casualty losses

The deduction for *personal* casualty losses is now generally limited to losses attributable to *federally declared disasters* for 2018 through 2025. This limitation does not apply to the extent the taxpayer has personal casualty gains; that is, *any* personal casualty loss may be deducted to the extent of the personal casualty gain.

Eligible personal **casualty losses that exceed 10% of AGI** may be deducted on Schedule A. A casualty loss is a *sudden event* (eg, theft or destruction) that causes the taxpayer to lose an asset or for its value to seriously drop over the course of a time period not exceeding 30 days. Accidental breakage of items in the home by family members is not considered a casualty event. Progressive deterioration is also not included (eg, *termite, moth, or drought damage*).

The loss is measured by the **drop in FMV** caused by the event but is limited to the **tax basis** of the asset. Costs incurred by the taxpayer to repair damaged property increase the tax basis of the property, but do not affect the drop in FMV loss measurement.

> Assume the taxpayer purchased their home for $100,000, it was worth $200,000 prior to a fire caused by a federally declared disaster, and the fire reduced the property's value to $120,000. The taxpayer spent $50,000 to repair the damage resulting from the fire. The drop in FMV from the event was $200,000 - $120,000 = $80,000. The tax basis of the property is $100,000 + $50,000 = $150,000. The loss that may be claimed is $80,000, the lower of the loss in FMV ($80,000) or tax basis ($150,000).
>
> Now assume all the same facts, except that the taxpayer bought the home for $10,000 in an auction. In this case, the taxpayer's basis in the property is $10,000 + $50,000 = $60,000. Thus, even though the loss in FMV is still $80,000, the loss that may be claimed is limited to the taxpayer's $60,000 basis.

Once the loss is determined, it must be reduced by **all** of the following:

- Insurance and government **reimbursements** that the taxpayer is entitled to receive (if reimbursements exceed the loss, an involuntary conversion gain has occurred).
- **$100 per event**
- **10% of AGI per year**

Carryover Rules		
	Carryback	Carryforward
Charitable Contributions	No	5 years
Net Operating Losses (NOL)	No	Indefinitely
Net Capital Losses: Corporations (0 net Cap. loss)	3 years	5 years
Net Capital Losses: Individuals ($3,000)	No	Indefinitely
Investment Interest	No	Indefinitely
Net Passive Losses	No	Indefinitely, or may be claimed when the investment is sold
Net Gambling Losses	No	No

1.09 Dependents & Filing Status

Personal Exemptions

The deduction for personal exemptions (including dependency exemptions) under IRC Section 151 is reduced to $0 for 2018 – 2025. This reduction will NOT affect any other deduction, credit, etc., based on the rules for determining a dependent under IRC Section 152 (below).

Dependents

Dependent if all requirements met for "Qualifying Relative" or "Qualifying Child":

- Qualifying Child – **JARRS**
  - No **J**oint Return with spouse
    - Unless filing only to get a total refund of taxes withheld or paid and weren't actually required to file.
  - **A**ge – A qualifying child, unless disabled, must be:
    - Under age 19, or 24 if a full-time student for at least 5 months of the year, and
    - Younger than the taxpayer or the taxpayer's spouse.
  - **R**elationship – Taxpayer's child, stepchild, foster child, sibling, step sibling, half sibling, or a descendant of any such individual (eg, nephew or grandchild).
  - **R**esidency – Child must live with the taxpayer more than half the year in the U.S.
  - **S**upport – Child must NOT have provided more than 50% of their own support, not including scholarships. (So, the taxpayer DOESN'T need to support over 50%.)

- *Qualifying* Relative - **C-IRS-J**ack you
  - **C**itizenship or Resident
    - U.S. citizen or
    - Resident of U.S., Mexico, or Canada.
  - **I**ncome – Limited to $4,400 for 2022
    - Social security ignored
  - **R**elative; or unrelated and a Household member for *entire year*
    - The following relatives don't have to live with taxpayer:
      - Children, stepchildren, foster children, or a descendant or spouse of any of them (eg, grandchildren and son-in-law) that do not qualify as a "qualifying child"
      - Siblings, including in-laws and half and step-siblings, and their descendants.
      - Parents, including step-parents and in-laws, or other direct ancestors.
      - Aunts and uncles, but does NOT include cousins.

Individual Taxation   REG 1

- Neither death nor divorce will dissolve any of the relationships established by marriage.
  - **Support** – Taxpayer must provide over 50% of total annual support.
    - Includes tax-exempt items like Social Security, AFDC
    - Multiple support agreement
      - If more than one person supports individual, but no one person pays more than 50%, can be dependent of any person who paid at least 10%.
  - No Joint Return (same as qualifying child rule)

Filing Status

On every return, the taxpayer(s) must select the filing status, which is used to determine the tax rates on income and the value of various deductions, thresholds, and limitations. In selecting the status, the following choices should be considered in order, using the first one for which all requirements are satisfied:

- Married Filing Jointly (MFJ)
  - Determined on last day of year or at time of death.
  - If divorced during year, not MFJ.
  - Taxpayers are considered unmarried for the whole year if, on the last day of the year, they are divorced or are legally separated under a divorce or legal separate maintenance decree.
  - Includes *same-sex married couples*, not registered domestic partnerships or civil unions (*Obergefell v. Hodges*); thus, any rules that apply to MFJ/MFS also apply to same-sex married individuals.
- Married Filing Separately (MFS)
  - Each spouse files their own return.
  - In community property state, everything is split 50/50.
- Qualifying widow (Surviving Spouse – SS) *with a dependent child*
  - Spouse died in prior 2 years and qualified to file a joint return in year of death
  - Provided over 50% of cost of maintaining principal residence of dependent child (or stepchild)
  - Not remarried as of end of current year
  - Same rate as MFJ
- Head of household (HOH) – To qualify – Both:
  - Taxpayer **not married** at year end (or considered unmarried because spouse left 6 months before year end), **and**
  - Taxpayer must **maintain** a **home** as the principal place of residence for over 50% of the year and provide more than 50% of costs of maintaining a household for:

- **Dependent "Qualifying Relative" living with the taxpayer,** including uncle, aunt, nephew, niece or certain step-relatives and in-laws. Other relatives and unrelated persons may be dependents if they live with taxpayer for the entire year, but NOT qualify them as HOH.
- **"Qualifying Child,"** stepchild, or grandchild living with the taxpayer (Must be a dependent. Note: Custodial parent who has released the right to claim the dependency exemption to the noncustodial parent by filing Form 8332 may still qualify for HOH status. Form 8332 does not qualify noncustodial parent for HOH status.)
- **Parent** must be a dependent but need not live with the taxpayer.

- **Single** - all others
  - Includes those who are married but legally separated under a decree of separate maintenance.

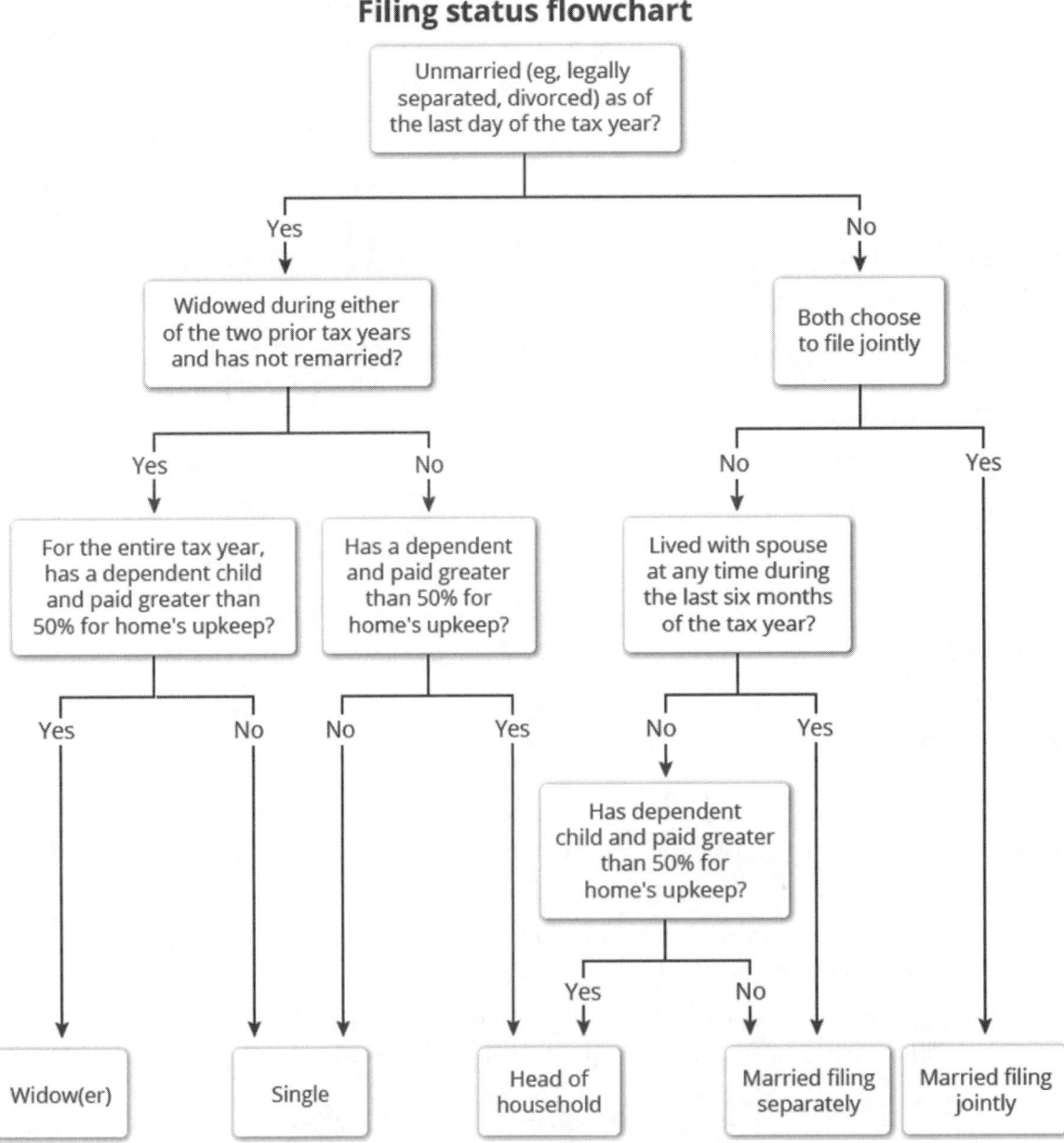

Filing status flowchart

1.10 Tax Credits & Other Taxes

Tax Credits

There are a few different credits **(dollar-for-dollar reduction of taxes payable)** related to having children and other dependents.

Family Tax Credit

- TCJA set the child tax credit at **$2,000 per qualifying child under age 17** for 2018 – 2025.
- The $2,000 child tax credit is phased out by $50 for each $1,000 (or fraction thereof) by which the taxpayer's MAGI exceeds $400,000 on a joint return, or $200,000 in all other cases.
- Once the amount of the allowable child tax credit is determined, that amount can be increased by **$500 for each U.S. citizen/resident dependent** that does not qualify as a child dependent; thus, the provision is collectively referred to as the "family tax credit."
- There is also a provision known as the "additional child tax credit" for certain low-income taxpayers with one or more qualifying children when the taxpayer is not able to claim the full child tax credit for each child (because their tax liability is less than the available credit). The maximum amount that is refundable is $1,400 per qualifying child (inflation adjusted after 2018).

    Note, however, that the actual amount of the refundable credit is determined under a somewhat complicated formula based on a number of factors, such as earned income and number of children and is, thus, beyond the scope of the CPA exam.

Child & Dependent Care Credit

- A child and **dependent care credit** is available if the taxpayer requires care for a child under age 13 or a disabled dependent in order to be gainfully employed. The credit is based on the smallest of three amounts:
    - Actual dependent care expenses
    - Earned income
    - $3,000 (for care of one dependent) or $6,000 (for care of multiple dependents)
- For married couples, the earned income limit is based on the income of the lower-paid spouse. If, however, one of the couple is gainfully employed and the other is a full-time student, the limit is based on the earned income of the spouse who is gainfully employed.
- The credit percentage is between 20% and 35%, depending on the AGI of the taxpayer. For taxpayers with AGI over $43,000, the credit is the minimum of 20%.
- A taxpayer may claim the child and dependent care credit (if all other applicable requirements are met) for a child who lives with the taxpayer for more than half the year, even if the taxpayer does not provide more than half the cost of maintaining the household.

- Any benefits received under an employer dependent care assistance plan and excluded from income must be subtracted from the maximum allowed credit before the percentage is applied.

Adoption Credit

The adoption credit is available for costs incurred in adopting a child under the age of 18. The credit is limited for 2022 to the first $14,890 of costs. Credits exceeding the tax liability may be carried forward up to 5 years. Phaseout exists.

Education Credits

- There are **two different credits** associated with the payment of **tuition and fees** to qualified educational institutions.
    - The **American Opportunity Tax Credit** – AOTC applies to the first 4 years of post-secondary school (ie, post-high school) education. The credit is equal to 100% of the first $2,000 and 25% of the next $2,000 in payments, for a maximum credit of **$2,500 per student**. The credit may be claimed by a taxpayer for tuition, textbooks and fees of the taxpayer, spouse, or dependent, and may be claimed for payments on behalf of each student in the family. The credit is also 40% refundable ($1,000).
    - The **lifetime learning credit** applies to any year of education and can include tuition paid to a qualified institution for education to improve job skills. The credit is equal to 20% of the first $10,000 paid on behalf of all family members, for a maximum credit of **$2,000 per family**.
- There are several restrictions placed on both credits, including:
    - The credits generally apply only to **tuition and fees** paid to qualified institutions, and no other costs. Taxpayer must have valid Form 1098-T from the institution.
    - The credits are not available to individual taxpayers with modified AGI exceeding certain amounts.
    - The credit cannot be claimed on the tax return of the dependent.
    - Cannot claim both AOTC and a Lifetime learning credit for the same student in the same year.
    - Cannot be MFS.

Saver's Credit

- The **saver's credit** is available for low to moderate income workers to enable and encourage them to make voluntary contributions to IRAs and 401(k) plans. The amount of the credit is up to $1,000 ($2,000 MFJ) for making contributions to an IRA or an employer-sponsored retirement plan.
- The credit may be claimed by:
    - MFJ with income up to $68,000 in 2022.
    - HOH with income up to $51,000 in 2022.
    - Single and MFS with income up to $34,000 in 2022.

Individual Taxation

- The amount of the credit can range from 10% to 50% of the amount of IRA contribution made based on income and filing status (Form 8880).

Foreign Tax Credit

The foreign tax credit is available for payments of foreign income taxes that are not being claimed as itemized deductions. The calculation of the credit is identical to that for corporations.

- One special exception for individuals, however, allows the taxpayer to claim a credit for up to **$300** ($600 on a joint return) for foreign income taxes paid on investment income without being subject to any other limits. This enables a taxpayer whose mutual fund had withholdings on foreign dividends to claim a credit for the taxes paid by the mutual fund without the need for complicated computations.
- Credit is limited to portion of U.S. tax on foreign income.
- The credit can be carried back 1 year and forward 10 years.

Credit for Elderly or Disabled

The credit for the elderly or disabled is available only to those *age 65 and older* or those who are *retired on permanent and total disability*. Such individuals must have AGI less than $17,500 (or $25,000 MFJ if both spouses qualify) and nontaxable Social Security or its equivalent less than $5,000 ($7,500 MFJ).

Earned Income Credit (EIC)

- If a taxpayer has some form of earned income, they may qualify for this **refundable credit.** Earned income for purposes of calculating EIC only includes taxable income.
- Since the EIC is a refundable credit, the excess of the credit over the tax liability is payable to the taxpayer in the form of a tax refund. In essence, a refundable credit is treated similarly to a payment of estimated tax or taxes withheld.
- A qualifying child does not have to meet the support test. Also, a qualifying child must have lived with the taxpayer in the United States for more than half the year and have a social security number that is valid for employment in the United States.
- If investment income is greater than $10,300 for 2022, the credit is denied.

 ARPA increased the investment income limit for the EIC to $10,300. The amount will be adjusted for inflation after 2021.

In general, tax credits may be offset, dollar for dollar, against a tax liability in the period to which the credit applies. When the amount of the credit exceeds the amount of applicable tax due, unused credits can be carried back or forward, depending on the provisions of the credit. They may only be used, however, to reduce taxes and, with the exception of refundable credits such as the EIC, cannot result in a refund to the taxpayer.

Other Taxes

Self-Employment Taxes (Schedule SE)

Individuals are subject to self-employment taxes on **net self-employment income**. This includes all business revenue reduced by all ordinary and necessary business expenses (except retirement plan contributions on behalf of the taxpayer).

- Tax rate double FICA rate
    - 6.2% OASDI (ie, Social Security) tax on amounts up to $147,000 for 2022
    - 1.45% Medicare (ie, Hospital Insurance—HI) tax—no maximum
        - Total 7.65% × 2 = 15.3%
    - 50% claimed as deduction for AGI.

    Note: Since ½ the self-employment tax is deductible, self-employment income must be multiplied by 92.35% (ie, 100% − 7.65% deductible portion of SE tax) before it is multiplied by the 15.3% SE tax rate to determine the SE tax due.

Increased Medicare Tax Rate (HI rate) for High-Income Earners

The Medicare tax rate is increased by 0.9% for individual taxpayers earning in excess of the threshold levels ($250,000 MFJ and $200,000 all others).

- For employees, the new rate is 2.35% (1.45% + 0.9%) on amounts in excess of the thresholds.
- For self-employed individuals, the rate is increased from 2.9% to 3.8% on amounts in excess of the thresholds.

Surtax on Unearned Income

A surtax called the **Unearned Income Medicare Contribution Tax** is imposed on the *unearned income* of individuals, estates, and trusts. This is part of the Patient Protection and Affordable Care Act (PPACA). For individuals, the surtax is **3.8%** of the **lesser of**:

1. The taxpayer's **net** investment income
    - "Net" investment income is investment income reduced by allowable investment expenses. Investment income includes interest income, dividends, annuities, royalties, rents (other than those derived from a trade or business), capital gains (other than those derived from a trade or business), trade or business income that is a passive activity with respect to the taxpayer, and trade or business income with respect to the trading of financial instruments or commodities. Retirement plan distributions are excluded. **OR**
2. The excess of modified adjusted gross income (MAGI), which is AGI before any foreign earned income exclusion, over the threshold amount **($250,000 for MFJ/SS)**, $125,000 for a married individual filing a separate return (MFS), and **$200,000** for all others)
    - This effectively makes the tax rate on L/T capital gains and qualified dividends 23.8% (20% + 3.8%) for high-income taxpayers ($517,200 MFJ, $459,750 single - 2022). Still applies if income under high-income threshold but over $250k, but rate would be 15% + 3.8% = 18.8%.

Roger and Louisa have investment income of $40,000 and MAGI of $300,000. The net investment income of $40,000 is lower than the excess of MAGI over the $250,000 threshold ($300,000 - $250,000 = $50,000). Therefore, they will be taxed on the lower amount of $40,000 vs $50,000, which is $40,000 × 3.8% = $1,520. If investment income had been $75,000, then they would be taxed on the lower of $50,000 vs. $75,000, or $50,000 × 3.8% = $1,900.

Note: Your **marginal tax rate** is the rate at which your last and your next dollar of taxable income are taxed. Your **effective rate** is the average rate of taxation for all your dollars (total tax / total taxable income).

REG 2
Corporate Taxation

REG 2: Corporate Taxation

2.01 C Corporation Overview	1
2.02 Formation of a C Corporation	2
2.03 Income & Ordinary Deductions	7
REVENUES	7
DEDUCTIONS	8
2.04 Charity, NOL & DRD Deductions	13
DEDUCTIONS (CONTINUED)	13
2.05 Penalty Taxes & Credits	17
ACCUMULATED EARNINGS TAX (AET)	17
PERSONAL HOLDING COMPANY (PHC) TAX	17
PERSONAL SERVICE CORPORATIONS (PSC)	18
FOREIGN TAX CREDIT	18
GENERAL BUSINESS CREDIT	19
2.06 Supplementary Schedules: M-1, M-2, M-3	21
M-1 RECONCILIATION OF BOOK INCOME TO TAXABLE INCOME	21
M-2 RECONCILIATION OF UNAPPROPRIATED BEG. RE TO END RE	21
M-3 RECONCILIATION OF FINANCIAL ACCOUNTING INCOME WITH TAXABLE INCOME	22
2.07 Corporate Distributions	26
NONLIQUIDATING DISTRIBUTIONS	26
STOCK REDEMPTIONS	27
LIQUIDATING DISTRIBUTIONS (TERMINATING THE CORPORATION)	27
CORPORATE REORGANIZATIONS	29
CONSOLIDATED RETURNS	30
2.08 Multijurisdictional Tax	31
STATE & LOCAL TAX ISSUES	31
INTERNATIONAL TAX ISSUES	32

2.01 C Corporation Overview

C Corporations are legal entities that are separate and distinct from its owners. They are formally created by filing Articles of incorporation. A corporation is taxed as a separate entity, and shareholders are generally taxed on corporate earnings that are distributed to them (ie, earnings are taxed twice).

- C Corporation
    - Created formally – Articles of incorporation
    - Limited Liability
    - Taxpaying entity (Form 1120)
    - Amended corporate return – 1120X
- 90% is GAAP which uses Accrual – rest are exceptions
    - **Calendar year** or **fiscal year**, which is chosen when the first tax return is filed. A **52-53-week** tax year is a fiscal tax year that varies from 52 to 53 weeks and ends on the same day (but does not have to end on the last day of a month).

 Return due dates and extensions are no longer tested on the CPA Exam.

Corporate Income Tax (1120)
Gross income (worldwide)
– Ordinary deductions
Income before "special deductions"
– Charitable deduction
– Net Operating Loss (NOL) Carryforward
– Div. Received Deduction (DRD)
Taxable Income
× 21% tax rate*
Gross Tax Liability
– Tax Credits (Foreign tax credit/gen bus credit)
Net Regular Tax Liability
+ Personal Holding Company (**PHC**) Tax
Tax Liability (self-assessed on 1120)
+ Accumulated Earnings Tax (**AET**), if audited
Total Corporate Tax Liability

*TCJA repealed the graduated tax rate system for corporations and instituted a flat 21% tax rate in its place.

Current versions of all Corporate tax forms can be found on the IRS website

2.02 Formation of a C Corporation

Formal (Articles of Incorporation)

No gain or loss is recognized if property is transferred to a corporation solely in exchange for stock and, immediately after the transfer, the transferors are in **control** of the corporation.

Tax-free exchange if contributors of cash and property gain 80% or more of the stock – control

- Cash or property 80% or more (control)
  - Tax free
  - Carryover basis
    - If property subject to debt, CV 40 –10 debt = 30 basis in stock
  - Carryover holding period
- **Services** (excluded from the definition of property) or **< 80% of stock**
  - Taxable income at FMV of stock
  - Wage expense for corporation
- If no control
  - Taxable to all parties, similar to services
- **Reorganizations** of corporation generally also tax free
  - Carryover basis

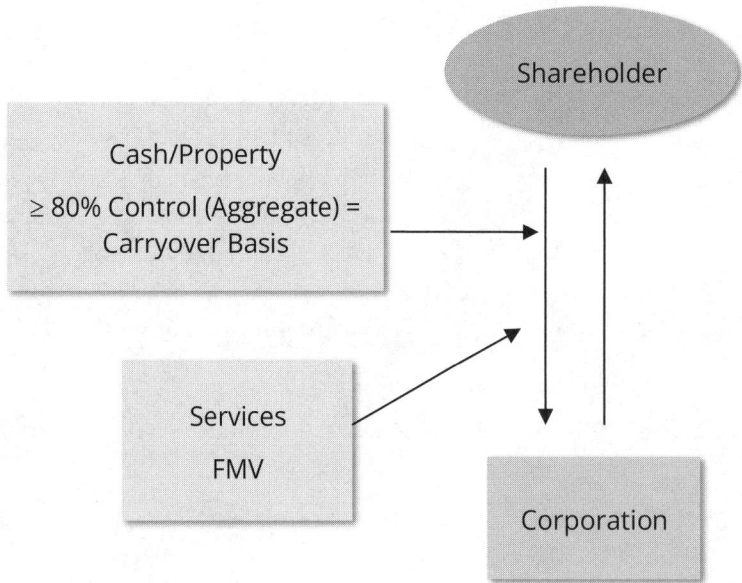

Shares issued for **cash** are handled in a straightforward manner: the shareholder's basis in the corporation is equal to the amount of cash paid.

Shares issued in exchange for the rendering of **services** to the corporation result in ordinary income to the service provider, since the shares are treated as compensation for the services. The service provider reports income equal to the estimated FMV of the shares.

> For example, if Saul Server is given 10% of the total outstanding shares of a company valued at $100,000 in exchange for Saul's services to the company, he will report $10,000 of ordinary income. This income is also subject to FICA or self-employment taxes, depending on whether Saul is considered an employee or independent contractor. His basis in the corporate stock is the same $10,000.

When a shareholder has contributed **property** to obtain stock, there are two possibilities as to the valuation of the investment:

- **Tax basis** of the property to the shareholder (80% or more—Control)
- **Fair market value** (FMV) at the date of contribution (less than 80%)

In most circumstances, Section 351 allows the *basis* of the property to be used, and FMV is ignored. For example, if land with an original cost to the shareholder of $100 and FMV of $300 is contributed, the shareholder will have a basis in the stock received of $100, and the corporation's basis in the land will be $100. As a result of this treatment, the transfer of the property is a *nontaxable* event to the shareholder as long as **80% or more** of the corporate stock is in the hands of shareholders that provided either cash or property to obtain their shares.

> Assume that a corporation is formed and 100 shares in total are issued to three different shareholders:
>
> - Carlos Cash paid $600 in cash to obtain 60 shares.
> - Paulette Property contributed land costing her $100 and valued at $300 for 30 shares.
> - Sadie Service received 10 shares in exchange for services.
>
> The total corporation was valued at $1,000 immediately after these actions.
>
> Carlos' 60 shares have a basis of $600, equal to the cash contributed. Sadie's 10 shares represent 10% of the total corporation, so Sadie's shares have a basis of $1,000 × 10% = $100, and Sadie must report ordinary income of $100 on her individual return. Since Carlos and Paulette (the shareholders contributing cash or property) received a combined 90% of the total shares, Paulette's 30 shares have a basis of $100, equal to the basis of the land she contributed, and the corporation has a tax basis of $100 in the land.

Although the tax basis of property is generally carried over from the shareholder to the corporation, a special rule applies to property contributions when **less than 80% (no Control)** of the total voting stock is in the hands of shareholders that contributed cash or property (meaning that more than 20% of the stock is in the hands of shareholders that received them in exchange for services). In such cases, the property contribution is reported at the *FMV* of the property on the date of contribution and is reported as a sale by the contributor.

Assume again that a corporation is formed and 100 shares in total are issued to three different shareholders. Carlos Cash paid $450 in cash to obtain 45 shares. Paulette Property contributed land costing her $100 and valued at $300 for 30 shares. Sadie Service received 25 shares in exchange for services. The total corporation was valued at $1,000 immediately after these actions.

Carlos' 45 shares have a basis of $450, equal to the cash contributed. Sadie's 25 shares represent 25% of the total corporation, so Sadie's shares have a basis of $1,000 × 25% = $250, and Sadie must report ordinary income of $250 on her individual return. Since Carlos and Paulette (the shareholders contributing cash or property) received a combined 75% of the total shares, Paulette's 30 shares have a basis of $300, equal to the FMV of the land she contributed, and the corporation has a tax basis of $300 in the land. Paulette must report a gain on sale of land of $200 on her individual tax return.

A corporation can be formed from an existing business operating in the form of a proprietorship or partnership. In such cases, the business interests transferred by the proprietor or partners are considered property, so the incorporation is nontaxable, and the assets and liabilities of the business are carried over to the corporation, as long as the owners of the previous business are given at least 80% of the voting stock of the corporation.

Nonrecognition of gain applies only to amounts transferred solely in exchange for stock. If the *shareholder receives cash or other property* (ie, boot) in addition to stock, gain is recognized up to the amount of cash or FMV of other property received. Securities are considered property for this purpose.

Charlotte transfers property with FMV of $20,000 and adjusted basis of $12,000 to Roberts Corporation in exchange for 80% of its stock. In addition to stock, she receives $3,000 in cash. Although the transfer qualifies under Section 351, Charlotte recognizes a gain of $3,000. Her basis in the stock is $12,000 (adjusted basis of property transferred, plus gain, less cash received). The corporation's basis in the property is $15,000 (transferor's basis plus gain recognized by transferor).

If a shareholder contributes *property subject to liabilities*, the shareholder's basis in the stock received is reduced by the amount of liability relief. If liabilities exceed the shareholder's adjusted basis in the property, gain is recognized on the excess, and the shareholder's basis in the stock is zero.

Corporate Taxation

Basis of Property Exchanged for Corporate Stock

Tax-free exchanges under Section 351
(Transferors have at least 80% control after the exchange)

Shareholder's basis in stock received equals:	*Corporation's basis* in property received equals:
+ Adjusted basis of property transferred + Recognized gain + Cash Paid + Liabilities assumed + Transaction costs and fees - Cash received - FMV of property received - Liabilities transferred	+ Adjusted basis of the property in the hands of the transferor + Gain recognized by the transferor

For Sec. 351 transactions, if the aggregate adjusted basis of transferred property (eg, C/O basis = $10,000) exceeds its aggregate FMV (eg, $7,000), the corporate transferee's aggregate basis for the property is generally limited to its aggregate FMV immediately after the transaction ($7,000). Any required basis reduction is allocated among the transferred properties in proportion to their built-in loss immediately before the transaction. (The Transferor's basis in the stock would still be the carryover basis of the property of $10,000).

Alternatively, the transferor and the corporate transferee are allowed to make an irrevocable election to limit the basis in the stock received by the transferor to the aggregate FMV of the transferred property. (The Transferor would then have a basis of $7,000, but the corporation would have a basis in the property of $10,000).

A corporation can also be created as the result of **reorganization** of an existing corporation. Corporate reorganizations are affected by the transfer of virtually all the assets and liabilities of one corporation to another in exchange for stock in the new corporation, and are generally nontaxable, with the shareholders having the same basis in the stock of the new corporation as they did in the old. Some examples of reorganizations that qualify for such **tax-free status** include:

- Changes in the place of organization (eg, the assets of a New York corporation are all transferred into a corporation with a Florida charter.)
- Mergers and consolidations of businesses
- Absorption of subsidiaries (ie, the assets and liabilities of a controlled subsidiary are transferred to the parent.)

In all of the examples cited, nontaxable status required that a standard of 80% ownership be met for parties providing consideration other than services for their stock. This 80% level is the standard of **control** for tax purposes, and is the minimum ownership level required to identify an investee company as a controlled subsidiary and allow the preparation of *consolidated tax returns*. The preparation of consolidated tax returns with controlled subsidiaries is *optional*.

In contrast, generally accepted accounting principles consider control to take place when a majority of the voting stock is owned, or when other acceptable standards are met, and require the preparation of consolidated financial statements when such circumstances arise. Be certain not to confuse the 80% standard of control for tax purposes with the majority rule (50%) for accounting purposes.

Once a corporation is formed, shareholders may subsequently transfer additional property to the corporation. In some cases, it will be in exchange for additional stock but, in others, no stock may be issued in exchange. When that is the case:

- The shareholder will recognize no gain or loss on the transfer and will increase the tax basis in the stock by the tax basis of the property transferred.

- The shareholder's tax basis in the transferred property will carry over to the corporation and become its tax basis in the property.

2.03 Income & Ordinary Deductions

Revenues

(same as individual tax with some exceptions)

General Rule

The general rule for the inclusion of income under Section 451 of the code is that income should be **recognized** in the **year received** unless it is properly accounted for in a different year under the taxpayer's method of accounting for tax purposes. While a corporation can use the cash basis method of accounting if it meets the gross receipts test, the majority of corporations are accrual-basis taxpayers, so our discussions will focus on accrual accounting rules.

- For cash-basis taxpayers, this means a taxpayer could earn the income but not include it in taxable income until it is actually received.
- For most corporations, however, revenue generally will be recognized at the **earlier** of when **earned or collected.**
    - Income is **earned** when all events have occurred that fix the taxpayer's right to the income and the amount can be *reasonably determined* (ie, the **all-events test** has been met). The all-events test is considered to be met no later than *when the income is included in revenue in the financial statements* (F/S) of the taxpayer.[1]
    - **Advance payments** (ie, unearned income) generally must be recognized in the year received. However, the taxpayer can elect to include only the part of the payment required to be recognized in the year of receipt (ie, the part included in revenue for F/S purposes) and the remainder in the following year. The election does not apply to certain advance payments, such as rent and insurance premiums received.

Capital Gains & Losses (Sch. D)

When a corporation sells assets that are held for investment, the difference between the tax bases and proceeds from sale are recognized as capital gains and losses, taxed at the regular **21% corporate tax rate** (ie, no special rates apply to corporate capital gains like they do for individuals).

- Capital losses for corporations, however, are deductible only to the extent of capital gains for a corporation (ie, **NET capital losses** are **not deductible**[2]).

CAP	GAINS
3	5
←	→

---

[1] *F/S for these purposes generally include only those certified as being prepared in accordance with GAAP/IFRS or those that are otherwise prepared for filing with certain regulatory or governmental agencies.*
[2] *Individuals can claim a net loss of $3,000 per year; the rest is carried forward indefinitely.*

- A corporation's net capital losses can be carried back *3 years* and then forward *5 years* to offset capital gains in those years.
- All loss carrybacks and carryforwards are considered **short term** (S/T).

- Noncurrent assets used in a trade or business are subject to special rules (discussed in more detail in the Property Tax Section):
  - If they are held for one year *or less*, gains and losses are treated as ordinary income or losses (ie, ordinary assets).
  - If they are held for *more than* one year, losses are treated as ordinary losses and gains are treated as long-term capital gains (ie, Sec. 1231 assets).

Deductions

(All reasonable operating expenses – must be ordinary and necessary)

General Rule

In general, deductions on a corporate tax return are claimed in accordance with the same matching principle used for GAAP purposes. As a result, expenses can be deducted in the period that they are accrued for financial reporting purposes. An accrual-basis taxpayer can accrue an expense if the transaction meets *both* an **all-events test** *and* an **economic performance test**.

- The all-events test is met when the existence of a liability is established, and the amount of liability can be determined with reasonable accuracy.

- Economic performance occurs when property and/or services have been provided. Certain accrued items that are expected to be paid within a short period of time after accrual may be deducted when accrued if they are paid within **2 ½ months** of the tax year-end. These items include the following payments to employees:
  - Wages
  - Bonuses
  - Vacation pay

Organizational Expenses

Organizational expenses are state incorporation fees (including legal and accounting fees related to the incorporation).

- A corporation may elect to deduct up to **$5,000 of organizational expenditures**. The $5,000 amount is reduced by the amount by which the organizational expenditures exceed **$50,000**. Any costs not currently deductible are amortized over 180 months (15 years), beginning with the month in which the active trade or business begins.
  - The entity must elect to amortize the organization costs in the period of organization.
  - If no election is made, the costs are capitalized and remain until the entity is liquidated.

- Costs of issuing, printing, and selling stock (including legal and accounting fees related to the offering of securities) are *not* organizational expenses (reduction of APIC).

Corporate Taxation

Start-up Costs

Start-up costs include pre-opening expenses, such as employee training; advertising expenses; travel and other costs of securing distributors, suppliers, and customers; salaries and fees for executives, consultants, or other professional services; and other costs incurred in the process of investigating the creation or purchase of a business.

- A corporation may elect to deduct up to **$5,000 of start-up costs**. The $5,000 amount is reduced by the amount by which the start-up costs exceed **$50,000**. Any costs not currently deductible are amortized over 180 months (15 years), beginning with the month in which the active trade or business begins.
    - The entity must elect to amortize the start-up costs no later than the filing date for the tax return, including extensions.
    - If no election is made, the costs are capitalized and remain until the entity is liquidated.
- Does *not* include deductible interest, taxes, research and experimental costs, or the actual expenses incurred in attempting to purchase a specific business.

Employee Compensation

- **Salaries, Wages, Bonuses, & Vacation pay** (if paid within **2 ½ months** of year-end), payroll taxes, fringe benefits
- Can deduct up to $1M of compensation expense for certain "covered employees." Covered employees include the principal executive officer, principal financial officer, and the three other highest paid executive officers of a public corporation.
    - Reported on Form 1125-E.
    - Compensation expense for these purposes includes commissions and other performance-based compensation.
    - Once an employee is considered a covered employee, their status as such never changes.
    - Pay to other employees is not limited.
- Premiums on **life insurance** to benefit an employee's family are deductible as a fringe benefit.
    - However, if the corporation is the beneficiary of a life insurance policy on an employee (aka, Company-Owned Life Insurance, or COLI), the premiums paid on such policies are *not* deductible since the proceeds are generally not taxable.
- **Employee Achievement Awards** for length of service or safety may be deducted *up to $400 under nonqualified plans* and *up to $1,600 for qualified plans* per employee.
    - Must be tangible personal property (eg, a watch).
    - "Tangible personal property" does *not* include any of the following items, and thus such items given are **not deductible** to the employer and are taxable to employee: cash, cash equivalents, gift cards, gift coupons, or gift certificates (unless only for certain tangible

personal property), vacations, meals, lodging, tickets to theater or sporting events, stocks, bonds, other securities, and other similar items.

Bad Debt, Warranty Expense, & Other Estimated Losses

Estimated losses are accrued for book purposes but cannot be claimed for tax purposes until they are actual losses; thus, they will cause temporary book-tax differences to be reported on Schedule M-1 or M-3 (discussed later).

- **Business bad debts** are deductible in the year they become *partially or wholly worthless*, but amounts cannot be deducted unless *actually written off the books* (aka, **direct write-off method**).
    - Allowance approaches are not permitted.
    - Note: *Nonbusiness* bad debt is deductible only once *wholly worthless*, and taxpayers *other than corporations* must claim them as short-term capital losses.
- **Warranty costs** cannot be claimed until *repairs are actually made*.
- **Lawsuits** – Unlike GAAP, the tax code does not permit the deduction of losses just because they are probable and estimable.
- **Marketable securities** – Changes in market value are not reported on the tax return. Gains and losses are only recognized for tax purposes at the time of sale.
- **Inventory** – Declines in market value are not deductible until disposal of the inventory takes place.

Interest Expense

- Not deductible if loan proceeds used for tax-exempt investments. Note: The investment income limitation on interest expense deductions does **not** apply to corporations.
- Unless the taxpayer meets the $26M gross receipts test (2020) or qualifies under another specific exemption for certain businesses, such as real property development, the *business interest deduction* is now limited to the sum of the following, with any disallowed interest expense being *carried forward* to the next tax year:
    - Business interest income (does not include investment interest/income),
    - 30% of the taxpayer's adjusted taxable income, and
    - The taxpayer's floor plan financing interest for the tax year. "Floor plan financing interest" means interest paid or accrued on debt used to finance motor vehicles held for sale or lease and which is secured by that same inventory.

Meals & Travel [3]

- 50% of meals if they are not lavish or extravagant and the taxpayer or an employee was present.
    - When reimbursed meals are treated by the employer as compensation and wages to an employee, they are fully deductible to the entity. In this case, the employee will be taxed

---

[3] *Entertainment expenses are generally no longer deductible after 2017.*

on the full amount of the reimbursement and will not be allowed to deduct 50% of the meals since employee business expenses are not currently deductible for individuals.

- All out-of-town travel costs
- *Lodging expenses* for non-away-from-home travel (ie, Local lodging)
  - If incurred for the convenience or personal benefit of the employee, such as additional employee compensation, to enable employees to avoid long commutes, to accommodate overtime, to provide temporary housing to a relocated employee, or for an employee's use indefinitely, it is deductible to the employer and taxable to the employee.
  - Safe Harbor Test: Deductible to employer and not taxable to employee as tax-free working condition fringe benefit if *4 conditions* are met:
    - Necessary for full participation in bona fide business meeting, conference, training activity, or other business function.
    - Does not exceed 5 calendar days nor once per calendar quarter.
    - Required by employer to remain at activity or function overnight.
    - Lodging is not lavish or extravagant.
    - Facts and Circumstances Test: Even if such expenses do not meet the requirements above, they may still qualify as deductible if they are considered ordinary and necessary business expenses based on the facts and circumstances. For example, the expenses may still be deductible if they are required by the employer for a bona fide business purpose; they are not for social or personal benefit to the employee; and the lodging is not lavish or extravagant.

Casualty losses

- Business property – Lesser of:
  - *Adjusted basis* immediately before the casualty, or
  - Decline in value.
- Note that the limitations that apply to *personal* casualty losses (ie, the $100 floor, 10% of AGI limitation, and federally declared disaster requirement previously discussed) for individuals do NOT apply to business casualty losses.

Goodwill, Franchises & Trademarks

- Amortized over 15 years for tax purposes.
- For book, tested annually for impairment.

Fines, Federal, FORGET IT!!

Some expenditures are never deductible.

- Since the intention of *government fines and penalties* is punishment, no deduction is allowed, even though such penalties may appear to be in the form of interest.

- *Federal income taxes* paid are treated as offsets against the federal tax owed (like a credit), and not as deductions.

Taxes

- Can deduct various state, local, and foreign taxes on the federal return (NOT federal income taxes).
- Note: Limitations applicable to individuals do NOT apply to corporate deductions of taxes.

Research & Experimental Costs (aka, R&D)

- Immediately or over a minimum of 60 months

Other Nondeductible Expenses

- **Costs of issuing stock** – These are treated as adjustments to the proceeds from sale.
- **Lobbying costs** – Corporations are discouraged from political involvement and may not claim any costs associated with influencing candidates and legislation.
- **Club dues** – These are considered too personal in nature to qualify as business expenses.

2.04 Charity, NOL & DRD Deductions

Deductions (continued)

Charitable Contributions

- Claimed after all ordinary deductions.
- Limited to 10% of income before claiming deduction (**10% ATI**).
- Adjusted Taxable Income (**ATI**) is Net Income before the following "special deductions" (Note that this is not the same usage of the term "special deductions" on Form 1120):
    - Charity
    - DRD
    - Capital loss carryback
- Unused amount carried forward **5 years**.
- Pledge may be accrued and deducted if paid within **3 ½ months** of year-end (ie, by the tax return due date—4/15 for calendar year corporations).

Assume that Roger Corp. has $200M in gross income, $50M in ordinary deductions, $20M in charitable contributions, a $35M DRD, and no capital loss carryback:

Gross income	$200
(Ordinary deductions)	– 50
Adjusted Taxable Income (ATI)	**150**
(Charity - $20M)	– 15*
(DRD)	– 35
Taxable Income	$100

*Roger Corp. has $20M in charitable contributions, but the maximum deduction is **10%** of its $150M ATI = $15M, so $5M is carried forward up to 5 years.

Net Operating Losses (NOL)

NOLs generally may only be carried forward *indefinitely* and are limited to **80% of taxable income** for the year to which it is carried. The NOL rules are essentially the same as for individuals, but the calculation for corporations is much simpler than for individuals; that is, one need only exclude NOL carryforwards from the corporate calculation.

- Gross income – excess allowable deductions + any NOLs carried forward to that year = Current Year NOL
- Carryforward NOL allowed = *Taxable income before NOL × 80%*

For example, assume that Roger Corp. has $100M in gross income, $115M in allowable deductions in year 1 (2022):

Gross income	$100)
(Allowable deductions)	– 115)
NOL year 1	(15)

Now assume in year 2 (2023) Roger Corp. has $110M in gross income and $115M in allowable deductions, which includes the $15M NOL carried forward from year 1:

Gross income	$110*
(Allowable deductions)	–115*
NOL carryforward	+ 15*
Taxable Income before NOL	10*
(NOL carried forward allowed from year 1)	– 8*
Taxable income	$ 2*

*Roger Corp. has a $15M NOL carryforward from year 1, but the maximum deduction is 80% of its $10M taxable income before the NOL = $8M, so $7M ($15M - $8M) of the NOL is carried forward to year 3.

The 2020 CARES Act provides that for taxable years beginning after 2020, the 80% limitation equals 80% of taxable income in *excess* of any pre-2018 NOL carryover. Therefore, any pre-2018 NOL carried forward to a tax year after 2020 is fully deductible, and any NOL created after 2017 and carried forward to a tax year after 2020 is subject to the 80% limitation.

Dividends (from other taxable domestic corporations)

- Reported fully in gross income
- **Dividends Received Deduction (DRD)** – Schedule C
    - To avoid triple taxation on dividends

Dividends Received Deduction (DRD)	
Percentage of ownership by corporate shareholder	Allowed DRD*
< 20%	50% - Unaffiliated Co.
≥ 20% but < 80%	65% - Unaffiliated Co.
≥ 80%	100% - **Affiliated Co. (Control)**

TCJA reduced the DRD deductions for interests in domestic corporations from 70% to 50% for less than 20% owned corporations, and from 80% to 65% for 20 - 80% owned corporations.

- If own at least 80%, may file consolidated tax returns and eliminate intercompany dividends – same effect.
- Investor doesn't qualify for DRD if:
  - Dividends are from a foreign corporation (since IRS didn't tax investee)
  - Borrowed the money to buy the investment (Interest expense)
  - Received from a tax-exempt organization (muni-bond interest, not taxable)
  - Owned for less than 46 days (ie, the taxpayer must hold the interest at least 46 days during the 91-day period beginning 45 days prior to ex-dividend date.)
- **Exception** if DRD < TI before DRD < Dividend
  There is a **rare limitation** on the DRD applicable to investments that qualify for the 50% or 65% DRD. It applies when the taxable income (TI) before DRD is less than the dividend itself, but not lower than the dividend multiplied by the applicable percentage. In these cases, the DRD percentage is applied to TI before DRD instead of to the dividend itself.

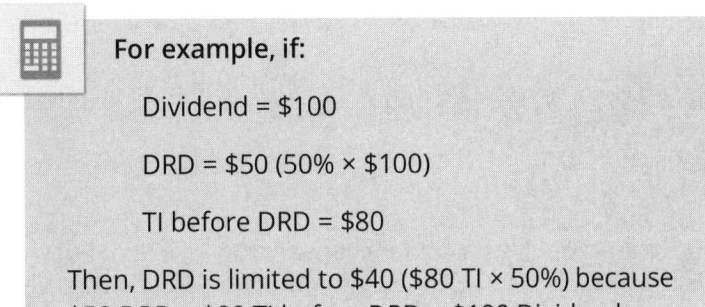

For example, if:

Dividend = $100

DRD = $50 (50% × $100)

TI before DRD = $80

Then, DRD is limited to $40 ($80 TI × 50%) because $50 DRD < $80 TI before DRD < $100 Dividend

Assume the corporation's gross revenue consists of sales and $100 in dividend income, and deductions other than the DRD total $490. Also assume the dividend was received from another taxable domestic corporation in which the investor holds a tiny 2% interest, so that the appropriate DRD is 50%. Let's look at five examples in which sales are (a) $530, (b) $500, (c) $470, (d) $420, and (e) $410. The calculation of taxable income is as follows:

	(a)	(b)	(c)	(d)	(e)
Sales	530	500	470	420	410
Dividend income	100	100	100	100	100
Gross income	630	600	570	520	510
Ordinary deductions	(490)	(490)	(490)	(490)	(490)
TI before DRD	140	110	80	30	20
DRD (50%)	(50)	(50)	**(40)**	(50)	(50)
Taxable income	90	60	40	(20)	(30)

Notice that the DRD is based on the dividend income ($100 × 50% = $50) in most examples. Only in example (c), in which TI before DRD is lower than $100 but not lower than $50, is the exception applicable, and the DRD is calculated on TI before DRD ($80 × 50% = $40). Because of the narrow range of income before DRD (between 50% and 100% of dividend income) in which the exception applies, this is a rarely tested item. In general, the percentage will simply be applied to the dividend income. The limitation does not apply when there is an NOL after subtracting the full DRD amount—examples (d) and (e).

2.05 Penalty Taxes & Credits

Accumulated Earnings Tax (AET)

To penalize corporations that accumulate earnings beyond the *reasonable needs* for expansion, retirement of debt and working capital needs.

- Excessive retained earnings in judgment of IRS
- Not self-assessed (by audit)
- Tax on undistributed income only **(20% rate)**
    - Reduce or eliminate if pay any of the following:
        - Actual dividend
        - Consent dividend – *hypothetical dividends* you pay taxes on, even though no money was actually received.
        - If already paid PHC tax (discussed later)
- **Safe harbor** allows certain amounts to be retained:
    - $250,000 for a manufacturing co. **or**
    - $150,000 for personal service corporations (PSCs)—provides personal services by owner-employees (eg, health, law, accounting, consulting);

    Plus: Additional sums retained for the purpose of paying federal income taxes owed.

    The sum of these two amounts is known as the minimum accumulated earnings credit.

Assume a manufacturing corporation in its first year of existence reports taxable income of $500,000 and has a federal income tax liability of $100,000. It is allowed to accumulate $250,000 + $100,000 = $350,000, so the maximum amount that might be subject to the penalty tax is $500,000 - $350,000 = $150,000. As long as dividend distributions of at least $150,000 are made, this corporation cannot be liable for the accumulated earnings tax.

- **Certain controlled groups** are limited to one $250,000 accumulated earnings credit, to be divided equally among its component members ($150,000 if any component member is a PSC).

Personal Holding Company (PHC) Tax

This tax was created to discourage the sheltering of certain types of passive income in corporations. This generally occurs when individuals in high tax brackets establish corporations to hold their personal investments to benefit from lower corporate tax rates on the income.

The tax applies only to **undistributed income** of the corporation, after deducting corporate taxes and net long-term capital gains to arrive at undistributed personal holding company income (UPHCI). The tax can be reduced or eliminated by sufficient dividend distributions, which of course results in the individual shareholders paying taxes on the dividends received.

- The **20% PHC tax** applies to UPHCI if both:
    - **5 or fewer** individuals own *more than 50%* of stock **and**
    - **60% or more** of revenue is from *passive sources* (eg, taxable interest, dividends, rental & royalty income).
        - Self-assessed by filing Sch. PH with return (Form 1120)
        - Can avoid if pay:
            - Actual dividend
            - Consent dividend (ie, a hypothetical dividend)

Personal Service Corporations (PSC)

A PSC is one that performs professional services and is predominantly owned by the parties providing those services. To qualify as a PSC, **two criteria** must be met:

- Substantially all activities involve the performance of health, law, engineering, architecture, accounting, actuarial science, performing arts, or consulting services; and
- 95% or more of the stock is owned by employees performing those services. Includes:
    - Retired employees who had performed such services;
    - Estates of employees or retirees who performed such services; and
    - Persons who acquired stock as a result of the death of such an employee or retiree for the 2-year period beginning on the date of the employee's or retiree's death.

Owner-employees of a PSC are considered related parties for purposes of the related party rules under IRC §267(a)(2), which requires a deduction to be matched with the related payee's recognition of income; thus, payments made to owner-employees may be deducted by a PSC only in the period in which they are taxable to the owner-employees.

Foreign Tax Credit

$$\text{U.S. tax liability} \times \frac{\text{Foreign income}}{\text{Worldwide income}} = \text{Foreign tax credit (never to exceed actual foreign taxes paid)}$$

Once the full tax liability is determined, it is reduced by available tax credits. The most frequently tested is the **foreign tax credit**. This credit is available to U.S. corporations for income taxes paid to foreign countries on income that is also reported on the U.S. return. The credit is limited to the portion of the U.S. gross tax that applies to the income on which the foreign tax was assessed.

For example, assume that the following facts apply:

Worldwide income	$100,000
Foreign income included in above	$30,000
U.S. gross tax before foreign credit	$20,000
Foreign income tax	$8,000

Since 30% ($30,000 / $100,000) of the total income is from a foreign country, 30% of the gross tax of $20,000, or $6,000, is the portion of the U.S. gross tax applicable to the foreign income and is the amount of the credit (the remaining $2,000 can be **carried back 1 year or forward 10** years). A corporation may elect to claim the entire amount of foreign taxes as a deduction from taxable income instead of claiming the credit.

General Business Credit

The general business credit (claimed on Form 3800) is made up of numerous individual tax credits, including but not limited to:

- Investment credit
- Work opportunity credit,
- Research credit,
- Low-income housing credit,
- Renewable electricity production credit,
- Orphan drug credit,
- Employer-provided child care credit,
- Differential wage payment credit,
- Small employer health insurance credit.

We will not cover the individual credits since they are often very specific to certain industries and subject to frequent legislative changes; thus, they are highly unlikely to be tested at the specific credit level.

Calculation of the Credit

- The general business credit for a tax year is equal to the sum of:
  - Business credit carryforwards for the year
  - Current year business credit
  - Business credit carrybacks for the year

- This amount is generally limited, however, to the excess of the taxpayer's net income tax (ie, regular tax + AMT[4]) over the greater of:
  - The tentative minimum tax for the year, or
  - 25% of the taxpayer's net regular tax liability over $25,000.
- Any general business credit that may not be claimed in the current year may be carried **back 1 year and forward 20 years**.

---

[4] *TCJA repealed the AMT for corporations, but this credit applies to other taxpayers as well.*

2.06 Supplementary Schedules: M-1, M-2, M-3

M-1 Reconciliation of Book Income to Taxable Income

The corporation must prepare a reconciliation of book income to taxable income (*before special deductions – DRD & NOL Deduction*) on the **Schedule M-1**. The purpose of this schedule is to identify to the IRS amounts that are reported differently for GAAP and tax purposes. The calculation begins with book income. It is then increased/decreased by items that cause taxable income to be higher/lower than book income.

- **Temporary** differences – bad debt expense, warranty expense, depreciation differences, etc.
- **Permanent** differences – municipal bond interest, 50% of meals (if not provided by a restaurant), fines, penalties, premiums paid on key person life insurance, etc.

Schedule M-1 Reconciliation of Income (Loss) per Books With Income per Return

Note: The corporation may be required to file Schedule M-3 (see instructions).

1	Net income (loss) per books		7	Income recorded on books this year not included on this return (itemize):	
2	Federal income tax per books			Tax-exempt interest $ _____	
3	Excess of capital losses over capital gains			_____	
4	Income subject to tax not recorded on books this year (itemize): _____		8	Deductions on this return not charged against book income this year (itemize):	
5	Expenses recorded on books this year not deducted on this return (itemize):		a	Depreciation $ _____	
a	Depreciation $ _____		b	Charitable contributions $ _____	
b	Charitable contributions $ _____			_____	
c	Travel and entertainment $ _____		9	Add lines 7 and 8	
6	Add lines 1 through 5		10	Income (page 1, line 28)—line 6 less line 9	

M-2 Reconciliation of Unappropriated Beg. RE to End RE

The corporation must also prepare a **Schedule M-2**, which is a statement of retained earnings (RE). The IRS examines this schedule to determine if any prior period adjustments might require amending returns of earlier years.

Schedule M-2 Analysis of Unappropriated Retained Earnings per Books (Line 25, Schedule L)

1	Balance at beginning of year		5	Distributions: a Cash	
2	Net income (loss) per books			b Stock	
3	Other increases (itemize): _____			c Property	
	_____		6	Other decreases (itemize): _____	
			7	Add lines 5 and 6	
4	Add lines 1, 2, and 3		8	Balance at end of year (line 4 less line 7)	

M-3 Reconciliation of Financial Accounting Income with Taxable Income

For corporations with total assets of $10 million or more, this schedule is prepared in lieu of Schedule M-1 and is, in essence, simply a more detailed form of that schedule. Unlike Schedule M-1, the Schedule M-3 income and expense differences are separately reported as *temporary or permanent differences*. Schedule M-3 also reconciles worldwide consolidated net income (loss) per the income statement to the net income (loss) per income statement of includible corporations. Income/Loss reconciliation Items are shown as single line items.

Corporate Taxation

SCHEDULE M-3 (Form 1120)
(Rev. December 2019)
Department of the Treasury
Internal Revenue Service

Net Income (Loss) Reconciliation for Corporations With Total Assets of $10 Million or More
▶ Attach to Form 1120 or 1120-C.
▶ Go to *www.irs.gov/Form1120* for instructions and the latest information.

OMB No. 1545-0123

Name of corporation (common parent, if consolidated return) | Employer identification number

Check applicable box(es): (1) ☐ Non-consolidated return (2) ☐ Consolidated return (Form 1120 only)
(3) ☐ Mixed 1120/L/PC group (4) ☐ Dormant subsidiaries schedule attached

Part I Financial Information and Net Income (Loss) Reconciliation (see instructions)

1a Did the corporation file SEC Form 10-K for its income statement period ending with or within this tax year?
  ☐ **Yes.** Skip lines 1b and 1c and complete lines 2a through 11 with respect to that SEC Form 10-K.
  ☐ **No.** Go to line 1b. See instructions if multiple non-tax-basis income statements are prepared.
 b Did the corporation prepare a certified audited non-tax-basis income statement for that period?
  ☐ **Yes.** Skip line 1c and complete lines 2a through 11 with respect to that income statement.
  ☐ **No.** Go to line 1c.
 c Did the corporation prepare a non-tax-basis income statement for that period?
  ☐ **Yes.** Complete lines 2a through 11 with respect to that income statement.
  ☐ **No.** Skip lines 2a through 3c and enter the corporation's net income (loss) per its books and records on line 4a.
2a Enter the income statement period: Beginning MM/DD/YYYY Ending MM/DD/YYYY
 b Has the corporation's income statement been restated for the income statement period on line 2a?
  ☐ **Yes.** (If "Yes," attach an explanation and the amount of each item restated.)
  ☐ **No.**
 c Has the corporation's income statement been restated for any of the five income statement periods immediately preceding the period on line 2a?
  ☐ **Yes.** (If "Yes," attach an explanation and the amount of each item restated.)
  ☐ **No.**
3a Is any of the corporation's voting common stock publicly traded?
  ☐ **Yes.**
  ☐ **No.** If "No," go to line 4a.
 b Enter the symbol of the corporation's primary U.S. publicly traded voting common stock . . . .
 c Enter the nine-digit CUSIP number of the corporation's primary publicly traded voting common stock . . . .

4a	Worldwide consolidated net income (loss) from income statement source identified in Part I, line 1 .	4a
b	Indicate accounting standard used for line 4a (see instructions): (1) ☐ GAAP (2) ☐ IFRS (3) ☐ Statutory (4) ☐ Tax-basis (5) ☐ Other (specify) _____	
5a	Net income from nonincludible foreign entities (attach statement)	5a ( )
b	Net loss from nonincludible foreign entities (attach statement and enter as a positive amount) . . .	5b
6a	Net income from nonincludible U.S. entities (attach statement)	6a ( )
b	Net loss from nonincludible U.S. entities (attach statement and enter as a positive amount)	6b
7a	Net income (loss) of other includible foreign disregarded entities (attach statement)	7a
b	Net income (loss) of other includible U.S. disregarded entities (attach statement)	7b
c	Net income (loss) of other includible entities (attach statement)	7c
8	Adjustment to eliminations of transactions between includible entities and nonincludible entities (attach statement)	8
9	Adjustment to reconcile income statement period to tax year (attach statement)	9
10a	Intercompany dividend adjustments to reconcile to line 11 (attach statement)	10a
b	Other statutory accounting adjustments to reconcile to line 11 (attach statement)	10b
c	Other adjustments to reconcile to amount on line 11 (attach statement)	10c
11	**Net income (loss) per income statement of includible corporations.** Combine lines 4 through 10 .	11

Note: Part I, line 11, must equal Part II, line 30, column (a), or Schedule M-1, line 1 (see instructions).

12 Enter the total amount (not just the corporation's share) of the assets and liabilities of all entities included or removed on the following lines.

		Total Assets	Total Liabilities
a	Included on Part I, line 4 . . . . ▶		
b	Removed on Part I, line 5 . . . . ▶		
c	Removed on Part I, line 6 . . . . ▶		
d	Included on Part I, line 7 . . . . ▶		

For Paperwork Reduction Act Notice, see the Instructions for Form 1120. Cat. No. 37961C Schedule M-3 (Form 1120) (Rev. 12-2019)

Schedule M-3 (Form 1120) (Rev. 12-2019) Page **2**

Name of corporation (common parent, if consolidated return) | Employer identification number

Check applicable box(es): **(1)** ☐ Consolidated group **(2)** ☐ Parent corp **(3)** ☐ Consolidated eliminations **(4)** ☐ Subsidiary corp **(5)** ☐ Mixed 1120/L/PC group
Check if a sub-consolidated: **(6)** ☐ 1120 group **(7)** ☐ 1120 eliminations

Name of subsidiary (if consolidated return) | Employer identification number

Part II Reconciliation of Net Income (Loss) per Income Statement of Includible Corporations With Taxable Income per Return (see instructions)

Income (Loss) Items (Attach statements for lines 1 through 12)	(a) Income (Loss) per Income Statement	(b) Temporary Difference	(c) Permanent Difference	(d) Income (Loss) per Tax Return
1 Income (loss) from equity method foreign corporations				
2 Gross foreign dividends not previously taxed				
3 Subpart F, QEF, and similar income inclusions				
4 Gross-up for foreign taxes deemed paid				
5 Gross foreign distributions previously taxed				
6 Income (loss) from equity method U.S. corporations				
7 U.S. dividends not eliminated in tax consolidation				
8 Minority interest for includible corporations				
9 Income (loss) from U.S. partnerships				
10 Income (loss) from foreign partnerships				
11 Income (loss) from other pass-through entities				
12 Items relating to reportable transactions				
13 Interest income (see instructions)				
14 Total accrual to cash adjustment				
15 Hedging transactions				
16 Mark-to-market income (loss)				
17 Cost of goods sold (see instructions)	( )			( )
18 Sale versus lease (for sellers and/or lessors)				
19 Section 481(a) adjustments				
20 Unearned/deferred revenue				
21 Income recognition from long-term contracts				
22 Original issue discount and other imputed interest				
23a Income statement gain/loss on sale, exchange, abandonment, worthlessness, or other disposition of assets other than inventory and pass-through entities				
b Gross capital gains from Schedule D, excluding amounts from pass-through entities				
c Gross capital losses from Schedule D, excluding amounts from pass-through entities, abandonment losses, and worthless stock losses				
d Net gain/loss reported on Form 4797, line 17, excluding amounts from pass-through entities, abandonment losses, and worthless stock losses				
e Abandonment losses				
f Worthless stock losses (attach statement)				
g Other gain/loss on disposition of assets other than inventory				
24 Capital loss limitation and carryforward used				
25 Other income (loss) items with differences (attach statement)				
26 **Total income (loss) items.** Combine lines 1 through 25				
27 **Total expense/deduction items** (from Part III, line 39)				
28 Other items with no differences				
29a Mixed groups, see instructions. All others, combine lines 26 through 28				
b PC insurance subgroup reconciliation totals				
c Life insurance subgroup reconciliation totals				
30 **Reconciliation totals.** Combine lines 29a through 29c				

Note: Line 30, column (a), must equal Part I, line 11, and column (d) must equal Form 1120, page 1, line 28.

Schedule M-3 (Form 1120) (Rev. 12-2019)

Corporate Taxation   REG 2

Schedule M-3 (Form 1120) (Rev. 12-2019)   Page **3**

Name of corporation (common parent, if consolidated return)   **Employer identification number**

Check applicable box(es): **(1)** ☐ Consolidated group   **(2)** ☐ Parent corp   **(3)** ☐ Consolidated eliminations   **(4)** ☐ Subsidiary corp   **(5)** ☐ Mixed 1120/L/PC group
Check if a sub-consolidated: **(6)** ☐ 1120 group   **(7)** ☐ 1120 eliminations

Name of subsidiary (if consolidated return)   **Employer identification number**

Part III   Reconciliation of Net Income (Loss) per Income Statement of Includible Corporations With Taxable Income per Return—Expense/Deduction Items (see instructions)

Expense/Deduction Items	(a) Expense per Income Statement	(b) Temporary Difference	(c) Permanent Difference	(d) Deduction per Tax Return
1 U.S. current income tax expense				
2 U.S. deferred income tax expense				
3 State and local current income tax expense				
4 State and local deferred income tax expense				
5 Foreign current income tax expense (other than foreign withholding taxes)				
6 Foreign deferred income tax expense				
7 Foreign withholding taxes				
8 Interest expense (see instructions)				
9 Stock option expense				
10 Other equity-based compensation				
11 Meals and entertainment				
12 Fines and penalties				
13 Judgments, damages, awards, and similar costs				
14 Parachute payments				
15 Compensation with section 162(m) limitation				
16 Pension and profit-sharing				
17 Other post-retirement benefits				
18 Deferred compensation				
19 Charitable contribution of cash and tangible property				
20 Charitable contribution of intangible property				
21 Charitable contribution limitation/carryforward				
22 Domestic production activities deduction (see instructions)				
23 Current year acquisition or reorganization investment banking fees				
24 Current year acquisition or reorganization legal and accounting fees				
25 Current year acquisition/reorganization other costs				
26 Amortization/impairment of goodwill				
27 Amortization of acquisition, reorganization, and start-up costs				
28 Other amortization or impairment write-offs				
29 Reserved				
30 Depletion				
31 Depreciation				
32 Bad debt expense				
33 Corporate owned life insurance premiums				
34 Purchase versus lease (for purchasers and/or lessees)				
35 Research and development costs				
36 Section 118 exclusion (attach statement)				
37 Section 162(r)—FDIC premiums paid by certain large financial institutions (see instructions)				
38 Other expense/deduction items with differences (attach statement)				
39 **Total expense/deduction items.** Combine lines 1 through 38. Enter here and on Part II, line 27, reporting positive amounts as negative and negative amounts as positive				

Schedule M-3 (Form 1120) (Rev. 12-2019)

2.07 Corporate Distributions

Nonliquidating Distributions

Is the distribution taxable, or is it a return of capital? Distributions made by the corporation to its shareholders generally are taxable as dividends to the extent of Earnings & Profits (E&P), and remaining dividends reduce the investor's basis in their shares.

More specifically, dividends are treated as dividend income up to the greater of:

- Current earnings & profits (CEP), or
- The Sum of Current & Accumulated E&P before distribution.
    - **Current Earnings & Profits (CEP)** – Similar to current year Net Income (NI).
    - **Accumulated E&P (AEP)** – The sum of all previous years' E&P, similar to retained earnings (RE) at the beginning of the year.

Calculation of CEP/AEP is no longer testable on the CPA Exam. If CEP or AEP is relevant to a problem (eg, a problem where the candidate must determine the taxability of corporate distributions), the CEP and/or AEP will simply be provided.

Current E&P – (NI)	+	–	+	–
Accumulated E&P – (RE)	–	+	+	–
Dividend (Taxable portion)	+	NET	++	0

Shareholder Receives $100 Cash Distribution →

Current E&P – (NI)	70	(40)	30	(20)
Accumulated E&P – (RE)	(30)	90	30	(20)
Dividend (taxable portion)	**70**	**50**	**60**	**0**
Return of Investment → (Nontaxable)	30	50	40	100

- In each case, the taxable dividend represents the higher of current E&P or total E&P. When both are negative, as in the last example, none of the distribution is treated as a taxable dividend.

- If total distributions during the year exceed current earnings and profits (CEP), the corporation's CEP must be prorated proportionately to each distribution. The ratio would be CEP/total distributions and would be applied to each distribution received throughout the year.
- **Property Distributions** as Dividend
    - Appreciated property dividends result in gain on sale.
    - Losses not deductible except in liquidation of company.
    - No gain or loss when subsidiary liquidates into parent.

    $ 100 FMV

    $ − 75 Basis

    $ 25 Gain → Increase E&P and usually already included in current E&P

Stock Redemptions

Redemptions (repurchase of shares from a shareholder) are treated as exchanges, generally resulting in capital gain or loss treatment to the shareholder if at least *one* of the following tests is met (constructive stock ownership rules generally apply in each case):

- Redemption is not essentially equivalent to a dividend;
- Redemption is substantially disproportionate (ie, after redemption, shareholder owns less than 50% voting stock and is reduced to less than 80% of previous ownership in voting stock and total FMV of stock);
- All of the shareholder's stock is redeemed;
- Redemption is from a noncorporate shareholder in a partial liquidation; or
- Distribution is a redemption of stock to pay death taxes under Sec. 303.

Liquidating Distributions (Terminating the Corporation)

Corporation discontinues operations and distributes all its assets—ie, Liquidating distribution.

- Corporation recognizes *both* gains and losses—usually ordinary (capital if related to the distribution of investments in stock).
- Shareholder's get capital gain/loss (proceeds − basis = gain/loss).

		Nonliquidating (dividend/return of capital)	Liquidating (treated as sale/exchange for stock)
Corporation	Gain	Capital	Ordinary (capital if stock)
	Loss	Not deductible	Ordinary (as if sold)
Shareholder	Gain	Ordinary/Dividend Income (Up to E&P)	Capital
	Loss	N/A	

When a corporation **distributes property** to a shareholder (aka, a dividend-in-kind), it is recognized by the individual shareholder at the fair market value (FMV) of the property received. The distributing **corporation** also must recognize a **gain** as if the property was sold if the FMV of the property exceeded its tax basis on the date of declaration. If the FMV of the property is lower than the tax basis, the corporation is **not** allowed a **loss** deduction (**unless** the distribution is in connection with a complete **liquidation** of the business).

For example, assume a corporation is carrying land with a tax basis of $100 and FMV of $500, and distributes it to its sole shareholder as a dividend-in-kind. The shareholder will report the distribution at $500, and the corporation will report a gain on sale of land of $400.

Keep in mind that the shareholder's tax treatment of the distribution depends on the same earnings and profits rules applicable to cash distributions, and that the gain (if any) on the property distribution is included in the determination of current earnings and profits.

If an asset is **subject to a liability**, and the corporation distributes the liability to the shareholder along with the asset, the liability reduces the amount of the distribution. Furthermore, if the basis of the liability exceeds the FMV of the asset, the corporation must report a gain on the excess in addition to the gain on sale discussed earlier.

For example, a corporation has land with a tax basis of $100 and FMV of $500, and an outstanding note payable secured by the land of $200. If the land is distributed and the shareholder assumes the note, the shareholder reports a distribution of $500 - $200 = $300, and the corporation reports a gain of $400 as if the land had been sold.

If the facts are the same, except that the note payable assumed by the shareholder is for $800 instead of $200, then the corporation has been relieved of a liability of $800 that exceeds the FMV of the land of $500, and the excess of $300 is an additional gain to the corporation. It reports a total gain from the distribution of $700, including the $400 for the excess of the FMV of the asset over the tax basis and $300 for the excess of the liability over the FMV of the asset. The total gain of $700 can also be computed directly as the excess of the liability ($800) over the tax basis of the asset ($100); that is, IRC Sec. 336 treats the excess liability as the true FMV of the asset.

When a corporation distributes all its assets and liabilities in a **complete liquidation** of the corporation, it reports gains *and* losses in full as if all the assets had been sold and may deduct all expenses associated with the corporation.

The only exception is if assets and liabilities are being transferred pursuant to a corporate **reorganization**, in which case, all assets and liabilities retain their tax bases in the new corporation.

When a noncorporate shareholder receives a distribution in exchange for their stock in a partial or total liquidation of the corporation, this is treated as a sale of the stock, and the gain or loss on redemption is reported as a capital gain or loss.

Exception to Liquidating Distribution

When subsidiary is liquidated into the parent:

- Tax-free reorganization
- No gain/loss for either parent or subsidiary
- Carryover basis

Corporate Reorganizations

Two corporations join together to form one corporation.

- Mergers & acquisitions
    - Stock for stock and must end up with control.
    - New shares at Carryover basis of old shares.
    - No gain or loss except to extent that cash/boot is received.
    - Reorganizations generally receive nonrecognition treatment under IRC Sec. 368.
- Types of Reorganizations
    - Type A: mergers or consolidations
    - Type B: Use of voting stock of the acquiring corporation to acquire at least 80% of the voting power and 80% of each class of nonvoting stock of the target corporation
    - Type C: Use of voting stock to acquire substantially all of the target's net assets
    - Type D: Transfer of assets by an acquiring corporation to acquire controlling interest in a target corporation
    - Type E: Recapitalization to change the capital structure of a single corporation
    - Type F: Mere change of identity, form, or state of incorporation
    - Type G: Transfer of assets of an insolvent corporation, including as part of bankruptcy proceedings, to former creditors

Consolidated Returns

An affiliated group of corporations may elect to file a consolidated tax return instead of filing separately.

- An **affiliated group** is one or more chains of includible corporations connected through stock ownership, with:
    - A common parent corporation (not individual shareholders) directly owning at least 80% of the voting power and total value of stock in at least one other corporation, and
    - All other includible members are at least 80% owned by the parent and/or other group members.
- That is, if one corporation has control (80%+), consolidated returns may be prepared, and intercompany profits, interest, and dividends will need to be eliminated.
- C corps and S corps may not consolidate their returns.

2.08 Multijurisdictional Tax

State & Local Tax Issues

In general, an entity is allowed to do business in states other than the one in which it was formed or is physically located. **Public Law 86-272**, referred to as the **Interstate Income Act of 1959**, allows a business to go, or send a representative, into a state to solicit orders for goods without being subject to a net income tax. The law applies exclusively to orders for tangible personal property and either:

- Orders solicited by employees are approved, and shipped from, outside the state; or
- Orders solicited by independent contractors that are shipped from outside the state.

A state may impose an income tax on an entity that is doing business in that state if the entity establishes **nexus** in a state, indicating that it has a presence in that state. Although the requirements for nexus vary from state to state, nexus is generally created for income tax purposes when an entity derives income from sources within the state, has employees in the state engaged in activities other than solicitation, or has capital or property in the state.

As a result of the various nexus laws, an entity may be taxable in various jurisdictions. To avoid being taxed on the same income in multiple jurisdictions, income will be allocated among the jurisdictions in which the entity is subject to income tax. The model that is used for allocating income is the **Uniform Division of Income for Tax Purposes Act** (**UDITPA**). The allocations are dependent on the **nature of the income**:

- Net rents and royalties from real property are generally allocated to the state in which the property is located, while net rents or royalties from tangible personal property is generally allocated to the state in which the property is used.
    - If the entity is not subject to income tax in the state in which property is used, net rents and royalties are allocated to the state in which the entity is domiciled (headquartered).
    - If the property is utilized in multiple jurisdictions, income will be allocated to each on the basis of the ratio of the number of days the property earned rents or royalties in that state to the total number of days on which rents, or royalties were earned from use of the property.
- The allocation of capital gains and losses is affected by the nature of the property.
    - Capital gains and losses on the sale of real estate are allocated to the state in which the real estate is located.
    - Capital gains and losses on the sale of tangible personal property are allocated to the state in which the property is located unless the entity is not subject to income tax in that state, in which case it is allocated to the state in which the entity is domiciled.
    - Capital gains and losses on the sale of intangible personal property are allocated to the state in which the entity is domiciled.
- Interest and dividends are allocated to the state in which the entity is domiciled.

- Royalties on patents and copyrights are allocated to the state in which they are used by the payer of the royalties or, when the entity is not subject to income tax in that state, it is allocated to the entity's state of domicile.
    - A patent is utilized in a state if the patented product is produced in the state.
    - A copyright is utilized in a state if printing or publication originates in it.
- Business income is multiplied by a ratio that is based on the entity's property holdings, payroll, and sales.

The entity calculates 3 ratios (property, payroll, sales):

1. The average value of the entity's real and tangible personal property owned, valued at its original cost, or rented, valued at 8 times net annual rent, and used by the entity in the state during the tax period is divided by the average value of all real and tangible personal property owned or rented and used by the entity for the period.
2. The total amount paid for compensation (payroll) in the state by the entity is divided by the total compensation paid everywhere.
3. Total sales by the entity in the state during the tax period are divided by the entity's total sales made everywhere.
    - The three ratios are added together and divided by three.
    - The result is multiplied by business income to determine the amount allocated to the state.

International Tax Issues

Income Taxes

Many companies try to minimize their taxes by locating operations in foreign countries with lower tax rates, known as "*tax havens*." The United States has a few rules to combat this abusive behavior, but the method depends on the type of foreign operation:

- **Foreign Branch** – a business operation carried on by a U.S. corporation, partnership, trust, estate, or individual, outside the United States. Such an activity must be considered a permanent establishment under the terms of a treaty between the United States and the foreign country.
    - Taxed on current U.S. income and losses are deductible.
- **Foreign Subsidiary** – a company incorporated under the laws of a foreign country where it is located, but which is partially or wholly owned by a U.S. corporation.
    - U.S. income tax is generally deferred until profits are repatriated back to U.S. in the form of dividends, and losses are *not* deductible; however, TCJA has introduced new rules to help migrate the international tax system to more current taxation of foreign income

and permanent exclusion of certain dividends repatriated back to the U.S. (discussed later).

- **Controlled Foreign Corporation (CFC)** is a foreign corporation where U.S. shareholders own *more than 50%* of the total voting power or value of all classes of the corporation's stock.
- A shareholder is considered a **"U.S. shareholder"** if they own *10% or more* of total voting power of all classes of stock, or 10% or more of the total value of all classes of stock in the foreign corporation.
  - **Subpart F Income of a Foreign Base Company** – To prevent a taxpayer from deferring income tax on certain movable income and shifting such income to a controlled foreign entity that may be taxed at a lower tax rate, every shareholder who, on the last day of the tax year, owns, directly or indirectly, *10% or more* of the voting stock in a foreign corporation that was a CFC at any time during that taxable year will include the taxpayer's share of Subpart F income in gross income, regardless of whether the CFC actually makes a distribution. Subpart F income of a CFC is the sum of various factors that includes foreign base company income. There are 3 main categories of foreign base company income:
    - Foreign base company *sales* income – income received by a CFC from the purchase or sale of personal property involving a related person.
    - Foreign base company *services* income – income from the performance of services by or on behalf of a related person.
    - Foreign *personal holding company* income – investment income such as dividends, interest, rents and royalties.

Foreign base company income is essentially income earned by a CFC that results from the purchase/sale, from or on behalf of a related party, of property that is manufactured, produced, or extracted outside of the country of the CFC's organization and is sold for use, consumption, or disposition outside of the country of its organization. This might also be the case, for example, if a CFC provides services to an entity in another country as the result of a contract entered by the CFC's parent from the United States.

International Tax Reform

To shift from a deferred tax regime to more current taxation of foreign profits, TCJA has created a sort of hybrid system by enacting a few international tax rules to encourage the repatriation of foreign income. Among them, and perhaps the most important, is the "**Participation Exemption**"—a 100% dividends received deduction (DRD) that is generally available for the foreign-source portion of dividends received from a "specified 10% owned foreign corporation" by domestic corporations that are at least 10% shareholders.

- A holding period of more than 365 days is required, and no foreign tax credit or deduction is allowed for any taxes paid with respect to a dividend that qualifies for the deduction.
- Since a foreign corporation is already subject to tax in its country of incorporation, this provision generally eliminates any additional U.S. tax on such foreign profits.

In addition to this Participation Exemption, TCJA has provided new reduced tax rates for domestic corporations on *"Foreign-Derived Intangible Income (FDII)"* and *"Global Intangible Low-*

Taxed Income (GILTI)." For 2019 through 2025, these tax rates are effectively 12.5% and 10%, respectively.

- **Foreign-Derived Intangible Income (FDII)** is intangible income (ie, income from the ownership, sale, etc., of intangible assets), derived from serving foreign markets. For example, Disney receives FDII from licensing its characters to a European apparel company for printing on T-shirts to be sold in Europe.

    FDII = Deemed Intangible Income × $\frac{\text{Foreign-derived deduction eligible income (FDDEI)}}{\text{Deduction Eligible Income (DEI)}}$

    - Foreign-Derived Deduction Eligible Income (FDDEI) is any deduction eligible income from:
        - Property "sold," (ie, leased, licensed, exchanged, etc.), to any foreign person for a foreign use. Note: If a taxpayer sells property for further manufacture or modification within the U.S., it is not generally treated as sold for a foreign use, even if it is subsequently used for foreign use; however, there is an exception for property that is ultimately sold by a related party to a foreign unrelated party for foreign use.
        - Services provided to any foreign person, or with respect to any foreign property. Note: DEI from services provided to an unrelated person located within the U.S. is not treated as FDDEI, even if the other person uses the services in providing services resulting in FDDEI.
    - **Deduction Eligible Income (DEI)** is the excess of gross income over allocable deductions (including taxes).

        DEI = Gross Income − Allocable Deductions − Exceptions*

        *Exceptions:
        - Subpart F income
        - GILTI (see below)
        - Financial services income
        - Dividends from a CFC (Controlled Foreign Corp)
        - Domestic oil and gas extraction income
        - Foreign branch income

- **Global Intangible Low-Taxed Income (GILTI)** is a new, wide-ranging category of income designed to tax foreign income at a low rate immediately (rather than it being deferred).

    GILTI = U.S. shareholder's Net CFC Tested Income − Net Deemed Tangible Income Return.

    - **Net CFC Tested Income** = CFC Tested Income − CFC Tested Loss.
        - **Tested Income** = CFC's gross income − allocable deductions (including taxes). CFC gross income does **NOT** include:
            - Income derived from sources within the U.S.
            - Subpart F Income
            - Gross income excluded from the foreign base company income and the insurance income

- Dividends received from a related person
- Foreign oil and gas extraction income
  - **Tested Loss** is the excess of the CFC's allocable deductions over the CFC's gross income.
- Net Deemed Tangible Income Return – The excess of:
  - 10% of the aggregate of a U.S. shareholder's pro rata share of the *qualified business asset investment (QBAI)* of each CFC owned, over
  - The amount of interest expense in excess of interest income included in the shareholder's net CFC tested income.
    - **Qualified Business Asset Investment (QBAI)** – The average of a CFC's aggregate adjusted bases in "specified tangible property" as of the end of each quarter of the tax year that is depreciable and used in a trade or business of the CFC.
      - **Specified Tangible Property** – Any tangible property used in the production of tested income. Note that *dual use property*—property used both in the production of tested income and income which is not tested income—is considered specified tangible property in the same proportion as the tested income produced bears to the total gross income produced.

Even with the Participation Exemption and these new lower FDII and GILTI tax rates, corporation's will still have the incentive to shift their profits to countries with lower tax rates, thus, TCJA has also created an additional base erosion *minimum tax* called the **"Base Erosion and Anti-Abuse Tax (BEAT)"** to protect against erosion of the U.S. tax base. An example of U.S. tax base erosion is the placement of high-value functions and assets in low-tax countries to generate profits offshore.

- Only applicable to corporations with *$500 million or more* in average annual gross receipts over the previous 3 tax years.

    BEAT = 10% × Modified Taxable Income* – (Regular Tax Liability – Certain Tax Credits).

    Modified Taxable Income is taxable income adjusted for base erosion payments (ie, generally any amount paid or accrued to a foreign related party).

Withholding Taxes

Salaries, wages, etc., paid to a nonresident alien (NRA) are subject to withholding in the same way as for U.S. citizens/residents if they are effectively connected with the conduct of a U.S. trade or business. However, the following types of U.S.-sourced income paid to NRAs are generally subject to withholding at 30%, unless a tax treaty provides for a lesser rate, or exemption:

- Nonemployee compensation
- Athletes and entertainers
- Interest Income effectively connected with a U.S. trade or business
- Dividend income
- Royalties
- Pensions and annuities
- Alimony

- Taxable scholarships/fellowships
- Social Security pensions – 85% of the U.S. Social Security pension paid to an NRA is taxable at the rate of 30%, for an effective rate of tax of 25.5%. The Social Security Administration generally withholds 25.5% federal income tax on U.S. Social Security pensions paid to NRAs.

Source rules – The following rules determine whether certain types of income are considered to be U.S. or foreign-sourced:

- The country of the payor determines the source of interest Income and dividends.
- The location of property rented/used/sold determines the source of rents, royalties, and gain on the sale of real property.
- The location of services performed determines the source of payments for services.
- The location at which title to inventory passes determines the source of gain on the sale of inventory.

REG 3
S Corporations

REG 3: S Corporations

3.01 S Corporations: Formation & Operation — 1
- Eligibility — 1
- Formation of an S Corporation — 2

3.02 Separately Stated Items — 5

3.03 Distributions to Shareholders / S Status — 7
- Nonliquidating Distributions — 7
- Other Adjustments Account (OAA) — 7
- Liquidating Distributions — 8
- S Status Termination — 8
- Built-in Gains Tax (BIG) — 8
- Advantages & Disadvantages of S Status — 9

3.04 Qualified Business Income Deduction — 10
- Overview — 10
- Qualified Business — 10
- Qualified Business Income — 11
- Deductible QBI Per Business — 11
- Overall QBI Deduction Limit Per Taxpayer — 14

3.01 S Corporations: Formation & Operation

Corporations that pay income taxes directly are known as C corporations. Some corporations elect to be treated in a manner similar to partnerships, filing a tax return (**Form 1120-S**) but not paying taxes directly (ie, an S corporation). Instead, the income reported by an **S corporation** is allocated to the shareholders (**Sch. K-1**), who must report their shares of the S corporation's income on their personal tax returns (flow-through entity).

 Return due dates and extensions are no longer tested on the CPA Exam.

Eligibility

To be eligible to be an S corporation, certain conditions must be satisfied (**Simple & Small**):

- There can be no more than **100 shareholders** (family members with a common ancestor no more than six generations above and their spouses may be treated as a single shareholder for purposes of this rule).
- All shareholders must be **individuals** (or certain estates or trusts for the benefit of individuals).
    - No corporations, partnerships or big trusts allowed as shareholders.
        - But S corp can own stock in a C corp, S corp, or be a partner in a P/S.
    - Grantor & Testamentary trusts are Ok.
    - Spouses count as one until divorce is final.
- All shareholders must be either **residents or citizens** of the United States.
- The corporation must be a **domestic** corporation.
- There can be only **one class** of stock (no preferred stock).

The last requirement needs to be carefully understood. The requirement of one class of stock means only that each share must be allocated an equal amount of the income of the corporation. It is acceptable for some of the shares to have voting rights and others to be nonvoting, so long as the income allocation requirement is satisfied.

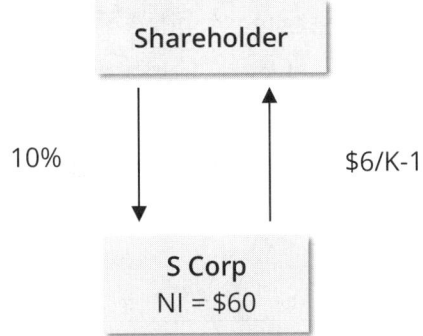

Formation of an S Corporation

Similar to a C corporation – **Formal**

- Cash or property 80% or more (control)
  - Tax free to both
  - Carryover basis
  - Carryover holding period
- Services or < 80%
  - Taxable at FMV of stock

S Election

The election to become an S corporation must be made **unanimously (100%)** by the shareholders (including those with nonvoting shares), since they are agreeing to be personally liable for the income taxes resulting from the election.

The election can be made at any time on **Form 2553**, but it must be made by the 15th day of the 3rd month of the tax year (3/15 for calendar corporations, **2 ½ Months**) in order to be effective for that year. Any election made after that cannot become effective until the start of the following tax year.

Tax Year

The tax year may be a calendar year or a fiscal year if it has an established business purpose.

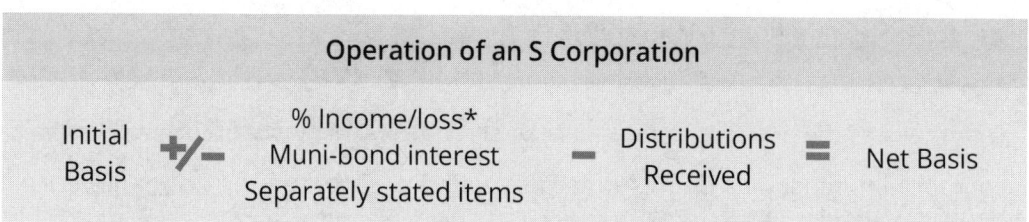

*Note: The following order applies in **calculating stock basis** to determine whether a distribution is taxable or whether a loss is deductible:

1. **+** Income items, including gains
2. **−** Distributions (does not include dividend distributions from C corp years)
3. **−** Nondeductible, noncapital expenses (eg, nondeductible portion of meals and entertainment expense) and depletion
4. **−** Items of loss and deduction (if amounts are greater than remaining basis, allocate them proportionally until basis is reduced to 0, and remainder is suspended until enough basis exists to absorb it)

Roger, the sole shareholder of an S corporation, has $10,000 of stock basis (and no debt basis) on January 1, year 1. Roger received a Schedule K-1 for year 1 with the following items:

Ordinary business income (loss)	(15,000)
Net §1231 gain	5,000
Nondeductible expenses	2,000
Charitable contribution	1,000
Distributions	9,000

1. Using the ordering rule, stock basis is first increased by items of income, so our initial stock basis of $10,000 is increased by the $5,000 net §1231 gain, for a stock basis before distributions of $15,000.

2. Then we reduce the $15,000 stock basis by distributions of $9,000, for a remaining basis amount of $6,000. Since the shareholder has adequate stock basis before distributions, the $9,000 distribution is not taxable.

3. Next, Roger's $6,000 stock basis is reduced by the $2,000 of nondeductible expenses, bringing stock basis to $4,000.

4. Finally, Roger has an ordinary loss of $15,000 and a $1,000 charitable deduction. Since Roger's loss and deduction items exceed his stock basis, we would look to see if he had any debt basis (money loaned to company). Since there is no debt basis, the loss and deduction items must be pro-rated to determine the amount currently allowable:

    - $15,000 loss/$16,000 total loss and deduction items × $4,000 remaining basis = $3,750 loss allowable in year 1

    - $1,000 deduction/$16,000 total loss and deduction items × $4,000 remaining basis = $250 allowable charitable deduction in year 1

Roger's remaining $11,250 ordinary loss and $750 charitable deduction are suspended until Roger has enough basis to absorb it.

Net Business Income (Ordinary Business Income)

- **Income** = Ordinary income/Loss + Muni-bond interest + Separately stated income items
    - Income computed on an *Average daily basis*.

Assume an S corporation with 100 shares outstanding reported $365,000 of income in 20X1 (a 365-day year). One shareholder purchased 5 shares on 11/30/X1 and held them through the end of the year. The income averages $365,000 / 365 days = $1,000 per day.

> With 100 shares outstanding, this comes to $1,000 / 100 shares = $10 per share per day. The shareholder making the purchase on 11/30/X1 held the shares for the last 31 days of the year and is allocated $10 × 5 shares × 31 days = $1,550.

- Losses
  - **Basis Limitation**—Losses are limited to amount invested (ie, **stock basis**) + amount loaned to company (ie, **debt basis**). Basis cannot go below zero; losses are suspended until the shareholder has sufficient basis to absorb the loss. Note: For S corporations, basis is often equal to the amount "at-risk."
  - **At-Risk Rules**—Losses are further limited by the investor's amount "at risk" under IRC Sec. 465 (similar to basis rules but amounts at-risk do not include amounts for which the investor bears no economic risk of loss—eg, certain nonrecourse loans and loans from certain related parties).
  - **Passive Activity Loss Limitation**—IRC §469 provides that passive losses are limited to passive income.

 For CPA exam purposes, you should be aware of the impact of the at-risk and passive activity loss limitations, but you are unlikely to be asked to calculate anything beyond the basis limitation.

Municipal Bond Interest

- Increases basis
- Not taxable

Distribution Received by Shareholder

- Reduces basis
- Not taxed

3.02 Separately Stated Items

Separately stated items can be income, losses, deductions, or credits that are reported separately from the S corporation's ordinary income/deductions to the shareholder because they are subject to different limitations/rules when reported on the individual tax return (ie, 1040). Examples include:

Separately stated item	Reason not included in ordinary income
Capital gains and losses	Limit on deductibility of net capital losses
Section 1231 gains and losses	Classification of net gain as capital gain
Investment Income (eg, Dividends and interest)	Needed for investment interest limitation
Passive income (ie, rents/royalties)	Passive activity loss limitations
Charitable contributions	Must itemize to deduct / % of AGI limitations
Section 179 depreciation election	Dollar limit on use of election per year
Tax credits	Limited to tax liability
Tax-exempt income	Affects shareholder basis but not taxable
Nondeductible expenses	Affects shareholder basis but not deductible

These items are passed through according to their percentage of ownership based on a **per-share/per-day method**. If there is no change in ownership during the year, then simply use the percentage of stock owned to determine the amount passed though. If a change in ownership occurred, then each shareholder's percentage is weighted for the number of days the stock was held (Like Weighted Average).

The S corporation prepares a **Schedule K** that summarizes the ordinary income and then separately lists all items that are not ordinary. Additionally, a Schedule K-1 is prepared for each shareholder, showing that owner's allocated share of all of the items on the Schedule K.

REG 3 — S Corporations

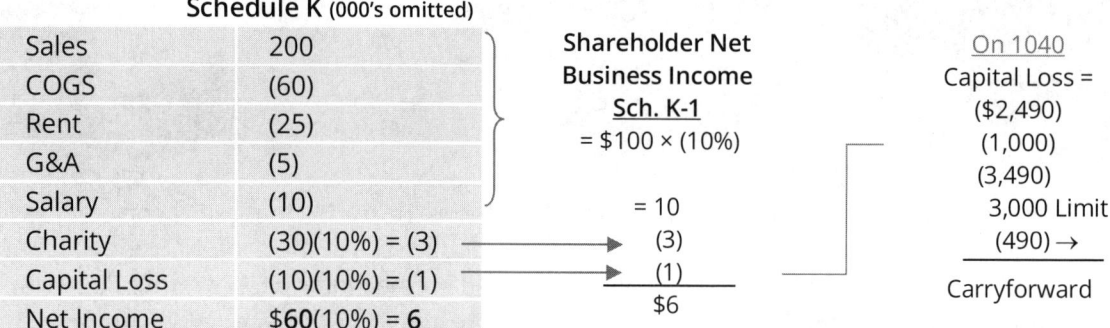

Schedule K (000's omitted)

Sales	200	
COGS	(60)	
Rent	(25)	
G&A	(5)	
Salary	(10)	
Charity	(30)(10%) = (3)	
Capital Loss	(10)(10%) = (1)	
Net Income	$60(10%) = **6**	

Shareholder Net Business Income
<u>Sch. K-1</u>
= $100 × (10%)

= 10
(3)
(1)
$6

<u>On 1040</u>
Capital Loss =
($2,490)
(1,000)
(3,490)
3,000 Limit
(490) →

Carryforward

 You should try and remember the list of items that are reported separately, as this has been tested. Also note that the calculation of income and identification of special items that need to be passed through to the shareholders separately are handled in the same way for S corporations as they are for partnerships, and such concepts are normally addressed on the CPA exam in partnership questions.

Refer to the IRS website for the most recent versions of the S-Corporation tax forms.

3.03 Distributions to Shareholders / S Status

Nonliquidating Distributions

Nonliquidating distributions to shareholders are nontaxable to the extent of the **Accumulated Adjustment Account** (AAA) and are applied to reduce the AAA and shareholder's stock basis. AAA represents the cumulative total of undistributed net income items for S corporation taxable years beginning after 1982.[1] A positive balance in AAA represents amounts that have already been taxed to shareholders during S years.

Accumulated Earnings and Profits (AEP) represent earnings and profits that were accumulated (and never taxed to shareholders) during C corporation taxable years.

S Election	
C corp	S corp
AEP	AAA

1. Distributions to the extent of the AAA are *not taxable*.
    - Distributions are generally treated as first coming from its AAA and then AEP; however, an S corporation may *elect* to distribute AEP before AAA.
2. Distributions in excess of the AAA are treated as *ordinary dividends* to the extent of the corporation's AEP.
3. Distributions are next *nontaxable* to the extent of remaining stock basis, as a tax-free return of capital.
4. Distributions in excess of stock basis are treated as *gain* from the sale of stock.

AAA	AEP	Basis	Excess
•Nontaxable •Reduce basis	•Taxable •Ordinary dividends	•Nontaxable •Reduce basis to zero	•Capital gain

Other Adjustments Account (OAA)

The AAA is generally increased by all income items and is decreased by distributions and all loss and deduction items. However, adjustments for tax-exempt income and related expenses, as well as adjustments for federal income taxes attributable to C corporation tax years are made to the **Other Adjustments Account (OAA)**, rather than the AAA.

---

[1] *Pre-1983 undistributed net income is referred to as Previously Taxed Income (PTI).*

Liquidating Distributions

The tax treatment for liquidating distributions is essentially the same for S corporations as it is for C corporations; that is, recognize gain/loss on the distribution of property to a shareholder as if the property were sold at its FMV in exchange for the shareholder's stock. However, gains/losses recognized by an S corporation are ultimately passed through to the shareholders.

S Status Termination

Election to Terminate

An election to terminate a corporation's status as an S corporation requires shareholders holding **more than half** of the shares (again, including those that are normally nonvoting shares) to agree (**>50% - Voluntary**). An S corporation's status will be revoked automatically (**Involuntary**) if an event occurs that causes it to violate one of the Small & Simple requirements (eg, if shares are sold to a nonresident alien). Once an S corporation's status has been revoked, it cannot reelect such status for **5 years**.

Unless a date is specified, a *voluntary* revocation made:
- Within the first 2 ½ months of the year is effective as of the 1st day of such taxable year.
- After the first 2 ½ months of the year shall be effective on the 1st day of the following year.

Involuntary Termination

Per Sec. 1362, termination will *involuntarily* occur if the S corporation has passive investment income exceeding *25% of its gross receipts* for each of 3 consecutive years and, if during these 3 years, the corporation was a corporation with AEP attributable to prior C corporation status. The termination is effective on the 1st day of the tax year following the 3rd consecutive year of violation. Passive investment income includes receipts from rents, royalties, dividends, interest, and annuities.

An S election termination can be effective at any time during a tax year, resulting in the need to allocate income between the resulting S short year and C corporation short year. If no special election is made, the income must be allocated on a daily basis between the two based on a 365-day year.

Built-in Gains Tax (BIG)

Built-in Gains Tax (BIG) applies if a C corporation elects S corporation status and the FMV of its assets exceeds their bases. The difference is a net unrealized built-in gain. If the assets are sold within **5 years**, a special built-in gains tax at the highest corporate rate applies. This is the tax that would be due if the assets were sold prior to the election of the S status. This would not apply if FMV is less than basis, because in this case no built-in gain is present in the transaction.

Advantages & Disadvantages of S Status

When the shareholders of a C corporation decide to elect S corporation status, there may be advantages and disadvantages.

- Shareholders will be **taxed on all income** of the S corporation, whether distributed or not.
- **Capital losses pass through** to the shareholders, instead of being carried back or forward to offset against corporate capital gains.
- Any net capital loss or net operating loss (NOL) carryforwards from an S corporation's time as a C corporation are not immediately deductible by shareholders; however, they may be used to offset any built-in gains tax that arises from the sale of appreciated assets during the recognition period.
- **Health insurance premiums** and other **fringe benefits** paid by an S corporation on behalf of a more than **2%** shareholder-employee are deductible by the S corporation as compensation and are includible in the shareholder-employee's gross income on Form W-2.

3.04 Qualified Business Income Deduction

Overview

In order to somewhat level the playing field for **flow-through entities** (through 2025) after reducing the corporate tax rate to 21%, Congress created a **20%** Qualified Business Income (QBI) Deduction for S corporations, partnerships, sole proprietorships, trusts, estates and even some Schedule E businesses. We say "somewhat" since the availability of the deduction depends on the *type of business* (eg, service/nonservice) and the taxpayer's *taxable income before the deduction (TI)*.

Level of TI	2022 MFJ Amounts	Eligibility for QBI Deductions
1. Below threshold	$0 – $340,100	• Full deduction allowed for any business
2. Between threshold & upper limit[2]	$340,101 – $440,100	• Wage/property limitation partially applies • If nonqualified business, another reduction applies
3. Above upper limit	Over $440,100	• Full wage/property limitation applies • Must be qualified business

[1] The threshold amount (adjusted for inflation) for other filing statuses is half as much.

[2] Upper limit = threshold + phase-in range (ie, $100,000 MFJ or $50,000 others).

When enacted, the original threshold was $315,000 for MFJ. Remember that one does not need to memorize inflation-adjusted amounts but should know the ballpark amounts. The examiners are likely to provide a threshold amount to be used when a precise calculation is necessary. Thus, it is important to be able to calculate QBI with any threshold amount given.

The QBI deduction can get quite complicated, so we will stick to the basics for CPA exam purposes.

Qualified Business

"Qualified Business" means any business **other than a Specified Service Trade or Business (SSTB)**. An SSTB is any business involving the performance of services:

- In the fields of health, law, accounting, actuarial science, performing arts, consulting, athletics, financial services, brokerage services, or any business where the principal asset of such business is the reputation or skill of one or more of its employees/owners.

- o Notice that this specifically **does not include engineering and architecture** since they are a part of building something. Contrast that to accountants, lawyers, etc., who only provide services. Thus, Congress decided payment for services generally should be taxed the same as wages (ie, without a 20% deduction).
- That consist of investing and investment management, trading, or dealing in securities, partnership interests, or commodities.

Qualified Business Income

"QBI" means the net amount of qualified items of income, gain, deduction, and loss, from a qualified business within the U.S. QBI does **not** include:

- Reasonable compensation paid to the taxpayer
- Guaranteed payments or other payments paid to a partner for services rendered
- Capital gains/losses
- Dividends (or the equivalent)
- Interest income (eg, investment interest income) *other than* business interest income

The QBI deduction is determined at the partner/shareholder level, so each partner/shareholder takes into account their allocable share of each qualified item of income, gain, deduction, and loss, and is treated as having W-2 wages and unadjusted basis of qualified property equal to their allocable share of such items.

Deductible QBI Per Business

Wage/Property Limitation

The deductible amount per business is equal to 20% of the business's QBI but is generally limited to the *greater of:*

- 50% of W-2 wages, or
- 25% of W-2 wages + 2.5% of unadjusted basis of qualified property
  (ie, the entity's depreciable tangible assets used in the production of QBI)

Lower Income Level 1 — Below Threshold

If the taxpayer's taxable income does not exceed the threshold ($329,800 MFJ/$164,900 others for 2021), the wage/property limitation above does not apply.

Sara, a sole proprietor, is married and will file a joint return in year 1. Sara has $300,000 of taxable income from a T-shirt business. W-2 wages were $100,000 and the unadjusted basis of qualified property is $60,000. What is the deductible QBI for the T-shirt business?

20% × $300,000 = **$60,000**

Wage/property limitation does not apply under the threshold*.

Unadjusted thresholds are used in examples for simplification purposes.

Middle Income Level 2 — Between Threshold and Upper Limit

For taxpayers with taxable income up to $100,000 MFJ ($50,000 others) over the threshold, the limitation will **partially apply** depending on where the taxpayer's income is in that $100,000/$50,000 phase-in range above the threshold. That is, the deduction is reduced by the amount equal to:

- [(TI – threshold)/$100,000] × (20% QBI – limitation) for MFJ taxpayers
- [(TI – ½ MFJ threshold)/$50,000] × (20% QBI – limitation) for other taxpayers

Now assume the same facts as the last example, except that in year 2 Sara increases her taxable income from the T-shirt business to $350,000. What is the deductible QBI for the T-shirt business when the threshold is $315,000* for joint returns?

- 20% × $350,000 = $70,000
- Wage/property limitation—Greater of:
  - 50% × $100,000 wages = $50,000
  - (25% × $100,000 wages) + (2.5% × $60,000) = $26,500
- Here the wage limitation of $50,000 applies because TI is greater than $315,000, but only partially since TI is below $415,000 (ie, $315,000 threshold + $100,000).
  - [($350,000 TI – $315,000 threshold)/$100,000] × ($70,000 – $50,000 limitation)
  - $35,000/$100,000 × $20,000 excess = $7,000 reduction
  - The deductible QBI is $70,000 – $7,000 partial limitation/reduction = **$63,000**

Unadjusted thresholds are used for simplification purposes.

S Corporations

Highest Income Level 3 — Above Upper Limit

Again, same facts, but Sara increases her taxable income from the T-shirt business to $450,000 in year 3. What is the deductible QBI for the T-shirt business?

- 20% × $450,000 = $90,000
- Wage/property limitation—Greater of:
  - 50% × $100,000 wages = $50,000
  - (25% × $100,000 wages) + (2.5% × $60,000) = $26,500
- Here the wage limitation of $50,000 would apply in full because Sara's TI is above the upper limit, so her deductible QBI is **$50,000.**

Exception for Specified Service Trade or Businesses (SSTB)

When the taxable income of a taxpayer is less than the upper limit—ie, the sum of the threshold amount plus $100,000 MFJ ($50,000 others)—then any specified service business of the taxpayer (ie, a nonqualified business) will be treated as a qualified business, but only the **applicable percentage** of qualified income/deduction items, W-2 wages, and the unadjusted basis of qualified property, is used in the calculations when TI exceeds the threshold.

- "Applicable Percentage" means:
  - 100% – [(TI – threshold)/$100,000] for MFJ taxpayers
  - 100% – [(TI – ½ MFJ threshold)/$50,000] for all others
- In other words, the deduction:
  - Is allowed in full for nonqualified businesses if the taxpayer's TI falls below the threshold amount
  - Is phased out for every dollar over the threshold, up to the $100,000 MFJ (or $50,000) limit

Randy is single and is the sole owner of an S corporation that provides home healthcare. In year 1, the business produces $175,000 of taxable income. W-2 wages were $500,000 and the unadjusted basis of qualified property is $25,000. What is Randy's deductible QBI for the home healthcare business when the threshold is $157,500* for single individuals?

- First, we find the applicable percentage: 100% – [($175,000 TI – $157,500)/$50,000] = 65%
- Then we apply it to the QBI calculation: 20% × ($175,000 TI × 65%) = $22,750
- Wage/property limitation—Greater of:
  - 50% × ($500,000 wages × 65%) = $162,500
  - (25% × $500,000 wages × 65%) + (2.5% × $25,000 × 65%) = $81,656.25
- Here the wage/property limitation does not apply, since the deductible QBI is **$22,750.**

> Note: If the wage/property limitation had been low enough to apply, the same partial application calculation that applies in the middle income category above would have to be applied on top of this applicable percentage reduction.
>
> *Unadjusted thresholds are used for simplification purposes.*

Overall QBI Deduction Limit Per Taxpayer

Let's throw in yet another limitation; the overall QBI deduction per taxpayer is generally limited to the *lesser of*:

- Combined deductible QBI for all businesses owned, or
- 20% × (TI – NCG)
  - TI = Taxable Income computed without QBI deduction
  - NCG = Net Capital Gain (includes qualified dividends)

> To demonstrate, let's assume Roger, who is married to Louisa, has taxable income* of $310,000 that includes $20,000 of Louisa's income from a part-time job, a net capital gain of $10,000 and $280,000 ordinary business income from Roger's CPA Review S corp. Since this is his only business, his $56,000 deductible QBI (ie, $280,000 × 20%) is considered his combined QBI amount. Thus, Roger's QBI deduction is limited to the lessor of:
>
> - $56,000 combined QBI amount, or
> - 20% × ($310,000 – $10,000 NCG) = $60,000
>
> *Remember, taxable income = AGI – standard/itemized deductions (ie, TI before QBI deduction).*

QBI Deduction Summary		
TI[1] < Threshold (Level 1)	TI > Upper limit[2] (Level 3)	Threshold < TI < Upper limit (Level 2)
1. Determine deductible QBI per business		
Deductible QBI before limitations = 20% × QBI		
SSTBs allowed	Wage/property limitation—Greater of: • 50% of wages, or • 25% of wages + 2.5% of unadjusted basis of qualified property No SSTBs	**Phase-in reduction of wage/property limitation** [(TI – Threshold) / Phase-in Range] × (Deductible QBI – limitation) **Applicable % for SSTBs =** 100% – [(TI – Threshold)/ Phase-in Range]
2. Determine QBI deduction		
Overall taxpayer limitation—Lesser of: • Combined deductible QBI for all businesses, or • 20% × (TI – NCG[3])		

[1] Taxable Income before QBI deduction.

[2] Upper limit = threshold + phase-in range (ie, $100,000 MFJ/$50,000 others).

[3] Net Capital Gain also includes qualified dividends.

REG 4
Partnership Taxation

REG 4: Partnership Taxation

4.01 Partnership Formation — 1
- Overview — 1
- Formation — 1
- Precontribution Gain — 2
- Organizational & Start-up Costs — 2

4.02 Partnership Taxation: Basis — 3
- Calculating Partner Basis — 3
- Recourse vs. Nonrecourse Liabilities — 5
- Capital (Equity) Accounts — 5

4.03 Operation of Partnership — 6
- Form 1065 & Schedule K-1 — 6
- Separately Stated Items — 6
- Guaranteed Payments — 7
- Partnership Tax Year — 7
- Transactions Between Partner and Partnership — 9

4.04 Partnership Distributions — 10
- Distributions to a Retiring Partner — 10
- Nonliquidating Distributions — 10
- Liquidating Distributions — 11

4.05 Partnership Termination — 13
- Sale of Partnership Interest — 13
- Termination for Tax Purposes — 14
- Election to Adjust Basis of Partnership Property — 15
- Similarities & Differences between LLPs and LLCs — 15

4.01 Partnership Formation

Overview

A partnership (P/S) is an association between two or more persons to operate a business as co-owners for profit.

- File an Information tax return since a P/S is a flow-through entity (**Form 1065**).

   Return due dates and extensions are no longer tested on the CPA Exam.

- Tax year generally must be the same as the partners, or a majority of partners.
- Accounting is similar to S corporations.

Formation

- **Informal** creation since all partners have unlimited liability (ie, everything is **"at risk"** in a general partnership).
    - Cash or Property
        - Tax-free exchange (No 80%/control rule!)
        - Carryover basis
        - Carryover holding period
    - Services
        - Taxable at FMV of capital interest received (ie, generally the FMV of Services provided).

The **holding period** of a partnership interest acquired in exchange for a contributed property:

- For capital assets or Sec. 1231 (noncurrent business) assets: includes period held by the partner
- All other property—when partnership interest acquired.

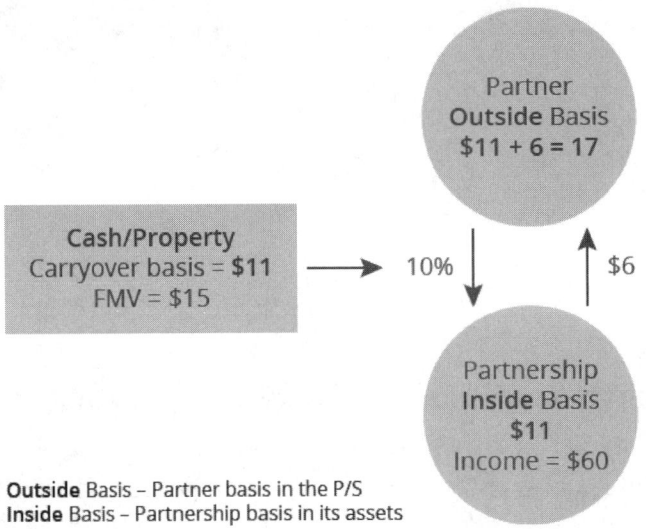

Outside Basis – Partner basis in the P/S
Inside Basis – Partnership basis in its assets

Precontribution Gain

An issue arises if a partner contributes **appreciated property** to a partnership. When the FMV of the property is greater than the partner's adjusted tax basis for the property, the property has an **unrecognized built-in-gain** for the difference between FMV and basis.

- To prevent the contributing partner from shifting the unrecognized gain to other partners in the future, the contributing partner is allocated the unrecognized gain when the partnership sells the property (or distributes the property to another partner within seven years).
- Any gain in excess of the unrecognized gain is allocated to all partners, generally based on their percentage of partnership interest.
- The contributing partner's outside basis is increased for the gain recognized.

Organizational & Start-up Costs

A partnership may deduct up to $5,000 of organizational expenditures and up to $5,000 of start-up costs for the tax year in which the partnership begins business. Any remaining expenditures are deducted ratably over the **180-month period** beginning with the month in which the partnership begins business. The $5,000 amount ($5,000 for each organizational and start-up costs) is reduced by the amount by which the organizational expenditures or start-up costs exceed $50,000, respectively.

- **Organizational costs** include partnership filing fees as well as legal and accounting fees incident to the organization of the partnership.
    - Syndication fees incurred to sell the interests are *not* organizational expenses and must be capitalized.
- **Start-up costs** include training, advertising and testing incurred before the start of active trade or business.

4.02 Partnership Taxation: Basis

Calculating Partner Basis

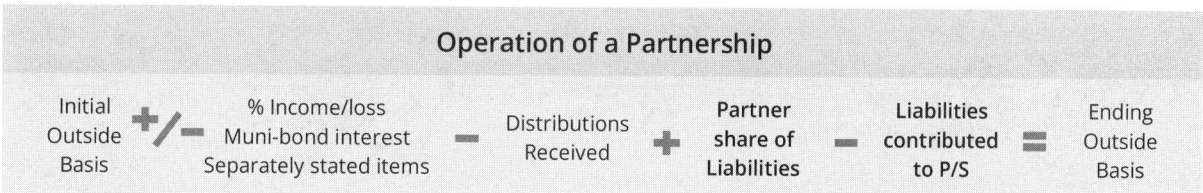

The most important concept in partnership tax law is that of basis, which generally equals the amount the partner has "at risk" in the partnership. A **partner's basis** is **not identical** to the **partner's Equity/Capital** in the business since a partner's basis includes the partner's share of partnership liabilities to creditors and the partner's capital account does not.

Note: Basis is generally equal the amount at-risk unless a reason is given as to why the partner is not at-risk for such amount (eg, a partner is not personally liable for repayment of a liability).

When a partnership is created, the partners normally make contributions of **cash or property**.

- When a partner contributes cash, their basis is increased by the amount paid.
- When a partner contributes property, their basis in their partnership interest is increased by the partner's tax basis in the contributed asset (FMV is ignored).
- If the asset being **contributed is subject to a liability**, the partner's net contribution is reduced because of the contributed liability, but then each partner's basis is increased by their individual shares of the liability the partnership has assumed.

Partner's Basis	
Increases for:	Decreases for:
• Contributions of assets by the partner to the partnership • Borrowings and other debts incurred by the partnership • Allocation of partnership income (distributive share) to the partner	• Distributions of assets from the partnership to the partner • Allocation of partnership losses (distributive share) to the partner • Repayments and other reductions of debts of the partnership

Determining Whether Losses Are Deductible

In determining whether a partner's distributive share of loss is deductible, *distributions are required to be taken into account before losses* due to the IRC Sec. 704(d) basis limitation. Any excess of such loss over basis is allowed as a deduction when the excess is repaid to the partnership (ie, there is sufficient basis to absorb the loss). Similarly, losses are also limited by the *at-risk rules* under IRC Sec. 465 and the *passive activity loss rules* under IRC Sec. 469, as previously discussed.

Assume that the ABC Partnership is formed with three equal partners: Andy, Billie, and Cindy. Andy and Billie each contribute $100 of cash. Cindy contributes land with a tax basis of $80 and a fair market value of $130, subject to an unpaid mortgage of $30 that is being assumed by the partnership. In terms of fair value, each partner has contributed an equal $100, but the tax determination of basis is as follows:

	Initial Contribution	± Income/Loss	- Distribution Received	+ % Partnership Liabilities	- Contributed Liabilities	= Net Basis (outside)
AA	$100			+$10		= $110
BB	$100			+$10		= $110
CC	$ 80			+$10	- $30	= $60

Partners	A	B	C
Contributed Asset	100	100	80
Contributed Liability	—	—	(30)
Net Contribution	100	100	50
Share of Liability	10	10	10
Basis (At Risk)	110	110	60

Notice that the $30 liability contributed by Cindy first decreases her basis due to the contributed debt but then increases it by $30 / 3 = $10, which is her share of the new partnership liability.

Partner Renders Services

When a partner renders **services** to the partnership in exchange for an interest in the business, the partner reports ordinary income equal to the FMV of the partnership interest being granted, and the partner's basis is increased by the same amount.

Gains and Losses

Partner basis never declines below $0.

- Losses in excess of basis are not deductible.
- Cash distributions in excess of basis results in gain.
- Contributed asset subject to higher liability results in gain.
- If an asset distribution exceeds basis, the basis of the distributed asset will be adjusted.

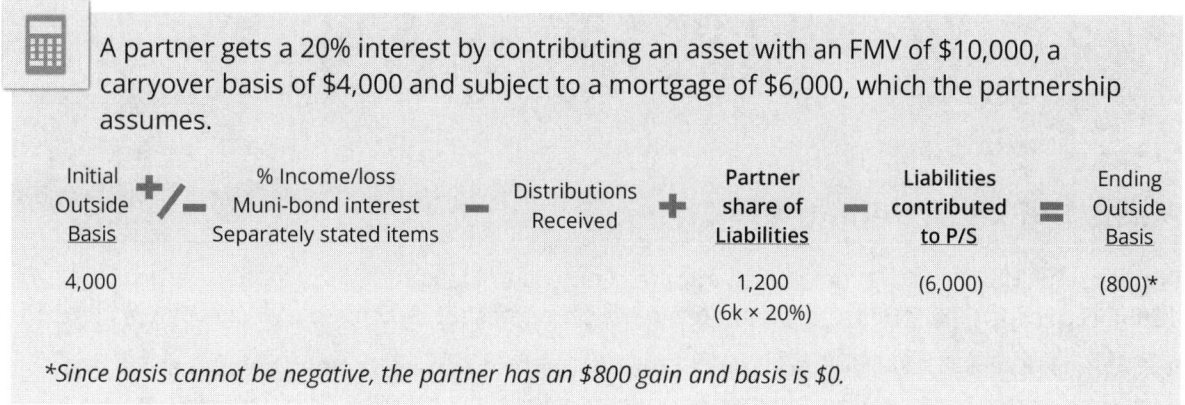

Since basis cannot be negative, the partner has an $800 gain and basis is $0.

Recourse vs. Nonrecourse Liabilities

- **Recourse Liabilities** – Debtor bears an economic risk of loss.
  - Partners generally share in recourse liabilities to the extent they are personally liable for repayment.
  - Since limited partners in a limited partnership are not generally liable for the repayment of debt, *recourse liabilities are allocated only to general partners*, unless otherwise specified.
- **Nonrecourse liabilities** – Debtor does NOT bear an economic risk of loss.
  - Partners (general and limited) generally share in nonrecourse liabilities in relation to their profits interest in the partnership. If a profits interest is not stated, it is the same as the capital interest.
    - Profits interest – Partner's share of future profits/losses.
    - Capital interest – Partner's share of net assets if partnership liquidates.

Capital (Equity) Accounts

Capital (Equity) accounts represent the partners' shares of partnership equity (partnership assets minus liabilities). A separate capital account for each partner is maintained. The partnership keeps track of each partner's capital account and presents an analysis of the capital account on Schedule K-1. Note: the capital account is different than the partner's adjusted basis. For example, the capital account does not include a partner's share of partnership liabilities, whereas basis does.

4.03 Operation of Partnership

Form 1065 & Schedule K-1

Partnerships do not pay income taxes but are required to file annual information returns (**Form 1065**), reporting partnership income and the allocation of that income to the various partners.

Since the items will be reported on the tax returns of the partners, the partnership must segregate items that have special treatment on individual tax returns. The partnership prepares a **Schedule K** that summarizes the partnership ordinary income and then separately lists all items that are not ordinary (ie, separately stated items). Additionally, a **Schedule K-1** is prepared for each partner showing that partner's allocated share of all items on the Schedule K.

 One should try and remember the list of the items that are reported separately as this has been tested.

Separately Stated Items

The purpose of separately stating items is to allow any special treatment on individual returns to be applied. Thus, any item that is always included in the gross income of an individual without restriction or limitation need not be separately stated. A few examples of separately stated items include:

Separately stated item	Reason not included in ordinary income
Capital gains and losses	Limit on deductibility of net capital losses
Section 1231 gains and losses	Classification of net gain as capital gain
Dividends and investment interest	Investment interest expense limitation
Passive activities	Passive activity loss limitations
Charitable contributions	Must itemize to deduct/ Up to 50% of AGI
Section 179 depreciation election	Dollar limit on use of election per year
Tax credits	Limited to tax liability

Note: Tax-exempt income and nondeductible expenses are also separately stated on the partner's Schedule K-1 since such items affect the partner's basis.

Examples of items that are included in partnership ordinary income are sales, depreciation, supplies, and salaries.

Guaranteed Payments

One item that is unusual and unique to partnerships is guaranteed payments to partners. These payments are based on separate contractual relationships between a partner and a partnership for **services rendered** by a partner (like wages) or for the **use of a partner's capital** (like interest). They may be a fixed dollar amount or a percentage of a partner's capital investment but can never be based on the amount of partnership income or loss.

For tax purposes, guaranteed payments are treated as if they were made with a nonpartner. Therefore, the payments are:

- **Deductible** as a separate expense on the **partnership's tax return** in the determination of net income or net loss
- **Taxable** as **ordinary income** to the partner receiving the payment (reported on Schedule K-1)

Other things to know about guaranteed payments include the following:

- Although guaranteed payments for services are not subject to withholding requirements by the partnership, they are subject to **self-employment tax** on the partner's tax return.
- Guaranteed payments for interest may be subject to the net investment income tax at the partner level.
- Because these payments are made to partners, neither type of guaranteed payment is included in the calculation of the QBI deduction.
- Unlike separately stated partnership items (eg, capital gains, dividends), guaranteed payments **do not directly affect a partner's outside basis**.

Partnership Tax Year

Per IRC Sec. 706(a), a partnership is **generally** required to adopt the same tax year as that of the partners (or a **majority** of partnership interests). Thus, if the partners are all individuals that report income using calendar years, the partnership itself should have a December 31 year-end.

- If there is **no majority** interest tax year, the tax year of the **principal** partners (ie, those owning **5%+**) is used.
- If there are no principal partners or their tax years are not the same, the year with the **least aggregate deferral** is used. Least aggregate deferral means the year that defers the least amount of the partners' income for the least amount of time, which is determined by adding together for each year: deferral period per partner × partner's % ownership.

Partner A (50% interest) reports income on the fiscal year ending 6/30 and Partner B (50% interest) reports income on the fiscal year ending 7/31.

Year-end 6/30

Partner	Year-end	% Interest in partnership	Months of deferral	Interest × deferral
A	6/30	.5	0	0
B	7/31	.5	1	.5
Aggregate deferral				.5*

Year-end 7/31

Partner	Year-end	% Interest in partnership	Months of deferral	Interest × deferral
A	6/30	.5	11	5.5
B	7/31	.5	0	0
Aggregate deferral				5.5

*A 6/30 year-end must be used since it results in the least aggregate deferral of income.

A partnership can use a tax year other than the normally required year if it **either**:

- Provides a valid **business purpose** for the alternate tax year.
    - A retail store with a natural business year ending on January 31.
    - Ski resort with a natural business year ending May 31.
    - Income deferral can exceed 3 months; business reason is the only criterion.
- Makes a **Section 444 election** – no business reason needed, but no more than 3 months' income deferral allowed. For example, a partnership that is normally required to use December 31 can, upon making a Section 444 election, choose November 30, October 31, or September 30. The result is to make it possible for up to 3 months of partnership income to be deferred into the following year before being taxed on the returns of the partners.

When the tax year of the partnership doesn't coincide with the tax year of a partner to whom the partnership is making guaranteed payments, the reporting of the payment received will be based on the tax year of the partnership.

Assume ABC partnership paid a regular $2,000 monthly salary to one of its partners, Andy Anderson, during calendar 20X1, and increased it to $3,000 monthly in calendar year 20X2. Andy's individual tax return is filed using a calendar year, but ABC is using the valid business reason exception and has a September 30 fiscal year.

The salary that will be reported by Andy on his individual tax return for 20X2 is **not** the $36,000 ($3,000 per month × 12 months) that he received in 20X2. He will be getting his 20X2 salary from the partnership K-1 for the year ended September 30, 20X2, and the partnership only paid $33,000 during the 12 months ended September 30, 20X2 ($2,000 per month × 3 months in 20X1, plus $3,000 per month for 9 months in 20X2).

Transactions Between Partner and Partnership

Transactions between a partner and the partnership generally are considered as occurring between two completely independent entities. The exception is if the partner owns over a majority interest in the partnership.

- **Losses** from sales of property between the controlling partner and the partnership are not allowed (related party transactions).
- **Gains** from the sale of property are characterized as *ordinary* income. This is the case whether the interest is owned directly or indirectly.

If, for example, partner A has a 40% ownership and related partner B has a 20% ownership, partner A would be considered to have a 60% controlling interest, thus, losses on transactions between partner A and the partnership would not be deductible.

Refer to the IRS website for the most recent versions of the Partnership tax forms.

4.04 Partnership Distributions

A distribution of assets from the partnership to a partner reduces that partner's basis in the partnership. The amount by which the partner's basis is reduced depends on several different factors. First, it must be determined if the distribution is:

- **Nonliquidating (Current or Operating Distributions)** – The partner continues in the business after the distribution.
- **Liquidating** – The distribution is in settlement of the partner's entire interest in the business.

Distributions to a Retiring Partner

Distributions to a retiring partner are generally treated as received in exchange for that partner's interest in partnership property, and as such are generally treated under the rules that apply to **liquidating distributions**. Payments made by a personal service partnership to a retired partner that are determined by partnership income are treated as income by the retired partner for tax purposes.

Nonliquidating Distributions

Normally, a nonliquidating distribution reduces the partner's basis in the partnership by the tax basis of the distributed asset in the partnership (the fair market value of distributed property is ignored, just as it is for contributed property). Since a partner's basis cannot be reduced below zero, however, a distribution in which the asset's basis exceeds the partner's basis must be handled specially:

- **Cash distributions** – The excess of the cash distribution over the partner's basis is reported as a gain on the partner's individual tax return.
- **Property distributions** – The basis of the distributed asset in the hands of the partner is reduced to equal the partner's basis in the partnership prior to the distribution.

Assume a partnership makes a nonliquidating distribution of $10 to a partner. If the partner's basis in the partnership was $17 before the distribution, the effect of cash distributions and property distributions is the same:

Type of asset	Cash	Property
Partner's basis before distribution	17	17
Distribution	(10)	(10)
Partner's basis after distribution	7	7
Gain or loss	0	0

If the partner's basis before the distribution was $8, the treatment varies:

Type of asset	Cash	Property
Partner's basis before distribution	8	8
Distribution	(10)	(8)
Partner's basis after distribution	0	0
Gain or loss	2	0

Notice that the basis of the property is simply reduced to $8 so that it will not exceed the partner's basis. Since cash cannot be adjusted, a gain must be reported.

Liquidating Distributions

A liquidating distribution is in some ways simpler, since the partner's basis in the partnership must be reduced to $0 in all cases. The difference between cash and property distributions is as follows:

- **Cash, inventory and unrealized receivable distributions –**
  - The total of cash, unrealized receivables, and inventory distributed to a partner is compared to the partner's basis in the partnership before the distribution and any excess basis is reported as a *loss* on the partner's individual tax return.
  - Only cash (and marketable securities) is used to determine a *gain*.
- **Property distributions** – The basis of the distributed asset is always equal to the partner's basis in the partnership before the distribution, so *no gain or loss* is recognized.

If a $10 **liquidating distribution** is made to a partner with a $17 basis in the business, the treatment is as follows:

Type of asset	Cash	Property
Partner's basis before distribution	17	17
Distribution	(10)	(17)
Partner's basis after distribution	0	0
Gain or loss	(7)	0

If the partner's basis in the partnership before the distribution was $8, the treatment is as follows:

Type of asset	Cash	Property
Partner's basis before distribution	8	8
Distribution	(10)	(8)
Partner's basis after distribution	0	0
Gain or loss	2	0

Note: If receive both cash and property, do cash first, the remainder is allocated to property.

To summarize the amount used for distributed property other than cash when the basis to the partnership of the distributed asset is different from the partner's basis in the partnership:

	Nonliquidating Distribution (Lower of inside or outside basis)	Liquidating Distribution (Outside basis)
Partner's basis > Asset's basis	Asset	Partner
Partner's basis < Asset's basis	Partner	Partner

4.05 Partnership Termination

Sale of Partnership Interest

When a partner wishes to sell their interest to another party (either another partner or an outsider), the *amount realized is the sum of*:

- Cash and property received
- + Relief from debt

For example, assume that Ronnie Remainder and Sammy Seller are equal partners in the R&S Partnership, and that the partnership, which reports on a cash basis for income tax purposes, has the following balance sheet:

	Tax Basis	Fair Market Value
Cash	150	150
Accounts receivable	---	300
Goodwill	---	400
Total assets	150	850
Liabilities	100	100
RR, capital	25	375
SS, capital	25	375
Total liabilities & capital	150	850

Bobby Buyer purchases Sammy's 50% interest in the partnership, paying Sammy $375 cash (based on the fair value of the partnership) and assuming Sammy's share of partnership liabilities.

In this transaction, the sales proceeds to Sammy are $425, including the cash received of $375 and the debt relief of $100 × 50% = $50. Sammy's basis in the partnership before the sale was $75, including the capital account's tax basis of $25 and Sammy's share of liabilities of $100 × 50% = $50. The gain on sale reported on Sammy's individual tax return is $425 - $75 = $350.

Actual Cash Proceeds	375
+ Debt Relief	+50
= Amount Realized	425
- Partner's Basis (Outside)	-75
= Gain/Loss	350

Normally, the gain on sale reported by a partner is a capital gain since it results from the sale of an investment asset (the interest in the business) rather than a business asset itself. There is, however, one possible complication. When a partner sells their interest, the amount the buyer is willing to pay is based on the FMV of the assets/liabilities (including goodwill), and not on the tax bases of these assets/liabilities.

If the partnership has **unrealized ordinary income assets (inventories and accounts receivable – "Hot Assets")** at the time of sale, the partner has effectively converted income that would have been ordinary to capital gains (since the partner sold the interest before the assets were realized). To prevent this, the gain on sale of a partnership must be reported as **ordinary income** to the extent of unrealized ordinary income assets at the time of sale. The rest is considered a capital gain.

Ordinary Gain/Loss for inventory and receivables → **Capital** Gain/Loss for everything else.

Again, assume Bobby Buyer purchases Sammy's 50% interest in the partnership so that Sammy realizes a gain of $350. In this example, the tax basis fails to reflect accounts receivable of $300 that result in ordinary income once the receivables are collected. Since Sammy's share of that receivable is $300 × 50% = $150, the first $150 of the gain on sale to Bobby is reported as **ordinary income**, and only the remaining $350 - $150 = $200 qualifies as a **capital gain**.

Termination for Tax Purposes

A partnership generally terminates for tax purposes under IRC §708(b) when no part of the business, financial operations, or venture of the partnership is carried on by any of its partners in the form of a partnership (ie, two or more partners).

A terminated partnership must file a final return that covers the period up to the date of termination. If the business continues, the new business must obtain a different tax identification number and file an initial return that begins from the date of the termination of the previous partnership. The end of the previous partnership and start of the new business are treated as distributions of all assets from the terminated partnership, followed by contributions of all the assets to the new business.

If a partnership divides into two or more separate partnerships, the partnership into which a majority of the interests of the old partnership are transferred is considered a continuation of that partnership, and the other partnerships are treated as brand-new businesses with new contributions of the transferred assets. If none of the separate partnerships holds a majority of previous interests, all are treated as new partnerships and the previous partnership is terminated.

If two or more partnerships merge and the partners in one of the businesses are given a majority of the interests of the merged entity, then the merged entity is considered a continuation of that previous partnership and the other previous partnerships are terminated. If no one former partnership gets a majority of interests in the new merged partnership, then all previous partnerships dissolve and the merged partnership is a new partnership with new contributions of the transferred assets.

Election to Adjust Basis of Partnership Property

A partnership may file a Sec. 754 election to adjust the basis of partnership property whenever there is a transfer of a partnership interest (ie, sale/exchange or when a partner dies). When this election is in effect, the partnership must increase/decrease its inside basis in partnership assets to make the new partner's outside basis equal to their share of inside basis in partnership property.

The election applies to all such transfers until the election is revoked by the partnership with IRS consent. (Note that the Sec. 754 election also covers basis adjustments in the event of a distribution of property, but this is likely beyond the scope of the exam).

Similarities & Differences between LLPs and LLCs

Limited Liability Company (LLC)

Some states allow for a type of business entity referred to as a Limited Liability Company (LLC). Owners of LLCs, which generally can be individuals, corporations, other LLCs, or foreign entities, are referred to as **members**. In most cases, all members have the right to participate in the management of the LLC and are treated as agents. Certain types of companies, such as banks and insurance companies, may not be structured as LLCs.

Unless the members elect otherwise, an LLC is **taxed** as a **flow-through entity**.

- If there is one member, it is considered a "disregarded entity" and the activities of the LLC are reported on the individual's tax return, using Schedule C to report income from a business or profession.
- If there are multiple members, the entity is usually treated as a partnership and is required to file an information return (1065). Profits, losses, and other pass-through items, however, may be allocated as the members see fit and not necessarily on the basis of ownership percentages.
- The entity may choose to be taxed as a corporation by filing an election (Form 8832). It may then elect to be taxed as a C corporation or an S corporation.

In addition to being able to elect how it is taxed, LLCs provide several other **advantages**. An LLC is considered an entity that is separate from its owners. It may sue or be sued. In addition, it provides the members with liability that is limited to the amount of their investments, although a distribution to members that renders the LLC insolvent will cause the members to be personally liable.

One **disadvantage** of the LLC is that, in most states, if a member leaves the LLC, the business is required to be dissolved. The remaining members must fulfill any business obligations and close the business, although they may start a new LLC if they so desire. Another disadvantage is that members of an LLC are considered self-employed and are subject to self-employment tax on their share of the entire earnings of the LLC.

Limited Liability Partnership (LLP)

Another form of entity is the Limited Liability Partnership (LLP), in which some or all partners, depending on the state of jurisdiction, have limited liability. It is like a general partnership in that all partners have the right to participate in management of the partnership.

Unlike general partnerships, partners in an LLP are not liable for the misconduct or negligence of other partners. In addition, an obligation of a partnership that is incurred while it is an LLP is generally the sole obligation of the partnership and the partners are not personally liable. [RUPA §306(c); adopted by a majority of states]

LLPs are popular among professionals, such as lawyers, accountants, and architects, to provide protection to partners from liability for ill advice that may be given by other partners within the firm.

Although an LLP provides its partners limited liability, it is **taxed** similarly to a general partnership.

- Taxed as a Partnership (Form 1065), unless elect to be taxed as a Corporation.
- If taxed as a Partnership:
  - A general partner, if there are any, is subject to both income tax and self-employment tax.
  - A limited partner's share of an LLP's income or loss is reported as passive income or loss, subject to the passive activity loss limitations.

Formation

- Both require an enabling statute in the state of formation.
- Both are easier to form than a corporation.
- Both require filing a certificate with an appropriate state authority, such as the secretary of state.
- An LLC may be formed with one or more owners, referred to as members, while an LLP requires 2 or more partners.

Taxation

- Both are pass-through entities.
- Both may report their operations by filing information returns (Form 1065) and distributing K-1s to its members or partners.
  - An LLP is, by default, treated as a partnership.
  - An LLC with more than one member is treated as a partnership, and those with one member are treated as sole proprietorships (Schedule C).

Liability

Both provide owners with some degree of protection.

- LLCs generally limit the liability of members to their investments, plus the costs resulting from their own negligence or malpractice.
- Partners of LLPs are generally not liable for the actions of copartners but are liable for the obligations and debts of the LLP in some states.

LLC	LLP (Accounting Firms)
Formal creation	Formal
≥ 1 Person	≥ 2 people
- Limited Liability for Contracts and debts - Unlimited Liability for Malpractice or Negligence	- Limited Liability for Malpractice or Negligence - Unlimited Liability for Contracts/Debts in some states
Agents/Member	Agents
Taxed as a P/S (or Corp or Sch. C)	Taxed as a P/S (or Corp)

REG 5
Trusts, Gift Taxes & Tax-Exempt Organizations

REG 5: Trusts, Gift Taxes & Tax-Exempt Organizations

5.01 Trusts   1
    Overview   1
    Creation of a Trust   2
    Types of Trusts for Income Tax Purposes   2

5.02 Gift Tax   4
    Overview   4
    Lifetime Transfers   5
    Lifetime Exclusion   5
    Generation-Skipping Tax   6
    Overview – Types of Organizations   8

5.03 Tax-Exempt Organizations   8
    Unrelated Business Income   8

5.01 Trusts

Overview

Trusts are typically established by a **trustor** for the purpose of benefiting specific individuals or charities (ie, **beneficiaries**) without giving them current **control** of the principal (**corpus**) of the trust. There are two types of beneficiaries: **income** and **remainder** beneficiaries.

The allocation of assets between the beneficiaries can be tricky. The corpus of the trust will eventually go to the remainder beneficiaries, and the income will go to the income beneficiaries.

- Income includes most of the items that are reported as income on accrual financial statements (regardless of whether it is reported for tax purposes).
- Notice, however, that the proceeds from the sale of corpus are allocated entirely to corpus, so that gains and losses on asset sales are **not** income to the income beneficiary.

Trustor (grantor, settlor, creator)	Trustee*	Beneficiaries (2 types)*	
		Income (I/S)	Remainderman (B/S)
Puts assets in trust	Controls assets	Receives trust **earnings**: • Interest income/payments • Dividends • Municipal bond interest • Rental income/expense • Cash dividends • Property taxes • Depreciation • Royalty income • Insurance premiums	Receives trust **principal**: • Assets contributed to the trust (ie, trust property) • Principal (corpus) • Capital gains • Stock dividends/splits • Proceeds/property received in exchange for trust corpus • Principal payments • Capital improvements • Insurance proceeds • Bonds (accrued interest)

*Must separate control and benefit of assets. Beneficiary can be co-trustee but not sole trustee.

 If a trust is formed with a contribution of $100,000 cash, the cash is classified as corpus. When the cash is used to purchase common stock, the stock is corpus. A cash dividend paid on the common stock is income (a stock dividend or split remains in corpus, though, since it is not reported on an accrual basis income statement). If the stock is subsequently sold for $350,000 cash, all the cash is corpus as it represents the proceeds from the sale of corpus.

Creation of a Trust

There are two points at which a trust can be created—during life or at death:

- **Inter vivos trust** – Assets transferred into a trust by a living person.
- **Testamentary trust** – Created through the execution of a will.

Valid Express Trust

For a trust to be a **valid express trust**, it must satisfy **five conditions (BRATS)**:

- **Beneficiary** – The trust must identify who will receive the benefits deriving from the trust. As discussed, a trust often identifies an *income beneficiary* to receive the earnings of the trust, and a *remainder beneficiary* to receive the principal of the trust when it terminates.
- **Reasonable intent** – There must be a valid purpose (tax savings do not qualify) for the existence of the trust. This is usually the separation of control of the assets from their benefits, so a trust with a single individual serving as both trustee and sole beneficiary will usually fail. A trust will also fail when its purpose is impossible to fulfill.
- **Assets** – The trust must contain some *corpus* or property. A trust without corpus has no earnings for the income beneficiaries or principal for the remainder beneficiaries.
- **Trustee** – A trustee must be in place to exercise control over the assets in the trust. This person does not need to be named in any legal document; however, they can be selected by the court or personal representative of the estate in the case of a testamentary trust. A successor trustee is not needed and can simply be selected in the event the trustee can no longer serve.
- **Specified life** – A trust must have an identifiable termination point, expressed in years or in the length of a life in being at the time the trust is created, plus a maximum of 21 years.
    - **Private trust** = cannot live forever – lives until purpose is satisfied (eg, if established for college, the trust ends after graduation)
    - **Charitable trust** = lives forever (**perpetuity**)

Types of Trusts for Income Tax Purposes

Revocable vs. Irrevocable Trusts

Trusts are **irrevocable**, unless:

- Reserve rights
- End of term
- Occurrence of an event (death)
- Purpose is accomplished
- Consent of trustor and all beneficiaries, remainderman, and courts

A **revocable** trust whose creator (grantor) reserves the right to withdraw assets at any time is called a **grantor trust**. The tax code ignores these trusts since the **transfer** of assets is considered **incomplete**. Thus, transfers to a revocable trust are not subject to gift tax, and any income is taxed on the grantor's Form 1040 as if the trust did not exist. Upon the death of the grantor, a revocable trust becomes irrevocable.

Simple vs. Complex Trusts

There are two types of nongrantor (irrevocable) trusts that are subject to taxes.

- **Simple trust** – A simple trust is one that distributes all of its **trust accounting income** (TAI), but no corpus, to **taxpaying beneficiaries** (not charities) each year. TAI is determined under the trust's governing documents and local law (not the IRC).
    - Taxable income is normally reduced to $0 by distributions.
        - Net capital gains can result in retained income.
        - Personal exemption is $300.*
    - TAI, the amount required to be distributed, may exceed **distributable net income** (**DNI**)—the maximum amount taxable to beneficiaries. The excess is considered a distribution of principal.
- **Complex trust** – Any nongrantor trust that fails to meet the criteria for a simple trust.
    - This means that a complex trust will meet at least one of the following three conditions during the tax year:
        - **Less than TAI** is **distributed** and some current income is retained within the trust.
        - Amounts are permanently set aside for **charitable gifts**.
        - An amount allocated to trust **corpus** was **distributed**.
    - Complex trusts often pay taxes on undistributed income.
        - Personal exemption is only $100.*

*Note: Trusts cannot claim standard deductions.

5.02 Gift Tax

Overview

Taxes may be owed by those who transfer large amounts of their wealth to others during their lifetime and upon their death, based on the **unified transfer tax**. Transfers made during their lifetime are reported on **gift tax returns (Form 709)**. The estate tax return (Form 706) then combines all reported gifts and the value of the estate at death to determine if any additional taxes are due. Note, however, that the estate tax is no longer tested.

Gifts may involve:

- Transfers of cash or property
- Sales of property at a bargain price to another family member
- Loans to family members on which a fair rate of interest is not charged (ie, imputed interest)
- Irrevocable trusts established for others in which income and/or corpus will eventually go to someone other than the taxpayer

Gifts do not include:

- Transfers to **spouses** (must be married at the time of transfer)
    - Gifts given in contemplation of marriage (eg, engagement rings) are not exempt.
- Support for minor children
- Transfers to qualified charitable organizations
- Political contributions
- Payment of medical expenses or tuition of another (must be made directly to the health care or education provider)
- $16,000 annual gift exclusion to any one person

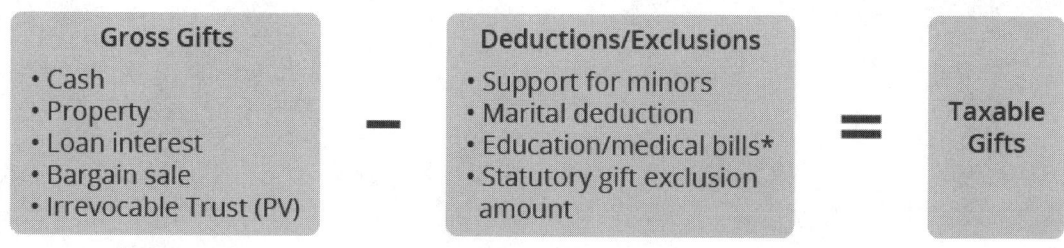

*Must be paid directly to the institution.

Lifetime Transfers

There are three types of transfers that may take place during a person's lifetime:

- **Gift of a present interest** – An immediate transfer of wealth that can be accessed by the recipient immediately. A **gift of a present interest** normally must be reported in years in which the taxpayer transfers more than **$16,000** in wealth to a single individual ($32,000 for MFJ with gift-splitting election).

  Can you start enjoying the gift now?

  - A present interest exists if there is:
    - An annuity starting now
    - Outright ownership of the property
    - A guaranteed right to immediately receive the periodic dividends, rents, or other income stream the property generates
  - A delayed right to property does not qualify.
  - Depositing cash into a *joint bank account* with an intended beneficiary (noncontributing tenant) only becomes a gift when the beneficiary withdraws funds from that account for their own benefit.

- **Gift of a future interest** – An irrevocable transfer of the right to access wealth at a future time. A gift of a future interest must be reported, regardless of size, at the present value of the future interest.
  - Any gift in which the amount is not immediately available to the gift beneficiary (cannot enjoy now).
  - Does not qualify for the $16,000 annual exclusion.

- **Uncompleted gift (no interest)** – A revocable transfer of the right to access wealth at a future time. An uncompleted gift (no interest) is not reported, and the wealth is still considered a part of the taxpayer's estate as long as they retain their right to revoke the transfer (eg, revocable trust).

It is possible for the interests in a trust to be split. If the trust income goes immediately to *one beneficiary* each year, and the corpus will go to another when the trust terminates, then the grantor is making a gift of a present interest to the *income beneficiary* each year and a gift of a future interest (if it is irrevocable) to the *remainder beneficiary*.

Lifetime Exclusion

The fact that a gift must be reported on a gift tax return does not, however, automatically mean that any tax liability will be owed. Each individual is permitted to make taxable gifts up to their lifetime limit before owing any tax. The lifetime exclusion amount is **$12,060,000 for 2022**[1].

Since gift taxes are applied to each individual donor, a husband and wife may each use the annual and lifetime exclusions mentioned. They can also agree to split large gifts made by one of them and treat each as having given half of the amount.

---

[1] *TCJA doubled the lifetime exclusion amount (adjusted for inflation) for estates of decedents dying and gifts made after 2017 and before 2026.*

Each gift tax return represents one individual donor. **Portability** between spouses, however, permits a surviving spouse to apply the decedent's unused exclusion amount to the surviving spouse's own transfers.

Note: The top tax bracket for the gift tax is **40%**.

Assume that Gerald Generous, a single individual, files a gift tax return on 4/15/X2 for the first time, reporting gifts made to three different persons in 20X1:

- Fran Friend – Gerald gave $1,000,000 cash to Fran.
- Pat Parent – Gerald sold Pat his condo in Florida for $500,000 (its appraised value was $2,000,000 at the time of sale).
- Nellie Niece – Gerald established an irrevocable trust that paid all income to Gerald for 10 years, then transferred the trust corpus to Nellie at the end of that period. The value of the corpus was $4,500,000 when the trust was established, and the present value of the gift was determined to be $2,000,000.

The gift to Fran is $1,000,000, of which $985,000 must be reported after the annual exclusion. The gift to Pat is $1,500,000, of which $1,485,000 must be reported after the annual exclusion. The gift to Nellie is $2,000,000, and doesn't qualify for an annual exclusion since the corpus is not immediately available to Nellie (ie, gift of future interest).

The total gifts reported on the return are $985,000 + $1,485,000 + $2,000,000 = $4,470,000. This uses $4,470,000 of the lifetime exclusion, but no tax is owed at this time. If, for example, Gerald makes reportable gifts of $8,000,000 more in his lifetime (assuming the lifetime exclusion of $12,060,000 - 2022), however, he will have to pay gift taxes, since he will have exceeded the cumulative lifetime exclusion.

Generation-Skipping Tax

There is one additional component to the unified transfer tax that is reported on the gift tax return known as the **generation-skipping transfer (GST) tax**. This tax is imposed when the donor transfers substantial property to beneficiaries at least two generations below the donor.

The GST tax applies when amounts exceeding the lifetime exclusion are transferred. The lifetime exclusion is **$12,060,000 for 2022**. This exclusion is separate from the lifetime exclusion on gift and estate taxes, and any tax resulting from transfers exceeding this amount is owed in addition to those taxes.

The intent of the GST tax is to prevent taxpayers from avoiding the transfer taxes on a generation by giving, for example, to grandchildren instead of children. The amount of the GST tax is usually reasonably close to the additional transfer taxes that would have been paid if the taxpayer had transferred the property to their children and then the children had transferred the property to the grandchildren.

The GST tax does **not** apply to transfers to a grandchild if the taxpayer's child who is the parent of the grandchild is already deceased, since the grandchild is actually the first generation in that line below the taxpayer.

Refer to the IRS website for the most recent Gift tax forms

5.03 Tax-Exempt Organizations

Overview – Types of Organizations

Certain organizations are eligible to be classified as **exempt organizations** once approved by the IRS. To be considered exempt, the organization must be one of those specifically identified in the tax code and must apply for and receive an exemption. There are more than 19 different classifications under IRC Sec. 501(c) that are eligible for exempt status. Some examples include:

- Organizations with specific charitable, educational, or scientific intent
- Religious organizations
- Social and recreation clubs (fraternity or country clubs)
- Credit unions
- Condo associations
- Labor unions

Charitable organizations are classified as **private foundations** if they receive less than 1/3 of support from the general public, and **public charities** if they receive more. An organization does **not** qualify as an exempt charity if it is merely a **feeder organization**. A feeder organization is an organization operated as a business for profit but that transfers all its net earnings to charitable organizations.

Unrelated Business Income

Any exempt organization will have to file a business income tax return (Form 990-T) and pay income taxes if it has more than **$1,000** of **unrelated business income (UBI)**. UBI refers to income obtained from the operations of business activities not associated with the exempt purpose of the organization (eg, a tattoo parlor at a church). The definition of UBI specifically **excludes**:

- Legal games of chance used to raise funds, such as **bingo**
- Activities only carried out on an intermittent basis, such as annual charity auctions
- Business activities **related to the organization's purpose,** such as sales of educational materials to members of an organization established to maintain/improve the skills of its members
- Most investment income
- Activities that are staffed entirely by volunteers working without pay
- The sale of merchandise that was received as a gift or contribution
- Convenience of members, employees, or students (eg, cafeteria or bookstore)

REG 6
Depreciation

REG 6: Depreciation

6.01 Depreciation: Real vs. Tangible Personal Property — 1
Real property (Section 1250 Property) — 1
Tangible personal property (non-realty) (Section 1245 Property) — 2

6.02 Section 179 & Other Cost Recovery Deductions — 5
Additional First-Year Depreciation (Bonus Depreciation) — 6
Intangibles (Section 197) — 7
Other Depreciable Assets — 7
Depletion — 8

6.01 Depreciation: Real vs. Tangible Personal Property

Federal tax law uses a method of depreciation called Modified Accelerated Cost Recovery System (**MACRS**) for property placed in service after 1986. This system **differs** from GAAP depreciation in three significant ways:

1. The cost of the asset is deducted over a stated recovery period that is shorter than the estimated useful life of the asset in most cases.
2. The recovery period for **new and used** property is identical.
3. Salvage values are **ignored.**

Real property (Section 1250 Property)

The recovery period is:

- **27.5 years** – Residential rental property
- **39 years –** Most other buildings, aka, Nonresidential real property (business and investment realty)
    - Land is not depreciated.
    - *Straight-line* method is used (MACRS).
    - Salvage value of building is ignored.
    - Mid-month convention is required.
        - Only depreciate real property for ½ the month when placed into service and ½ in the month of disposal. In other words, all real estate bought and sold during a particular month are treated as having been bought and sold in the middle of the month.

> Assume that the client purchases an office building on 11/1/X1 for $500,000, which includes land with a value of $32,000. The cost of the building itself is $500,000 – $32,000 = $468,000, and this is recovered over a 39-year period, resulting in MACRS deductions of $468,000 / 39 years = $12,000 per year. In 20X1, the year of acquisition, the property is treated as having been purchased in the middle of November, so that only 1 ½ months of depreciation are claimed that year. Depreciation of $12,000 / 12 months = $1,000 per month is multiplied by 1 ½ months, resulting in a $1,500 MACRS deduction in 20X1.

Tangible personal property (non-realty) (Section 1245 Property)

- **3 years** – Small tools, off-the-shelf (OTS) software*
- **5 years** – Automobiles, light trucks, copiers, computers & printers
- **7 years** – Most other personal property, equipment, office furniture, desks
- **10 years** – Barges, tugs, vessels, water transportation equipment

- **15 years** – Municipal wastewater treatment plants
- **20 years** – Municipal sewer and farm buildings
    - MACRS
        - *Double Declining Balance* (DDB/200% DB—3, 5, 7, 10-year property)
            - Switch to straight line (S/L) when it results in a greater deduction.
            - Straight line may be elected instead of DDB.
              Note: DDB does not apply to OTS software—S/L depreciation only with no half-year convention.
        - 150% Declining Balance (15, 20-year property—rarely tested)
    - Salvage value is ignored.
    - Half-year convention
    - Mid-quarter convention
        - If acquired at least 40% of its assets in the final three months of the year, it is assumed that every asset purchased occurred at the mid-point of the quarter in which it was purchased.

Unless the business makes a specific election to use straight-line depreciation, the method of depreciation used for personal property is **double-declining balance**. In addition, purchases and sales are normally handled using the **half-year** convention, so that all transactions are treated as taking place in the middle of the year.

 Assume the client purchases office furniture for $490 on 2/1/X1. Furniture, like most personal property, has a 7-year recovery period. Assuming straight-line depreciation of 1/7 of cost per year is not elected, the client will use double-declining balance, and claim 2/7 of the remaining basis each year. In the year of acquisition, 20X1, the half-year convention is applied, so the MACRS deduction is $490 x 2/7 x ½ = $70. In 20X2, the remaining basis of $490 - $70 = $420 is used, and the MACRS deduction is $420 x 2/7 = $120.

The half-year convention may not be used in all cases. In order to prevent businesses from getting a half-year of depreciation on an excessive number of assets acquired late in the year, businesses acquiring 40% or more of their personal property in the final quarter of the year are required to use a **mid-quarter** convention, meaning that items are treated as having been purchased in the middle of the quarter in which they were purchased, instead of the middle of the year.

Depreciation

Assume the client purchased small tools for $300 on 12/29/X1, and that this was the **only** purchase of tangible personal property that took place during 20X1.

Small tools have a 3-year recovery period, and the MACRS deduction using double-declining balance and the half-year convention would have been $300 × 2/3 × 1/2 = $100. This is not allowed, however, since more than 40% (actually, 100%) of personal property was acquired in the last quarter of the year. As a result, the small tools are treated as having been acquired in the middle of November (the middle of the last quarter), and only 1 ½ months of depreciation may be claimed in 20X1. Since 1 ½ months is equal to 1/8 of a year, the MACRS deduction using the mid-quarter convention in 20X1 is $300 × 2/3 × 1/8 = $25.

A depreciation table may be used to calculate depreciation expense for MACRS Personal Property. This table is assuming 200% declining balance (Double Declining Balance), switching to straight-line when it is beneficial to do so. Remember that we are assuming half-year convention and salvage value is ignored.

If a computer (5-year property) is purchased for $100, depreciation expense for the first 2 years would be calculated as follows:

- Year 1 = $100 × 1/5 yrs × 200% = $40 × 1/2 (half-year convention) = $20 dep exp in the 1st year
- Year 2 = $100 – $20 yr 1 dep = $80 x 1/5 yrs x 200% = $32 dep exp in the 2nd year

One could also simply use the factors from the table (20% and 32%) to calculate the same results.

This table is set up for 3, 5 and 7-year property.

MACRS Depreciation 200% DDB Table
Half-Year Convention for Personal Property

Year	3 Year	5 Year	7 Year
1	33.33%	20.00%	14.29%
2	44.45%	32.00%	24.49%
3	14.81%	19.20%	17.49%
4	7.41%	11.52%	12.49%
5		11.52%	8.93%
6		5.76%	8.92%
7			8.93%
8			4.46%
			100%

6.02 Section 179 & Other Cost Recovery Deductions

TCJA permanently increased the Section 179 deduction amount and the phaseout limit to $1,000,000 and $2,500,000, respectively. These amounts will be indexed for inflation after 2018. TCJA also expanded the definition of "qualified real property" eligible for the deduction.

As a way to stimulate investment in small businesses (and, in turn, the economy), simplify tax compliance, and reduce the burden of recordkeeping for depreciation purposes, the federal tax code permits businesses to make a **Section 179 election** to immediately expense certain *New and Used* depreciable property (ie, "Section 179 Property") used in the business, instead of capitalizing and depreciating it.

- Maximum expense amount is **$1,080,000 for 2022.**
- The phase out begins at **$2,700,000**; that is, the $1,080,000 limit is reduced $1 for every $1 spent over $2,700,000 on Section 179 property. Thus, the election is not available if such purchases exceed $3,780,000.
- **Section 179 Property** – Property eligible for the deduction includes:
  - The property must be acquired by purchase from an unrelated party for use in an active trade or business.
  - Tangible personal property (ie, 3, 5, 7-year depreciable property used in the business—Section 1245 property)
  - Off-the-shelf Computer Software
  - Qualified Real Property
    - *Qualified improvement property* – Generally, any improvement to an interior portion of nonresidential real property after the building was first placed in service (eg, remodeling the dining area of a restaurant when it has become outdated)
      - Note that the following types of improvements do *not* qualify:
        - Enlarging the building
        - An elevator or escalator
        - The internal structural framework of the building
    - Any of the following improvements to nonresidential real property after the building was first placed in service:
      - Roofs
      - Heating, ventilation, and air-conditioning property
      - Fire protection and alarm systems
      - Security systems
- Property acquired by purchase from a related party does *not* qualify.
- Deduction *not* allowed if a net loss exists or if taking the depreciation expense would create a net loss. Disallowed amounts can be carried forward.

- *Not* generally available on intangibles or real property (except for certain improvements as discussed above).
- The cost of a heavy SUV that may be expensed is limited to $27,000 (2022).

With respect to S corporations and partnerships, 179 limitations are applied at both the entity and owner level.

For example, if the maximum election permitted for the tax year is $1,000,000*, this maximum is phased out on a dollar-for-dollar basis if the purchases of qualified property during the tax year exceed $2,500,000. As a result, a business that purchases $3,500,000 or more in tangible personal property may not use this election. A few examples of the maximum election follow:

Qualified purchases	30,000	1,080,000	2,800,000	3,700,000
Maximum election	30,000	1,000,000	700,000	0
Remaining basis	0	80,000	2,100,000	3,700,000

Notice in the case of qualified purchases of $2,800,000, the purchases exceed the threshold of $2,500,000 by $300,000, so the maximum election is reduced from $1,000,000 to $700,000 ($1,000,000 - $300,000). In other words, a dollar-for-dollar reduction of $300,000 is equal to the amount by which the total purchase price exceeds the $2,500,000 threshold. In each example, the remaining basis (if any) is used to determine additional MACRS deductions based on the normal 3, 5, or 7 years, etc.

Unadjusted amounts are used for simplification purposes.

On the CPA Exam, tax threshold amounts subject to frequent change will often be provided within the related problems.

Additional First-Year Depreciation (Bonus Depreciation)

Bonus depreciation is an additional allowance of depreciation in the first year certain property is placed in service. Like the Section 179 deduction, this is yet another tool the government uses to stimulate business investment, simplify tax compliance, and reduce the burden of recordkeeping. As such, it is frequently adjusted by Congress to suit the needs of the current economic environment. Unlike the 179 deduction, this provision is not capped at a certain dollar amount.

TCJA increased and extended the bonus depreciation deduction to 100% through 2022, at which point it will begin to phase out again by 20% each year until it is no longer available. The deduction was also expanded to include purchases of used property in addition to new property.

- **100-percent** bonus depreciation is available through 2022.

- Applies to qualified *new or used* assets (ie, tangible Sec. 1245 property with a MACRS life of 20 years or less) in the year they are placed in service.
- Claimed after the Section 179 expense deduction, if elected, but before the Regular depreciation expense deduction. Note: This order makes more sense in years where less than 100% bonus depreciation is allowed (eg, when the percentage is reduced to 80% in 2023).
- If the taxpayer does not wish to take the bonus depreciation allowed in the first year the property is placed in service, the taxpayer must make an election to opt out.

Intangibles (Section 197)

Qualifying intangibles include franchises, trademarks, customer-based intangibles, and acquired but not self-created goodwill. Certain intangibles qualify only if acquired in connection with the acquisition of a trade or business. These include covenants not to compete, patents, and copyrights. *Straight-line amortization* is used.

- 15 years – most intangibles (including goodwill)
- 15 years (180 months) ($5,000 immediately) – organization expense – must begin amortization in first year of operations.
- Life of contract – franchises
- Must begin amortization in month of acquisition.

Other Depreciable Assets

There are a handful of other assets rarely mentioned on the exam:

- 10 year – Water transportation equipment, single-purpose agricultural (constructed to house, raise and feed livestock) and horticultural structures (a greenhouse for Farmers) – Double-declining balance
- 15 year – Wastewater treatment plants & cement-producing assets – 150%-declining balance
- 20 year – Sewers and farm buildings – 150%-declining balance

Most of these assets are not eligible for the Section 179 election but can claim the additional first-year depreciation.

Depletion

Depletion is used for natural resources that are exhaustible or wasting assets, such as timber, minerals, oil and gas. There are 2 methods allowed:

Cost method = $\dfrac{\text{Adjusted basis (cost-acc depletion)}}{\text{Estimated recoverable units}}$ × Units sold = Depletion exp/yr

Percentage method = A statutory percentage × Gross income = Depletion exp
 (Percentage generally ranges from 5% to 20% but can never exceed 50%.)

Refer to the IRS website for tax forms relating to depreciation and amortization.

REG 7
Property Tax Transactions

REG 7: Property Tax Transactions

7.01 Property Types: Ordinary, 1231, & Capital Assets   1
- OVERVIEW   1
- CAPITAL ASSET HOLDING PERIOD   2
- NETTING PROCESS & TAX TREATMENT   2

7.02 Depreciation Recapture   5
- SECTION 1245 DEPRECIATION RECAPTURE FOR TANGIBLE PERSONAL PROPERTY   5
- SECTION 1250 DEPRECIATION RECAPTURE FOR REAL PROPERTY   5

7.03 Capitalization Rules   7
- UNIFORM CAPITALIZATION RULES (UNICAP – SECTION 263A)   7
- CAPITALIZATION VS EXPENSE OF ACQUIRING, MAINTAINING, IMPROVING, REPAIRING & REPLACING TANGIBLE PROPERTY (SECTION 263)   7

7.04 Gifts & Inheritances   11
- INDIVIDUAL PROPERTY TAX TRANSACTIONS – OVERVIEW   11
- INHERITANCES   11
- GIFTS   12
- SPECIAL RULES APPLICABLE TO INDIVIDUALS & CORPORATIONS   15

7.05 Special Property Tax Transactions   15
- SPECIAL RULES APPLICABLE TO INDIVIDUALS ONLY   19

7.01 Property Types: Ordinary, 1231, & Capital Assets

Overview

- **Ordinary income assets** (current assets of a business, aka, "Hot Assets") – Generally refers to assets that were acquired or produced with the intention of being sold in the ordinary course of business.
  - Includes:
    - Inventory
    - **Receivables** arising from sales
    - Self-created **artistic work** (eg, copyrighted material)
    - Self-created **intangible assets** (eg, patents, inventions, secret formulas)
  - Tax Treatment: All gains/losses are taxed at ordinary tax rates. No special rate/treatment or limitations apply (assuming no related parties are involved).
  - Note: Assets used in a business for 1 year or less also generate ordinary gains/losses since they do not qualify as Sec. 1231 assets or capital assets.
- **Sec. 1231 assets** (noncurrent business assets) – Assets used in the trade or business and **held longer than one year**, whose eventual sale or disposal is only incidental to the business.
  - Includes:
    - Depreciable and amortizable property
    - Land used in business, PP&E
  - Must be held over 1 year:
    - Net 1231 **loss** is ordinary loss. (Form 4797)
    - Net 1231 **gain** is Long Term Capital Gain. (Schedule D)
      - Prior depreciation is recaptured as ordinary income on tangible personal property.
    - Tax treatment: **Best of both worlds**! Since a net 1231 gain is treated as a capital gain, it can be used to offset net capital losses that otherwise might not have been deductible in the current year. Since a 1231 loss is treated as an ordinary loss, it is fully deductible.
  - If held ≤ 1 year – Ordinary gains/losses
- **Capital assets** (nonbusiness assets) – Assets that do not qualify as ordinary income or Sec. 1231 assets.
  - Includes:
    - Investment assets
    - **Personal use** assets (ie, used by taxpayer or family/household)
    - **Goodwill**—Although goodwill is amortizable, it is not actually used by a business in a meaningful sense, since it doesn't diminish in value from usage, therefore, it is also treated as a capital asset.
  - Nonbusiness bad debts write offs are always S/T capital losses.

- *Not* capital assets:
    - Property normally included in inventory or held for sale to customers in the ordinary course of business
    - Depreciable property and real estate used in business
    - Accounts and notes receivable arising from sales or services in the taxpayer's business
    - Copyrights, literary, musical or artistic compositions
    - Patents, inventions, models, designs, and secret formulas and processes
    - Treasury stock

Notice that the tax character of the item depends on the handling by the taxpayer. A *personal computer* would be an ordinary income asset to the manufacturer of the computer, a Sec. 1231 asset to an accounting firm which acquired the computer for use by its employees, and a capital asset to a person who bought it to run educational software for their children at home.

Capital Asset Holding Period

In general, short-term capital transactions refer to sales that take place within a year of the acquisition date, and long-term transactions are those held for longer than one year. There are two exceptions:

- **Inherited assets** – Sales are always classified as long-term (**L/T**).
- **Nonbusiness bad debts** – Write-offs are always classified as short-term capital losses (**S/T**).

Note: When a security becomes worthless, the holding period is calculated by treating the property as if it was sold on the last day of the tax year in which it becomes worthless. *Worthless securities* generally receive capital loss treatment; however, if the loss is incurred by a corporation on an investment in an affiliated corporation (80% or more ownership), the loss is treated as an ordinary loss item.

Netting Process & Tax Treatment

- Long-term capital gains (LTCG) and losses (LTCL) are combined to determine the net long-term capital gain or loss for the year.
- Short-term capital gains (STCG) and losses (STCL) are combined to determine the net short-term capital gain or loss for the year.
- If the results of these combinations are both gains, stop, they are reported separately.
    - **STCG**—Ordinary tax rates apply.
    - **LTCG**—Special tax rates apply (0%, 15% and 20%) for individuals, but not corporations.
- If both are losses, stop, they are reported separately.
    - Loss Treatment for Individuals
        - Net capital loss of **$3,000 ($1,500 MFS) is deductible against ordinary income**. Short-term losses are claimed first.
        - No carryback is allowed but can carry forward **indefinitely**. Carryforwards retain their character as short term or long term.

- A net loss in any rate group is applied to reduce the net gain in the highest rate group first (eg, 28% collectibles gain, 25% Unrecaptured Sec. 1250 gain, then 15% capital gain).
  - Loss Treatment for Corporations
    - Net capital loss **not deductible** against ordinary income.
    - May be carried back to offset net capital gains in one of **previous 3** tax years, and then carried forward to offset net capital gains in the **next 5** tax years.
    - A carried back loss cannot create a net operating loss in a prior year. In such a case, the carryback would be limited to taxable income.
- If one is a net gain and the other is a net loss, they are combined to produce a single net capital gain or loss for the year, which will be treated as having the character of the larger of the two numbers being combined. See the examples that follow.

	Netting Process and Tax Treatment Examples					
	Both Gains	Both Losses	Opposites			
Net LTCG & LTCL	LTCG $10	LTCL ($10)	LTCG $10	LTCL ($3)	LTCL ($10)	LTCG $3
Net STCG & STCL	STCG $3	STCL ($3)	STCL ($3)	STCG $10	STCG $3	STCL ($10)
Report	LTCG $10 STCG $3	LTCL-($10) STCL-($3)	LTCG $7	STCG $7	LTCL ($7)	STCL ($7)
Treatment for Individuals	LTCG—special rate STCG—ordinary rate	Deduct up to $3k against ordinary income; S/T is used first; Carryforward retains character.	Special rates	Ordinary rate	Deduct up to $3k against ordinary income; L/T Carryforward	Deduct up to $3k against ordinary income; S/T Carryforward
Treatment for Corps	Ordinary rate	Carryback 3 years; carryforward 5 years—all S/T.	Ordinary rate		Carryback 3 years; Carryforward 5 years—all S/T.	

Long-term capital gains of individuals generally benefit from a special tax rate of 15%. Lower-income individuals (ie, up to $80,000 MFJ and $40,000 for single individuals for 2020) may qualify for a 0% long-term capital gains tax rate while high-income taxpayers ($496,600+ MFJ, $441,450+ single for 2020) are subject to a 20% rate.

Note: No special capital gains rate applies for corporations.

A special long-term tax rate of 28% applies to all gains and losses on **collectibles** reported on Schedule D. Collectibles include works of art, rugs, antiques, metals (gold), gems, stamps, coins, alcoholic beverages and other certain tangible property.

Capital Assets Summary – Schedule D/ 8949

- Holding period
    - Long term > 1 year
    - Short term ≤ 1 year
- How net
    - Net L/T and L/T = $10 gain
    - Net S/T and S/T = $(3) loss....net again to L/T $7 gain
        - A net loss in any rate group is applied to reduce the net gain in the highest rate group first (eg, 28%, 25% then 15%).
- Rates
    - Short-Term Capital Gain
        - No special rates, ordinary tax rates
    - Long-Term Capital Gain
        - Individuals 20% / 15% / 0% rates (Not applicable to corporations.)
        - Collectibles @ 28%
    - Capital losses
        - Corp's—no **net** deduction (back 3yrs, forward 5yrs – all S/T)
        - Individuals up to *$3,000* per year; rest carried forward *indefinitely.*
- In most cases, an individual must report capital gains and losses on **Form 8949** and then report the totals on **Schedule D**.

Note: Refer to the IRS website for the most recent property transaction tax forms.

7.02 Depreciation Recapture

Section 1245 Depreciation Recapture for Tangible Personal Property

For Sec. 1245 property (generally 3-, 5-, or 7-year property), the calculation of the Sec. 1231 gain may be affected by depreciation recapture. These assets are written off so quickly (especially when the Sec. 179 election is utilized to expense costs) that they often result in gains on sale. Since the depreciation deductions were ordinary deductions, the tax code requires that the **gains be reported as ordinary income to the extent of prior depreciation**.

Note that Sec. 1245 recapture is computed the same way for both individuals and corporations.

 Assume Sec. 1245 equipment costing $10,000 has had MACRS deductions of $4,000 to date, and then is sold. The adjusted basis of the asset on the date of sale is $6,000.

- If the equipment is sold for more than $6,000, the first $4,000 of gain will be recaptured as ordinary income, with the remainder, if any, qualifying as a Sec. 1231 gain.
- If the asset is sold for less than $6,000, there is no recapture needed, since all the depreciation was justified.

Here is a schedule computing the ordinary and Sec. 1231 portions of the sale with different selling prices:

Original cost	10,000	10,000	10,000
MACRS deductions	4,000	4,000	4,000
Adjusted basis	6,000	6,000	6,000
Selling price	11,000	8,000	5,000
Gain (loss)	5,000	2,000	(1,000)
Depreciation recapture (ordinary)	4,000	2,000	0
Sec. 1231 (**capital**)	1,000	0	0

Section 1250 Depreciation Recapture for Real Property

Corporations

When depreciable real property, consisting of buildings and structural components, is sold at a gain, it is subject to Sec. 1250 depreciation recapture. Like Sec. 1245 property, the depreciation deductions are ordinary deductions, so the tax code requires that a portion of the gains be subject to recapture. Sec. 1250 recapture generally no longer applies as it's based on the excess of accelerated depreciation over straight-line and current law requires the use of straight-line depreciation.

Individuals

A modified version, unrecaptured 1250 gain, applies to individuals, however. For individuals, the **lesser of either depreciation taken or the recognized gain** is reclassified as unrecaptured 1250 gain, taxed at a maximum rate of **25%**. Any remaining gain is Sec. 1231 gain, which is generally long-term capital gain (LTCG).

Roger, an individual, sells an office building for $600,000 that has an adjusted basis of $60,000, resulting in a gain of $540,000. The original cost of the building was $500,000 and $440,000 of straight-line depreciation has been recorded. Roger will reclassify $440,000 (lesser of gain or depreciation) as unrecaptured 1250 gain. The remaining $100,000 (ie, $540,000 total gain – $440,000 unrecaptured 1250 gain) is Sec. 1231 gain, treated as a LTCG.

Section 291

When a **C corporation** sells Sec. 1250 property at a gain, a portion of the gain is treated as ordinary income. Under Section 291, a C corporation must **recapture** as ordinary income **20% of the lesser of the recognized gain or depreciation taken**. Any remaining gain is Sec. 1231 LTCG.

Assuming the same facts as the above example, except that Roger is a corporation, $440,000 depreciation × 20% = $88,000 Sec. 291 gain. The remaining $452,000 (ie, $540,000 gain – $88,000 Section 291 gain) is Section 1231 LTCG.

Note: Corporations do not qualify for special capital gain rates, but corporate capital losses offset corporate capital gains. Any net corporate capital gain is taxed at the ordinary corporate tax rate, while any net corporate capital loss is not deductible against ordinary income but may be carried back 3 years and forward 5 years.

7.03 Capitalization Rules

Uniform Capitalization Rules (UNICAP – Section 263A)

When a corporation, partnership or sole proprietorship has manufactured or constructed an asset for use, sale or resale, it must follow the **uniform capitalization rules (UNiCAP – Sec. 263A)**, which require the capitalization into inventory of virtually all direct costs, and part of the indirect costs, associated with the manufacture or resale of the asset (this differs from GAAP so as to increase tax liability to the government). The UNICAP rules apply to costs incurred in manufacturing or constructing real or personal property, or in purchasing or holding property for sale.

Any trade or business that:

- Produces real or tangible personal property.
- Acquires property for resale with average annual gross receipts for past 3 years of more than $26 million.
    - Capitalized costs will be recovered through either depreciation/amortization, or if inventory, through cost of goods sold.
    - **Capitalized costs include**:
        - Pre-production: design, bidding exp, purchasing
        - Production costs: direct materials, labor, & production, indirect production costs (factory overhead)
        - Pre-Sale costs: storage, handling, excise tax (if levied before sale)

For inventory, the company must also *capitalize* most general, administrative, engineering, and overhead costs associated with holding the assets (such as storage costs, repackaging, warehousing) prior to sale. However, nonmanufacturing costs such as selling, advertising, marketing, research and development expenditures would be *expensed* as incurred. Also, businesses with **$26 million** (2020) or less in average gross receipts for the past 3 years are not required to follow these rules.

The capitalized costs are the basis for depreciation of assets used in the trade or business and also determine the gain or loss on sale for all assets subject to these rules.

Capitalization vs Expense of Acquiring, Maintaining, Improving, Repairing & Replacing Tangible Property (Section 263)

Sec. 263 of the Internal Revenue Code (IRC) requires the capitalization of costs incurred in the acquisition, production, or improvement of property, like buildings. **Sec. 162**, on the other hand, allows certain costs to be deducted, such as materials, supplies, repairs, and maintenance. These rules were established to distinguish, for example, between a repair and a renovation and also created safe harbor elections for small amounts being spent for acquisitions, materials and supplies. The regulations help to specify when a cost must be capitalized versus when it can be expensed.

Acquisition or Production Costs

As a general rule, under Regulation Sec. 1.263(a)-1, an entity may deduct (expense) the cost of an item of property for each invoice or the cost of an item that is substantiated by an invoice. There is a de minimis annual **expense** election safe harbor amount of $5,000 per invoice or $5,000 per item, but an entity may be able to justify a greater amount if a higher threshold is used for financial reporting purposes (eg, if a taxpayer has a $6,500 de minimis rule in its audited financial statements, the taxpayer may use the $6,500 threshold for tax purposes).

- To qualify for the **$5,000 per item or invoice** deduction:
    - The entity must prepare audited financial statements and must have a similar policy, effective as of the beginning of the year, for financial reporting purposes.
    - An annual election is required.
- Taxpayers who do not prepare applicable audited financial statements are subject to a limit of **$2,500**, rather than $5,000.
- Property with a useful life of **12 months or less** may also be deducted. This deduction also requires a comparable policy, as of the beginning of the year, for financial reporting purposes.

An entity electing to take this deduction must also apply the de minimis safe harbor limitations to expenditures for repairs and maintenance.

Deductible amounts are considered on an "all or nothing" basis. If the cost of an item exceeds the limit, no portion of the cost is deductible under the safe harbor and must be capitalized. An entity may not divide the cost of property into components to keep amounts within the limitations.

Improvements (BAR)

Amounts paid to improve tangible property are required to be **capitalized** if the costs incurred result in a *Betterment* to the property, or an *Adaptation* of the property for a different use, or a *Restoration* of the property.

- If a taxpayer disposes of property in a circumstance where no gain or loss is recognized, the cost of removal is deducted.
- Otherwise, the cost of removal of property is capitalized to the property.

In order for a cost to result in a **Betterment**, the expenditure must be used to correct a defect that existed prior to acquisition or occurred during production; must be intended to provide an addition to the property, such as by making it larger; or intended to cause an increase in usefulness of the property, such as increased capacity, productivity, or efficiency.

An **Adaptation** of the property is considered a new or different use that is inconsistent with the taxpayer's intended, ordinary use of the property at the time it was originally placed into service. These costs are capitalized. An example would be converting a manufacturing facility into a showroom or converting part of a pharmacy into a clinic. These would qualify as adaptations.

Costs of **Restoration** (restores basis, replaces part or a major component of the property) are required to be capitalized if they would be required to be capitalized if incurred for purposes other than restoring property. Other costs of restoration are also capitalized up to the excess of the reduction in the asset's carrying value that resulted from the casualty or other event requiring the restoration over the amount paid for costs that would otherwise be required to be capitalized.

Assume a building was seriously damaged in an earthquake, resulting in a casualty loss of $300,000. The entity incurs $225,000 to reconstruct the 3rd story and to replace the roof and an additional $275,000 for cleaning up the site and for general repairs.

- The $225,000 cost of reconstructing the 3rd story and replacing the roof would be capitalized.
- Since the basis of the building was reduced by $300,000, the excess of that over capitalized costs of $225,000, or $75,000, would also be capitalized.
- The remaining $200,000 incurred for cleanup and general repairs would be deductible.

Materials and Supplies

Under Regulation Sec. 1.162-3, materials and supplies are generally defined as items other than inventory that are used or consumed in the entity's business operations. They may be classified as either incidental or nonincidental. **Incidental** materials and supplies that can be **expensed** immediately (in the year **paid**) include:

- Property with a cost of less than **$200**
- Tangible property with a useful life of **12 months or less**
- Spare parts or other items used to repair tangible property but that was not acquired for a specific piece of property
- Fuel, lubricants, paper, staplers and other maintenance supplies that are expected to be consumed within 12 months of acquisition
- Other items specifically identified in IRS guidance

Nonincidental materials and supplies (other than those that are incidental) are generally deductible (**expensed**) in the period **used or consumed**. There is, however, an optional alternative treatment that is available for rotable spare parts and for temporary or standby emergency spare parts. Under the alternative, costs are *capitalized and depreciated* as separate assets.

- Rotable spare parts are items, such as a stapler attachment on a photocopy machine that may be attached to one item of property, removed and either reattached to the same property, attached to another, or stored for future use.
- Standby emergency spare parts are parts acquired for a specific piece of property to make certain that delays for repairs can be minimized.

Repairs and Maintenance

Cost of routine repairs and maintenance under Sec. 162 are **expensed** when they are incurred to keep existing property operating efficiently and effectively.

- The taxpayer, at the time the property is placed in service, must expect the repair or maintenance activity to occur *more than once* over the life of the property.
- For buildings and structural components of buildings, the activity must be expected to occur more than once over a 10-year period.
- Qualified Small taxpayers (Average gross receipts of $10 million or less over the preceding 3 tax years) can **expense** repairs and improvements to a building, under Regulation Sec. 1.263(a)-3, up to the *lesser of*:
    - $10,000, or
    - 2% of the building cost (original cost of less than $1 million)
        - If the amount of repairs and improvements exceed $10,000, then all improvements must be *capitalized*.

A taxpayer may elect to *capitalize and depreciate* repairs and maintenance if they are treated similarly on the taxpayer's books and records. This requires an annual election.

7.04 Gifts & Inheritances

Individual Property Tax Transactions – Overview

Sales of business assets by an individual are identical to those by corporations. Sales of capital assets (assets held for investment purposes or personal use) have many complicated rules specific to individuals.

The basic rule is that a capital asset that is sold results in a gain or loss equal to the difference between the sales proceeds and the basis of the asset (usually its original cost). The tax basis of property normally refers to its cost, adjusted for any depreciation previously claimed. A special problem arises, however, when property is received by an individual as either a **gift** or **inheritance**.

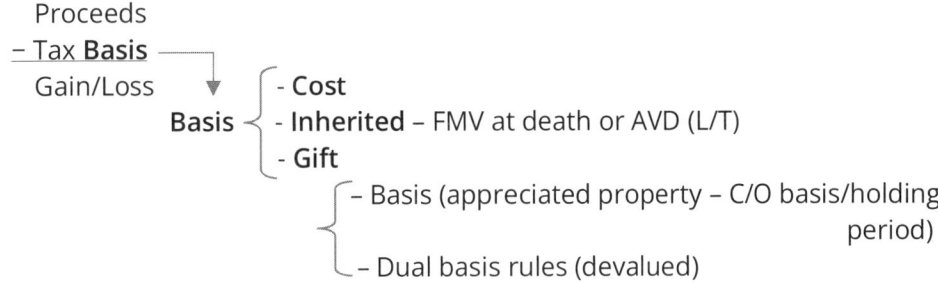

Inheritances

The receipt of an inheritance is nontaxable. The basis for inherited property is the basis used to determine estate taxes for the decedent. Usually, this is **fair market value** (FMV) on the date of **death**. If, however, an election is made in the filing of the estate tax return to use the **alternate valuation date**, then the basis will be the earlier of:

- The date the property was **transferred** to the beneficiary.
- **Six months** after the date of death.

 Assume the decedent died on 2/1/X1 and that two different assets were distributed to the beneficiary: one on 4/24/X1 and the other on 10/25/X1. The basis of both assets would normally be the fair market value on 2/1/X1, the date of death. If, however, the executor of the estate elected the alternate valuation date, then the first asset's basis to the beneficiary is the value on 4/24/X1, and the second asset's basis to the beneficiary is the value on 8/1/X1, determined as follows:

Asset	First	Second
Date of death	2/1/X1	2/1/X1
Date of distribution	4/24/X1	10/25/X1
Six months after death	8/1/X1	8/1/X1
Earlier of last two dates	4/24/X1	8/1/X1

On a subsequent sale, the gain or loss is **always** reported as **long term**, regardless of the actual holding period. The original cost and acquisition date by the decedent are ignored in all determinations, in part because there may be no practical way to determine these items and in part because the government wants to assess estate taxes on current values instead of original purchase costs.

Gifts

Gifts are excluded from gross income. Although the donor of a gift may have to report and pay gift taxes in some cases, the recipient (donee) of the gift generally does not report any taxable income on the receipt of the gift. If the gift is in the form of **appreciated property**, the cost basis and acquisition date of the property to the donee is the same as for the donor (**Carryover basis & Carryover Holding Period**).

> If Greta Giver purchased stock in 20X1 for $10,000 and gave it to her son Ron Recipient in 20X8 at a time the stock was worth $30,000, Ron would report no income from the receipt of the stock. If Ron sold the stock for $29,000 later in 20X8, he would have to report a long-term capital gain on the sale of $19,000. Both the gain and the long-term status result from carrying over Greta's purchase price of $10,000 in 20X1.

If the donor pays gift taxes on a gift, the portion of the tax paid attributable to the appreciation in the property's value at the date of the gift over the donor's basis, is added to the donee's basis.

> Assume Tara gives Sam land worth $200,000 and pays $27,000 in gift taxes. Tara bought the land for $150,000. Sam's basis in the gift from Tara includes Tara's $150,000 basis in the property plus the portion of the gift taxes paid that is attributable to the increase in value at the date of the gift, calculated as follows: $200,000 FMV on date of gift – $150,000 basis = $50,000 increase in value. $50,000 increase/$200,000 FMV = 25% × $27,000 gift tax paid = $6,750 applicable portion of gift tax + Tara's $150,000 basis = $156,750 for Sam's basis.

When the value of the property on the date of the gift is lower than the donor basis (**dropped in value**), the donee must keep track of both the donor's basis and the FMV (**Dual-Basis Rules**).

- The **higher donor basis** is used to calculate a subsequent **gain** on sale.
- The **lower FMV** on the gift date is used to calculate a subsequent **loss** on sale.
- If the selling price is between the two amounts, no gain or loss is recognized. The effect is to not tax the donee on gains to the extent the donor suffered a nondeductible loss.

The acquisition date for the donee is the date from which the amount used as basis was derived.

Property Tax Transactions   REG 7

Assume Greta's stock was purchased in 20X1 for $30,000, and she gave it to Ron in 20X8 after it had declined to $10,000. The following examples assume Ron resold the stock later in 20X8 for (a) $9,000, (b) $20,000, (c) $29,000, and (d) $39,000:

20X1 Donor cost	30,000	30,000	30,000	30,000
20X8 FMV gift date	10,000	10,000	10,000	10,000
20X8 Selling price	9,000	20,000	29,000	39,000
Donee basis	10,000	20,000	29,000	30,000
Acquisition date	**Gift date**	Sale date	Sale date	**Purch date**
Gain (loss)	(1,000)	0	0	9,000
Status	**Short term**	Short term	Short term	**Long term**

What is Cost or Tax Basis?

1. Inherited → FMV at date of death or AVD → L/T
2. Gift → Carryover basis → Carryover holding period
   o Add portion of gift taxes paid to basis for appreciation in property value.
   o If dropped in value (**dual-basis rules**) – What do you eventually sell it for?

```
                $ 12 Selling Price  ⎫
Between         $ 10 Carryover basis ⎬  $ 2 GAIN
= No G/L        
                $ 6 FMV             ⎫
                $ 3 Selling Price   ⎬  $ (3) LOSS
```

Page 7-13

Types of Property — Summary		
Property Category	Included in Category	Tax Treatment
Capital Assets	All assets **except:** • Inventory • Business receivables • Self-created artistic works • Depreciable or amortizable business assets, and land used in a business (1231) • Treasury stock	<u>Individuals:</u> LTCG: Special rates STCG: Regular rates • Net loss: Maximum of $3,000 during the current year. • Carryforward indefinite. <u>Corporations:</u> • Net loss: Not deductible • Carryback 3 years • Carryforward 5 years • Considered S/T
Ordinary Assets	• Inventory • Business Receivables • Self-created artistic works • Assets used in a business 1 year or less	• Regular tax rates
Sec. 1231 Assets	• Depreciable or amortizable business assets over 1 year • Land used in a business over 1 year (parking lot and shed)	• Net gains are generally considered to be LTCG. • Net losses are generally considered to be ordinary losses.

7.05 Special Property Tax Transactions

Special Rules Applicable to Individuals & Corporations

Wash Sales

A wash sale occurs when an asset (eg, stock) has been **sold at a loss** and a substantially similar asset is **purchased within 30 days** before or after the sale.

- Such a loss is **not deductible**, but is **added to** the **basis** of the repurchased asset.
- If the number of shares reacquired are less than the shares originally purchased, the disallowed loss must be prorated (ie, based on the shares reacquired).

Assume the client purchased 100 shares of stock in XYZ Corporation for $300 in 20X1. On 12/20/X2, the client purchased an additional 100 shares in the company for $200. On 12/27/X2, the client sold the 100 shares acquired in 20X1 for $210. Since a purchase of substantially identical securities occurred only 7 days earlier, the loss of $90 on 12/27/X2 cannot be deducted. Instead, the basis of the shares acquired on 12/20/X2 is increased by $90 to $290.

Sales to a Related Party

Losses from related-party sales are not deductible. These are sales between:

- Husband and wife
- Sister and brother
- Parent to child
- Grandparent to grandchild
- Ancestor and descendant
- Majority shareholder and corporation
- Majority partner and partnership (including a partnership interest owned directly or indirectly)
    - Not uncle, aunt, nephews, in-laws.

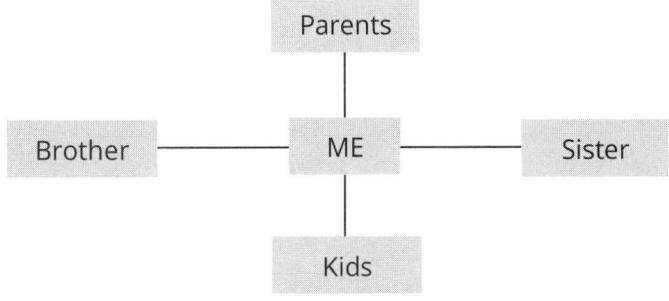

The buyer is not taxed on gains to the extent of the denial of the seller's deduction for the loss.

- **Gains** resulting from related-party sales are fully taxable.
- **Losses** are treated in a similar manner to gift tax rules (dual-basis rules).

If a grandfather sells an asset he originally acquired for $800 to his granddaughter for $500, he cannot deduct the $300 loss, since it is a sale from ancestor to descendant. If the granddaughter later sells the asset for $900, she only reports a $100 gain, since grandfather's basis was $800.

Like-Kind Exchanges

TCJA limited the Like-Kind Exchange rules to real property for exchanges occurring after 2017. Thus, for 2018 and beyond, business property such as delivery trucks, equipment, etc. no longer qualify for like-kind exchange treatment.

Sec. 1031 allows **real property** held for investment or productive use in a business to be exchanged tax free (ie, neither gain nor loss is reported) when it is exchanged for similar property. If, however, the taxpayer receives monetary consideration (boot) as part of the exchange, a gain for the excess of the fair value over the tax basis of the property relinquished is recognized up to a maximum of the amount of boot received.

- **Boot** can result from the following:
    - Cash received
    - Unlike property received
    - Relief from debt that exceeds debt assumed
- If boot is received, **gain** is lesser of:
    - FMV of boot received
    - Realized gain
    - **No loss** deduction.
    - The like-kind exchange provisions do not apply to exchanges of real property held primarily for sale.
    - Most exchanges of real property qualify as like-kind, except the exchange of U.S. property for foreign property, or vice versa.

Assume that the taxpayer owned real estate with a basis of $200,000 and fair market value of $500,000, and this was exchanged for other real estate with a fair value of $400,000. In addition, the taxpayer was relieved of a mortgage on the old property of $150,000, assumed a mortgage on the new property of $80,000, and received $30,000 in cash.

Although the facts are complicated, the transaction makes financial sense, since the value given and received equal:

	Value Given	Value Received
Property	500,000	400,000
Debt Relief	80,000	150,000
Cash		30,000
Total	580,000	580,000

Since the relinquished property had a basis of $200,000 and fair market value of $500,000, the realized gain was $300,000. The recognized gain is limited to the boot received, however, which includes the cash of $30,000 and the net debt relief of $70,000 ($150,000 debt relief - $80,000 debt assumption), for a total gain reported on the tax return of $100,000.

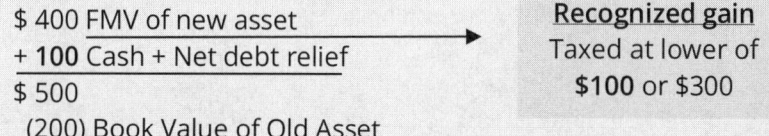

$ 400 FMV of new asset
+ 100 Cash + Net debt relief
$ 500
 (200) Book Value of Old Asset
$300 Realized Gain / Recognized Gain = $100 (for book 100/500 × 300 = $60)

Recognized gain
Taxed at lower of
$100 or $300

The basis in the new asset will be: the basis of the old (200) + liability assumed (80) + gain recognized (100) – Liability on old (150) – cash/boot received (30) = 200 New basis. **Note:** This formula would include "+ cash/boot given" if cash/boot was given rather than received.

New - basis		200 (plug)	
Cash		30	
Liability old		150	
Liability new			80
Old (Basis)			200
Gain			100

It is possible to execute a like-kind exchange and defer some or all taxes in the manner just discussed even when the sale of property and acquisition of similar property are in separate transactions. To do this, *all of the following conditions* must be satisfied:
- The proceeds from the sale of property must not be received by the taxpayer but must instead be paid into a separate escrow account held by a **qualified intermediary**.

- The replacement property must be identified within 45 days after the sale (the qualified intermediary must be notified in writing).
    - The taxpayer may identify more than one property as the potential replacement, as long as either of the following is satisfied:
        - No more than 3 properties are identified, or
        - The total fair value of all identified properties doesn't exceed 200% of the fair value of the property that was sold.
- The replacement property must actually be acquired *within 180 days* of the sale.

Involuntary Conversions

When the taxpayer realizes a gain from an involuntary conversion (**Sec. 1033 exchange**) of property, the gain may be deferred if the property is replaced within the statutory time limit established by law. The time limit is measured from the calendar year the taxpayer received the proceeds, and equals:

- **2 years** – Destruction or theft of property resulting in insurance recovery.
- **3 years** – Government condemnation or eminent domain award.
- **4 years** – Conversion in connection with a federally declared disaster.

Notice that the *time limit* is measured by calendar year, so the actual date for replacement is always December 31 of the year in which the *proceeds are received*.

> A taxpayer owns business property that is destroyed in a fire on 12/10/X1. The insurance company makes payment for the fair market value of the property (which exceeds its tax basis) on 1/20/X2. The taxpayer can defer the gain if all of the proceeds are used to replace the property by 12/31/X4. If the fire was part of a gigantic blaze that caused the president to declare the area a federal disaster area, the taxpayer has until 12/31/X6 to replace the property.

When proceeds are not fully reinvested in the new property, the gain is taxed to the extent of the unreinvested amount. Deferred gains reduce the basis of the replacement property. The deductibility of losses will depend on the taxpayer's use of the property (ie, business/investment vs. personal) and whether the loss occurred in a federally declared disaster area (remember, for 2018 – 2025, the deduction for personal casualty losses is generally limited to losses attributable to federally declared disasters.)

Stock Dividends

The basis of stock received as a dividend depends upon whether it was included in income when received.

- If included in income, basis is its FMV at date of distribution.

- If nontaxable when received, the basis of the shareholder's original stock is allocated between the dividend stock and the original stock in proportion to their relative FMVs (eg, own Common stock and get Preferred stock as a dividend). The holding period of the dividend stock includes the holding period of the original stock.

Stock Splits

A stock split is a nontaxable transaction. The original tax basis of the stock owned before the split is allocated among the new total shares held after the stock split.

Long-Term Construction Contracts

A long-term construction contract is a contract that cannot be completed within the taxable year to manufacture, build, install or construct property. Income under such contracts is generally recognized under the **Percentage-of-Completion method of accounting.** Income is based on the cost-to-cost method and recognized during the construction period. The calculation is contract costs incurred to date divided by total contract costs.

The **Completed Contract method** of accounting is permitted, however, for either:

- Home construction contracts, or
- Any other construction contract that will be completed within 2 years and the taxpayer's average annual gross receipts for the 3 previous years is $25 million or less.

Under the completed contract method, gross receipts and all allocable costs incurred are recognized in the *year of completion*.

Special Rules Applicable to Individuals Only

Sale of Personal Assets

Losses on the sale of assets held for personal, family, or household use at prices less than original cost are **not reported**, as they are presumed to represent consumption. For example, if a refrigerator is purchased for $1,000 and then sold 15 years later for $100, the drop in value is not a loss but the result of the use of the refrigerator for all those years (**consumption loss**).

- The only exception is for casualty losses attributable to federally declared disasters (2018 – 2025).
- **Gains** on the sale of personal assets, however, are **taxed**.

Sale of Personal Residence

There is also special treatment for individuals for a **gain on sale of personal residences**. Under IRC Sec. 121, if a taxpayer sells a home that served as the taxpayer's principal residence for at least 2 of the previous 5 years, the first **$250,000** of the gain on sale is not recognized (**$500,000** for a married couple filing a joint return). This can be done every 2 years.

- If a taxpayer does not meet the 2-year requirement but is forced to sell due to a change in place of employment (50+ miles), health, or other unforeseen circumstances (war, divorce, death), a pro rata amount of the exclusion applies.

- The exclusion of gain does not apply to periods of nonqualified use. When there is nonqualified use, the exclusion is reduced by a pro rata amount based on the ratio of the length of nonqualified use to the total time of ownership. **Nonqualified use** generally includes any use other than as a principal residence, except any use during:
    - The 5 years between the sale and when the taxpayer last used the property as a personal residence
    - A military service absence for up to 10 years
    - A temporary absence up to 2 years for certain unforeseen circumstances

> If Jim owned a home for the last 5 years and used it as a personal residence for the first year, rented it out for the next 3 years, and then moved back in for the last year, the exclusion would be reduced by 3/5 for the period of nonqualified use. Thus, if Jim has a gain of $100,000 on the sale, he can exclude only 2/5 of it from his gross income, or $40,000, and must recognize the other $60,000.

Installment Sales

Installment Sales Method (Form 6252) applies to gains (not losses) from the disposition of property where at least one payment is to be received after the year of sale. A portion of the gain is reported as each payment is received.

- A person sells property for periodic installment payments. The installment sale method is **not available** for sales of stocks or securities traded on an established market. Also not allowed for gains on property held for use in the ordinary course of business.
- All depreciation recaptured is reported in income in the year of sale, if applicable.
- A portion of the overall gain is recognized and reported on **Form 6252** and then transferred to either Schedule D or Form 4797, only as a person collects cash each year, as follows:

$$\text{Gross Profit \%} \times \text{Cash Collected} = \text{Installment Sale Income}$$

$$\text{Gross Profit \%} = \frac{\text{Gross profit}}{\text{Contract price}}$$

> Steve sells property with a basis of $80,000 to Bob for a selling price of $150,000. As part of the purchase price, Bob agrees to assume a $50,000 mortgage on the property and pay the remaining $100,000 in 10 equal annual installments together with adequate interest.
>
> - The contract price is $100,000 ($150,000 selling price − $50,000 mortgage).
> - The gross profit is $70,000 ($150,000 selling price − $80,000 basis).
> - The gross profit ratio is 70% ($70,000 gross profit ÷ $100,000 contract price). Thus, $7,000 of each $10,000 payment is reported as gain from the sale.

Losses on Deposits in Insolvent Financial Institutions (Banks)

A loss resulting from a nonbusiness deposit in an insolvent financial institution is treated as a nonbusiness bad debt, which is deductible up to $3,000 ($1,500 MFS) as a short-term capital loss on Schedule D.

Section 1244 Stock

Since most startups fail, Section 1244 of the tax code allows losses from the sale of small, domestic corporation stock that was sold directly to individual shareholders, to be deducted as ordinary losses up to $50,000 (MFJ $100,000), as opposed to treating the loss as a capital loss. The remaining loss will be treated as a capital loss subject to the $3,000 per year limit.

If a gain is realized, it would be taxed as a capital gain. To qualify, the aggregate capital must not exceed $1 million when the stock was issued, and the corporation must not derive more than 50% of its income from passive investments.

- If appreciates, gain is considered a *capital gain* (Schedule D).
- If value declines, loss is considered an *ordinary loss* (Form 4797, L/T business property).
- Up to $50,000 ordinary loss ($100,000 MFJ), rest is a capital loss.
- Only applies to the first $1 million of stock.
- Must be sold by original purchaser.
- The stock must be issued by a domestic (U.S.) corporation to an individual or partnership in exchange for money or property (other than stock or securities), and not for services.
- For the five most recent tax years ending before the date of the loss, the entity must have earned less than 50% of its revenues from royalties, rents, dividends, interest, annuities, and sales or exchanges of stocks and securities.
- Any type of stock can qualify, whether common or preferred; voting or nonvoting.

Section 1202 Stock

Section 1202 Qualified Small Business Stock (QSBS) is a similar provision. If certain requirements are met, gain on the sale of Section 1202 stock acquired after September 27, 2010, and held for more than 5 years, is 100% excludable from income, up to $10 million ($5 million if MFS) or, if greater, 10 times the total basis of such stock sold during the year. This exclusion also applies for purposes of the 3.8% surtax on unearned income.

- If acquired prior to February 18, 2009 – 50% exclusion
- If acquired after February 17, 2009, and before September 28, 2010 – 75% exclusion

Nonrecognition Transactions		
Transaction	Do Not Recognize	When it Applies
Sale of Personal Assets	Losses	A person sells personal-use property at a loss.
Wash Sale	Losses	A person acquires stock within **30 days** of selling the same stock at a loss.
Sale to Related Party	<ul><li>Losses – not deductible</li><li>Gains – taxed</li></ul>	A person sells property at a loss to a **related party**, which includes a:<ul><li>Parent, grandparent, child, grandchild, spouse or sibling</li><li>Majority-owned corporation</li><li>Majority-owned partnership</li></ul>
Like-Kind Exchange (1031 exchange)	<ul><li>Losses</li><li>Gain is recognized only to the extent that **"boot" is received:** cash + net debt relief + unlike property</li></ul>	A person exchanges real property for other real property.
Involuntary Conversion	Gain is recognized only to the extent that a person reinvests less in a replacement property than the proceeds received from the original property.	A person who lost property due to a casualty, theft, or condemnation, if:<ul><li>A similar replacement property is purchased within **2 years** from the end of the year in which the casualty or theft occurred (or within **3 years** from the year in which a condemnation occurred, or **4 years** if a federal disaster area).</li><li>An appropriate election to not report the gain is filed.</li></ul>
Installment Sale	A portion of the overall gain is recognized only as a person collects cash each year, as follows: Cash Collected × *Gross Profit* / *Contract Price*	A person sells property for periodic installment payments.

Nonrecognition Transactions		
Transaction	Do Not Recognize	When it Applies
Sale of Principal Residence	Up to **$250,000** of reportable gain is excluded ($500,000 MFJ)	Owned and lived in the home for at least **2 of the prior 5 years**
Section 1202 Stock	Up to $10 million ($5 million if MFS) or, if greater, 10 times the total basis of such stock sold	QSBS is acquired after September 27, 2010, and held for more than 5 years

REG 8
Ethics & Responsibilities in Tax Practice

REG 8: Ethics & Responsibilities in Tax Practice

8.01 Taxpayer Responsibilities   1
   CORPORATE REQUIREMENTS   1
   INDIVIDUAL REQUIREMENTS   2
   TAX EXAMINATIONS & PROCEDURES   3

8.02 Preparer Responsibilities   5
   TAX RETURN PREPARERS   5
   CONFIDENTIALITY REQUIREMENTS   5
   PREPARER PENALTIES   6
   SUBSTANTIATION & DISCLOSURE OF TAX POSITIONS   6
   FEDERAL TAX AUTHORITATIVE HIERARCHY   8

8.03 Treasury Department Circular 230   10
   SECTION 10.3 – WHO MAY PRACTICE   10
   SECTION 10.8 – RETURN PREPARATION & APPLICATION OF RULES TO OTHER INDIVIDUALS   11
   SECTION 10.20 – INFORMATION TO BE FURNISHED   11
   SECTION 10.21 – KNOWLEDGE OF CLIENT'S OMISSION   11
   SECTION 10.22 – DILIGENCE AS TO ACCURACY   11
   SECTION 10.27 – FEES   12
   SECTION 10.28 – RETURN OF CLIENT'S RECORDS   12
   SECTION 10.29 – CONFLICTING INTERESTS   12
   SECTION 10.30 – SOLICITATION   12
   SECTION 10.31 – NEGOTIATION OF TAXPAYER CHECKS   13
   SECTION 10.34 – STANDARDS WITH RESPECT TO TAX RETURNS & DOCUMENTS, AFFIDAVITS & OTHER PAPERS   13
   SECTION 10.37 – REQUIREMENTS FOR OTHER WRITTEN ADVICE   14
   SECTION 10.50 – SANCTIONS   14
   SECTION 10.51 – INCOMPETENCE & DISREPUTABLE CONDUCT   14
   SECTION 10.60 – INSTITUTION OF PROCEEDING   15

8.01 Taxpayer Responsibilities

Corporate Requirements

Estimated Tax Payments and Underpayment Penalties

A corporation is required to make quarterly estimated tax payments during the tax year and is subject to a penalty for underpayment of taxes if the tax liability has not been paid in four equal installments over the course of the tax year. The quarterly estimated tax payments are due by the *15th day of the 4th, 6th, 9th and 12th* months of its taxable year (1120-ES). The penalty doesn't apply, however, if one of the following **exceptions** occurs:

- **Small balance** - The total underpayment is less than **$500.**
- **Annualized income** – The installments each quarter cover the tax on the income to date, assuming total income will, for the full 12 months, be in proportion to the income to date (eg, the income for the first 3 months will be divided by 3/12 to estimate the full year income in determining the first quarter estimated payment).
- **Seasonal method** – The installments each quarter cover the tax on the income to date, assuming total income will, for the full 12 months, bear the same relationship to the income to date as it has, on average, in the previous 3 fiscal years (eg, if the income during the first quarter has averaged 40% of the total annual income over the previous 3 years, the income for the first 3 months of this year will be divided by 40% to estimate the full year income in determining the first quarter estimated payment).
- **Previous year** – The payments equal at least **100% of the prior year** tax liability.

Note: This last exception may not be used to escape a penalty, however, if either:

- There was no tax liability in the previous year, or
- The corporation had taxable income exceeding $1 million in any of the preceding 3 tax years.

If the entire tax liability is not paid by the original due date of the return, interest will be owed to the IRS on the unpaid balance. In addition, if the amount paid by the original due date is less than 90% of the total tax liability, a monthly delinquency penalty will be owed in addition to the interest charges. If part of a tax underpayment is the result of fraud, there is an additional penalty equal to 75% of the portion of the underpayment attributable to the fraud.

Individual Requirements

Estimated Tax Payments and Underpayment Penalties

Individual taxpayers who have withholding on salaries and wages may not need to make estimated tax payments to the IRS during the year. If estimated tax payments are required, they are due by the 15th day of the *4th, 6th & 9th* months of the taxable year and by the *15th of January* (1040-ES). An individual is only subject to an underpayment penalty if the balance due on the tax return is greater than **$1,000**. Even then, there are certain exceptions to the penalty that are available:

- **Prior year tax liability** – No penalty is assessed if the withholdings and estimated payments totaled at least **100%** of the prior year tax liability, unless the taxpayer had *more than $150,000 of AGI* in the prior year. In the latter case, payments must exceed *110%* of the prior year tax liability to utilize this exception in the current year.

- **Annualized income method** – No penalty is assessed if the cumulative payments for each quarter cover the tax on the income to date (assuming it continues at the same rate for the remainder of the year).

- **Current tax liability** – No penalty is assessed if the payments covered at least **90%** of the current tax liability.

Accuracy-Related Penalties

- An **accuracy-related penalty of 20%** of the underpayment applies under IRC Sec. 6662 if the underpayment of tax is attributable to negligence or disregard of rules and regulations, any substantial understatement of income tax (ie, generally, more than the greater of 10% or $5,000 for individuals), any substantial valuation overstatement, any substantial overstatement of pension liabilities, or any substantial gift or estate tax valuation understatement.

- Note that there are additional civil penalties related to negligence, and civil and criminal penalties for fraud on the return.

Late Penalties and Interest

Any balance due must be paid by April 15, the normal due date for the individual return. An individual can obtain an automatic extension of the due date for the return until October 15 (6 months), but the *extension is only for the filing, not the payment* of the entire tax.

- The **late filing penalty** is based on the net amount of unpaid tax by the tax return filing due date (April 15th). The penalty is 5% per month, or part of a month, that the return is late, up to a total of 25% of the unpaid tax.

- The **late payment penalty** is ½ of 1% (0.5%) for each month, or part of a month, after the due date (April 15th) that the tax is not paid, up to a total of 25% of the unpaid tax.

- If both penalties apply for any month, the late filing penalty is reduced by the late payment penalty so that the maximum penalty is 5% per month, or part of a month.

- Interest is charged from April 15 to the date of actual payment in addition to the penalties discussed above.

Filing Requirements

Unlike corporations, an individual is not **required to file a tax return** if the gross income during the year is clearly insufficient for any tax liability to result. This is the case if the gross income of the taxpayer for the year does not exceed the **sum of:**

- The basic standard deduction based on filing status.
- The additional standard deductions based on age (≥ 65)

Note: For purposes of determining whether a return has to be filed, the taxpayer cannot use the additional standard deduction based on blindness, since it is not automatically available without supporting evidence.

Even if the taxpayer does not have gross income exceeding the calculated limit, a return must be filed if the taxpayer's **net earnings from self-employment exceeds $400** since self-employment taxes will be due, even though income taxes are not. Note, however, that the taxpayer can actually have up to **$433.13** (ie, $400/.9235) of self-employment income before having to file a tax return. Since ½ the self-employment tax is deductible, self-employment income must be multiplied by 92.35% (ie, 100% – 7.65% deductible portion of SE tax) to arrive at net earnings from self-employment, which is then multiplied by the 15.3% SE tax rate to determine the SE tax due.

Tax Examinations & Procedures

Audits

While many tax returns are randomly selected for examination, tax returns also may be selected for examination for any number of reasons.

- A high score on the IRS computerized Discriminant Inventory Function System will not only cause a return to be selected for examination, but also indicates a high likelihood that the examination will result in a change in the tax liability.
- Returns are selected when information does not agree with that received from third parties in the form of W-2s or 1099s.
- Returns are examined when some source, including newspaper articles, public records, and individuals, provides information to the IRS regarding potential noncompliance.

The taxpayer is notified by letter that the return will be examined, at which time the examination begins. A taxpayer may wish to be represented in the examination proceeding, in which case a Form 2848 is completed.

If a taxpayer does not agree with a proposed adjustment that results from an examination of a return, one alternative is fast track mediation, **offers in compromise**, trust fund recovery penalties, and other collection actions. Offers in compromise can be filed by a taxpayer to obtain a reduction in the amount of tax owed. The IRS will consider an offer in compromise if one of the following applies:

- The amount owed, or whether it is owed, is in doubt.
- The taxpayer's ability to pay the amount owed is in doubt.

- The taxpayer would suffer an economic hardship if required to pay the entire amount.
- The IRS determines that the case presents compelling reasons that are a sufficient basis for compromise.

Upon completion of an examination, there will be a closing conference with the examiner or a supervisor, after which the taxpayer will receive a **30-day letter** with a copy of the examination report. This gives the taxpayer 30 days to accept or appeal proposed changes.

If an agreement is not reached, or if the taxpayer does not respond to the 30-day letter, a **notice of deficiency**, often referred to as a **90-day letter**, is sent. This allows the taxpayer 90 days (150 days if taxpayer's address is outside the U.S.) to file a petition with the Tax Court.

Appeals and Judicial Process

As an alternative to Tax Court, a taxpayer can bring the matter to an **IRS Appeals Office**, which is the only level of appeal within the IRS. If agreement is not reached, the taxpayer may be eligible to take the matter to a court, such as the U.S. Tax Court, the U.S. Court of Federal Claims, or a U.S. District Court. The U.S. Tax Court generally will not hear a case until after it has been considered for settlement by an Appeals Office.

Tax Court hears cases related to income tax; estate tax; gift tax; or certain excise taxes of private foundations, public charities, qualified pension and other retirement plans, or real estate investment trusts. Taxes may be assessed and paid before going to Tax Court, but it is not required. In addition, if a petition is not filed on a timely basis, the taxpayer forfeits the opportunity to go to Tax Court and will be billed.

The **District Courts** and the **Court of Federal Claims** will generally not hear a case until after the tax has been paid and a claim for credit or refund has been filed. A suit may be filed any time within 2 years after a claim has been rejected and as early as 6 months after a claim has been filed if the IRS has not delivered a decision. The Court of Federal Claims will not hear a case involving a claim for a refund of a penalty related to an abusive tax shelter or to aiding and abetting the understatement of tax on someone else's return.

In court proceedings, the burden of proof is on the IRS, provided the taxpayer:
- Introduced credible evidence supporting the position being taken;
- Complied with IRS substantiation requirements;
- Maintained required records; and
- Cooperated with all reasonable requests for information.

If, however, the taxpayer is a corporation, partnership, or trust, the burden of proof will be on the IRS only if net worth did not exceed $7 million and the entity had no more than 500 employees at the time the tax liability is contested in court.

An unfavorable decision in any of the 3 courts may be brought before the U.S. Court of Appeals. Circuit courts of appeals will retry cases from lower courts. If there is a conflict between different circuit courts of appeals, the case may be taken before the U.S. Supreme Court.

8.02 Preparer Responsibilities

Tax Return Preparers

A "tax return preparer" includes anyone who prepares **for compensation**, or who employs one or more persons to prepare, all or a **substantial portion** of any tax return or claim for refund.

- Need not be enrolled to practice before the IRS.
- Considered a preparer only if compensation is received, which can be either explicit or implicit.
- Performing the following acts does **not** classify a person as a tax return preparer:
  - Preparing a return for family or a friend free of charge
  - Simply typing, reproducing, or providing other mechanical assistance in preparing a return
  - Preparing a personal return for an employer (eg, an officer, partner, shareholder, etc.)

Tax return preparers are required to register for a Preparer Tax Identification Number (**PTIN**). This nine-digit number must be used by paid tax return preparers on all returns or claims for refunds. Paid preparers must renew their PTINs annually to legally prepare tax returns.

Confidentiality Requirements

Information that is obtained from a client in connection with the preparation of their tax return is confidential. The preparer is not permitted to use such information for personal benefit or reveal this information to third parties without the consent of the taxpayer, except in limited circumstances. The most important **exceptions** are:

- To respond to a valid government order (while discussions between CPAs and clients on federal tax matters are privileged, this does not apply to criminal matters and tax shelters)
- As part of a quality control peer review program
- To permit the electronic preparation or submission of the taxpayer's return
- To secure legal advice from an attorney

A CPA is not obligated to inform the IRS or any other taxing authority of a client's failure to file a prior year return without the client's permission, although there is an obligation to promptly inform the client upon becoming aware of such a circumstance. Also, a CPA must inform a client if there are material errors in a previously filed tax return so that the client may file an amended return.

Preparer Penalties

There are several special obligations imposed on paid tax return preparers. Penalties for failure to comply with such obligations apply under IRC Sec. 6695.

- The preparer must **sign** the preparer's declaration on the tax return and provide their preparer tax identification number (ie, **PTIN**).
- The return must be timely filed and a **copy** of the completed return must be **provided** to the taxpayer.
- The preparer must **retain** either **documentation** of the taxpayer's name and tax identification number or a copy of the prepared return for **three years**.
- The preparer need not obtain from the taxpayer documentation of information provided to prepare the return but must make **reasonable inquiries** about the existence of such support where appropriate. For example, the preparer should ask the client if travel and entertainment costs are supported by a log and if charitable contributions exceeding $250 are supported by receipts from the charities.

Penalties are assessed against preparers who knowingly or recklessly:

- Understate the tax liability of a client.
- Give erroneous advice or fail to advise a client of tax elections available.
- Endorse or negotiate a refund check for their own account.
- Adopt a frivolous position on a tax issue ($5,000 penalty).

In addition, a preparer may be held responsible for errors in the preparation of the return, but may escape liability based on exceptions for good faith or reasonable cause, when the error results from:

- Utilizing the services of a computerized tax preparation service.
- Obtaining advice from another professional on tax questions.
- Following inaccurate IRS form instructions or advice from an IRS employee.

Substantiation & Disclosure of Tax Positions

Certain activities are listed as **reportable transactions** under the federal tax code and **must be disclosed** when the return is filed. These include all registered **tax shelters** as well as any **special arrangement** that changes reportable income by more than **$10 million**.

Penalties apply for the failure to disclose such activities, even when there is no determination of an underpayment of taxes. Such activities must also meet the higher standard of "**more likely than not**" to succeed on its merits for the preparer to avoid penalty under IRC Sec. 6694 for understatement of a taxpayer's liability.

A preparer is subject to a penalty equal to the greater of $1,000, or 50% of the income derived by the preparer with respect to the return or refund claim if any part of an understatement of liability is due to an **undisclosed position** on the return for which there is not a reasonable belief that the position is backed by substantial authority (may be referred to as an **unreasonable position**).

- The **substantial authority** standard requires about **40% probability of being sustained** on its merits, in contrast to the *more likely than not* standard, which requires a 50% likelihood of success, and the *realistic possibility* standard, which requires a 33% likelihood of success.
- The penalty can be avoided by:
  - Adequate **disclosure** of the questionable position on the return or refund claim, and
  - Showing that there was a **reasonable basis** for the position (ie, 20% probability of being sustained on its merits).
- The penalty can also be avoided if the preparer can show there was a *reasonable cause* for the understatement and that the return preparer acted in *good faith*.
- **Form 8275**, *Disclosure Statement*, is generally used to disclose positions that lack substantial authority. However, **Form 8275-R,** *Regulation Disclosure Statement*, is used to disclose a tax position that is **contrary to Treasury Regulations**.

Probability of Success			Significance of Threshold
More likely than not	>	50%	• Understatement penalty applies for **reportable transactions** that do not meet this threshold.
Substantial authority	≈	40%	• Understatement penalty applies for **undisclosed tax positions** that do not meet this threshold.
Realistic possibility	≈	33%	• AICPA SSTSs* require members to meet this threshold as a minimum for undisclosed tax positions.
Reasonable basis	≈	20%	• $5,000 penalty applies for positions that do not meet this threshold (ie, **frivolous** tax positions). • Positions meeting this threshold must be disclosed to avoid penalty.

*Statements on Standards for Tax Services (no longer tested).

Any additional taxes and interest owed due to an error are entirely the responsibility of the taxpayer and not the preparer. The taxpayer also may be subject to negligence or fraud penalties in addition to any penalties the preparer is assessed if the taxpayer is determined to have committed a penalty offense of their own.

Federal Tax Authoritative Hierarchy

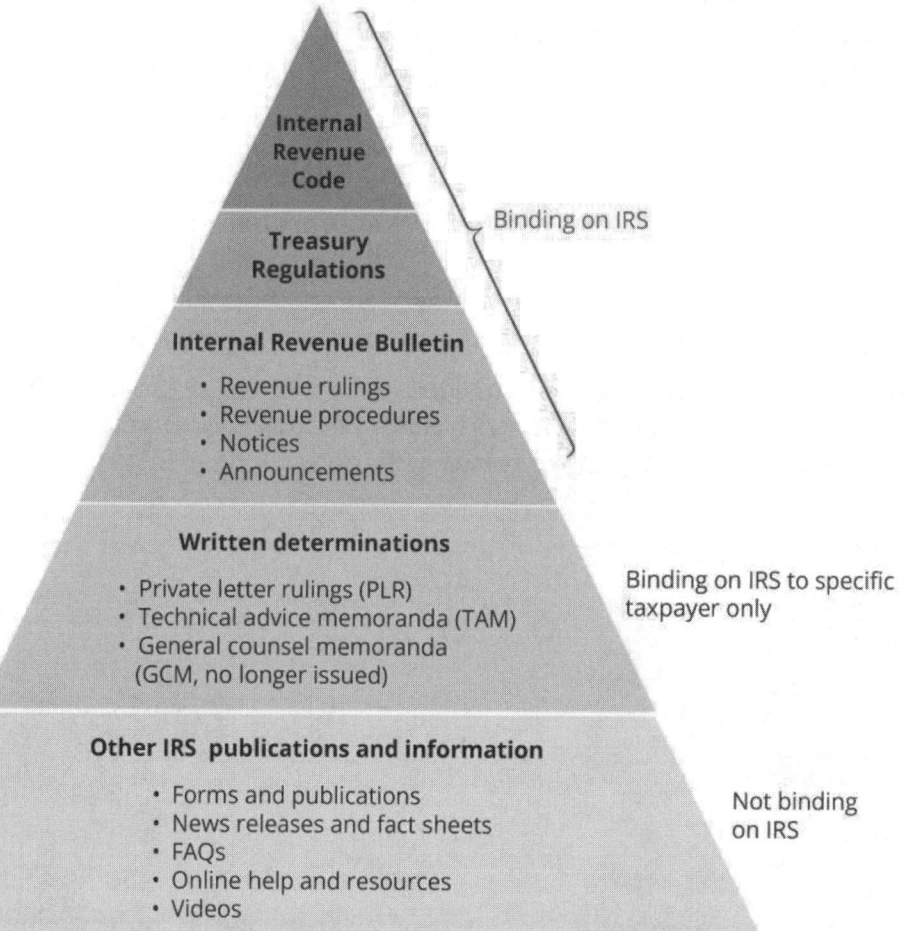

Income Tax Return Preparer Penalties	
Penalties Imposed for	**Amount of Penalty**
Understatement of tax caused by: • Undisclosed position lacking substantial authority • Preparer's reckless or intentional disregard of rules or regulations	> of $1,000 or 50% of return prep fee* > of $5,000 or 75% of return prep fee*
Failure to furnish copy of return to taxpayer	$50 per return/ up to $28,000 yr (2022)
Endorsing or negotiating taxpayer's refund check	$560 per check (2022) – unlimited

Income Tax Return Preparer Penalties

Penalties Imposed for	Amount of Penalty
Improper use or disclosure of return information	$250 for each instance/ up to $10,000 yr* • If minor criminal offense, $1,000 max penalty or 1 year in prison, or both* • If identity theft related, $1,000 each instance/ up to $50,000 yr*
Failure to sign return	$55 per return/ up to $28,000 yr (2022)
Failure to furnish identifying number of preparer on return	$55 per return/ up to $28,000 yr (2022)
Failure to retain a copy of return for 3 years or maintain a list of names and ID numbers of the taxpayers for whom the returns were prepared	$55 per return/ up to $28,000 yr (2022)
Failure to retain and make available a list of the tax return preparers employed	$55 per preparer/ up to $28,000 yr (2022)
Fraudulent or deceptive conduct, including misrepresentation of eligibility to practice before IRS	The courts may enjoin such person from further engaging in such conduct.

*Not adjusted for inflation.

8.03 Treasury Department Circular 230

Circular 230 is a set of U.S. Treasury *regulations that govern practice before the* IRS. It affects attorneys, CPAs, enrolled agents (EA), enrolled retirement plan agents, and others who prepare tax returns, represent taxpayers before the IRS, or provide tax advice. Circular 230 consists of 5 subparts. Within each subpart, certain sections are particularly applicable to CPAs:

- Subpart A provides rules related to the authority to practice before the IRS.
    - Sec. 10.3 – Who may practice
    - Sec. 10.8 – Return preparation and application of rules to other individuals
- Subpart B describes the duties and restrictions of those authorized to practice before the IRS.
    - Sec. 10.20 – Information to be furnished
    - Sec. 10.21 – Knowledge of client's omissions
    - Sec. 10.22 – Diligence as to accuracy
    - Sec. 10.27 – Fees
    - Sec. 10.28 – Return of client's records
    - Sec. 10.29 – Conflicting interests
    - Sec. 10.30 – Solicitation
    - Sec. 10.31 – Negotiation of taxpayer checks
    - Sec. 10.34 – Standards with respect to tax returns and documents, affidavits and other papers
    - Sec. 10.37 – Requirements for other written advice
- Subpart C indicates sanctions for violations.
    - Sec. 10.50 – Sanctions
    - Sec. 10.51 – Incompetence and disreputable conduct
- Subpart D provides rules for disciplinary proceedings.
    - Sec. 10.60 – Institution of proceeding
- Subpart E relates to the availability of public records.

Section 10.3 – Who May Practice

In order for a CPA to practice before the IRS, the CPA:

- Must not be currently under suspension or disbarment from practice before the IRS.
- Must file a declaration with the IRS indicating the CPA is currently qualified as a CPA and authorized to represent the party

A CPA not currently under suspension or disbarment may provide written advice without filing a written declaration.

Note: A district court held in *James C. Sexton, Jr. and Esquire Group, LLC v. Karen L. Hawkins, Director of Office of Professional Responsibility, IRS*, that an individual suspended from practice before the IRS could still engage in the preparation of tax returns or offer tax advice since these activities are not considered to be "practice before the IRS."

Section 10.8 – Return Preparation & Application of Rules to Other Individuals

A preparer tax identification number (PTIN) is required in order to prepare a tax return or claim for refund in exchange for compensation. Only attorneys, CPAs, EAs, and registered tax return preparers may obtain PTINs.

Section 10.20 – Information to be Furnished

Unless the practitioner believes records or information are privileged, records properly and lawfully requested by the IRS must be promptly submitted. When records are not in the possession of the practitioner:

- The IRS should be notified; and
- Inquiry should be made of the client as to who does have custody.

Section 10.21 – Knowledge of Client's Omission

If a practitioner becomes aware of an incident of a client's noncompliance with revenues laws, or of an error or omission on a filing with the IRS, the practitioner is required to:

- Promptly advise the client of the circumstance; and
- Advise the client as to the potential consequences.

Section 10.22 – Diligence as to Accuracy

While required to exercise due diligence in preparing or assisting in the preparation of filings with the IRS, and in determining the correctness of representations made by the practitioner to the IRS and to clients. This does not preclude the practitioner from relying on another person, provided the practitioner has exercised reasonable care and due diligence in engaging, supervising, training, and evaluating the individual.

Section 10.27 – Fees

A practitioner may not charge either an unconscionable fee or a contingent fee for matters before the IRS. A **contingent fee may be charged** in relation to:

- An administrative examination or a ***challenge to*** an original return, an amended return, or a claim for refund (not for preparing original return);
- Services related to a claim for credit or refund in connection with statutory interest or penalties charged by the IRS; or
- Services related to a judicial proceeding under the IRC.

Section 10.28 – Return of Client's Records

A practitioner is generally required to return any and all client records needed for the client to comply with tax obligations, although *copies may be retained*. A dispute over fees does not justify retention of client records.

Some states allow the retention of client records as a result of a dispute over fees. When they are retained under such circumstances, the practitioner must:

- Return those that are required to be attached to the client's tax return; and
- Provide reasonable access to the client to review and copy records necessary to comply with the client's tax obligations.

Section 10.29 – Conflicting Interests

A practitioner may not represent a client before the IRS when there is a conflict of interest, such as when representation of one client would be adverse to another, or there is a risk that representation will be limited as a result of responsibilities to other clients or others.

A practitioner may represent a client despite a conflict of interest if:

- It is reasonable for the practitioner to believe that representation will be competent and diligent;
- Representation is not prohibited by law; and
- All clients affected waive the conflict of interest, giving a written informed consent.

Section 10.30 – Solicitation

A practitioner may not make false, fraudulent, or coercive statements or claims; or misleading or deceptive statements or claims with respect to any IRS matter in any form of public communication or private solicitation. Nor may a practitioner make an uninvited solicitation to perform services in matters related to the IRS, whether written or oral, if doing so violates federal or state laws or another applicable rule.

Any lawful solicitation by or on behalf of a practitioner before the IRS must:

- Identify that it is a solicitation
- Indicate the source of information used to choose the recipient, if applicable

A practitioner may disseminate information about fees, including fixed fees for specific routine services, hourly rates, ranges of fees for particular services, and fees charged for an initial consultation. Fee information may be communicated in a variety of ways, including professional lists, telephone directories, print media, mailings, electronic mail, facsimile, hand-delivered flyers, radio, television, and any other method.

Section 10.31 – Negotiation of Taxpayer Checks

A tax preparer may not endorse or otherwise negotiate a government check issued in relation to a federal tax liability.

Section 10.34 – Standards with Respect to Tax Returns & Documents, Affidavits & Other Papers

A **tax return** should not be filed with a tax position that lacks a reasonable basis; is an unreasonable position; or represents a willful attempt to understate the liability or constitutes an intentional disregard for rules or regulations. A practitioner may **not** willfully, recklessly, or through gross incompetence:

- Sign a tax return or claim for refund when the practitioner knows or should know that it contains such a position; or
- Advise a client to take such a position or prepare a portion of a return or claim for refund containing such a position.

A tax practitioner may not advise a client to take a frivolous tax position on a **document, affidavit, or other paper** submitted to the IRS. Nor may a tax practitioner advise a client to submit a document, affidavit, or other paper to the IRS if:

- It is intended to delay or impede administration of federal tax laws;
- It is frivolous; or
- It contains or omits information indicating an intentional disregard for a rule or regulation, unless the practitioner also advises the client to submit a document indicating a good faith challenge to the rule or regulation.

A practitioner is required to **advise clients regarding potential penalties** that are reasonably likely to be assessed, and the opportunity to avoid penalty through disclosure, when those penalties have the potential of arising from:

- A tax position taken if the practitioner either signed or prepared the return or advised the client relative to the position
- A document, affidavit, or other paper submitted to the IRS

A practitioner may, in good faith, **rely on information obtained from a client** without verification. If information furnished by the client appears incorrect, incomplete, or otherwise unsatisfactory based on information known by, or furnished to the practitioner, that fact may not be ignored by the practitioner.

Section 10.37 – Requirements for Other Written Advice

A practitioner is prohibited from giving written advice that is based on unreasonable assumptions; unreasonably relies on representations, statements, findings, or agreements of the taxpayer or another; does not consider all relevant information that is known, or should be known, by the practitioner; or considers the possibility that the position, or the return on which it is taken, will not be audited or will be resolved through settlement.

A practitioner may rely on the advice of another, provided:

- The advice is reasonable, and
- Reliance is in good faith, considering all facts and circumstances.

Section 10.50 – Sanctions

The Secretary of the Treasury has the authority to **censure**, **suspend**, or **disbar** a practitioner from practice before the IRS if the practitioner:

- Is shown to be incompetent or disreputable;
- Violates requirements either willfully or as a result of gross incompetence; or
- Willfully and knowingly misleads or threatens a client or prospective client with the intent to defraud.

The Secretary of the Treasury also has the authority to impose a *monetary penalty* on any practitioner who engages in the prohibited conduct indicated above.

Section 10.51 – Incompetence & Disreputable Conduct

Some of the actions or events that indicate incompetence or disreputable conduct include:

- Conviction of a criminal offense under federal tax laws or involving dishonesty or breach of trust, or for any felony for conduct that renders the practitioner unfit to practice before the IRS.
- Knowingly giving false or misleading information, or participating in doing so, to the Department of the Treasury
- Solicitation prohibited by Section 10.30
- Willfully failing to make a federal tax return or evading, or attempting to evade, an assessment or payment of federal tax
- Willfully assisting, counseling, or encouraging a client or prospective client to violate a tax law or evade federal taxes or their payment
- Failure to promptly remit funds received from a client for the payment of taxes
- Attempting to influence an officer or employee of the IRS
- Disbarment or suspension from practice as an attorney or CPA
- Knowingly assisting another person in practicing before the IRS when disbarred or suspended

- Contemptuous conduct, such as using abusive language, knowingly making false accusations; or circulating malicious or libelous material in connection with practice before the IRS
- Knowingly, recklessly, or as a result of gross incompetence, giving a false opinion
- Willingly failing to sign a tax return when required
- Willfully disclosing or using a tax return or tax information inappropriately
- Willfully failing to file using electronic media when required to do so
- Providing covered tax services without a valid PTIN
- Willfully representing a taxpayer before the IRS when not authorized to do so

Section 10.60 – Institution of Proceeding

Any violation of laws relative to practice before the IRS may result in reprimand or a proceeding for sanctions. Instituting a proceeding requires that the respondent be advised in writing of the law, facts, and conduct warranting such action; and is given an opportunity to dispute facts, assert additional facts, and make arguments.

REG 9
Accountant Liability

REG 9: Accountant Liability

9.01 Common Law Liability — 1
- OVERVIEW — 1
- BREACH OF CONTRACT — 2
- NEGLIGENCE — 3
- FRAUD OR GROSS NEGLIGENCE — 4
- SUMMARY — 6
- CLIENT CONFIDENTIALITY — 7

9.02 Licensing & Disciplinary Systems — 8
- ROLE OF STATE BOARDS OF ACCOUNTANCY — 8
- REQUIREMENTS OF REGULATORY AGENCIES — 8

9.01 Common Law Liability

Overview

Common Law Principles

Accountants face liability under several different common law principles. Most exam testing deals with liability in connection with audits.

- **Contracts** – An audit is performed under a contract between the auditor and client. Thus, the most obvious liability facing an auditor is for **breach of contract** (nonperformance). Since the auditor promises to perform an audit in accordance with generally accepted auditing standards (GAAS), a lawsuit charging breach of contract by the auditor must usually show violation of at least one standard. The CPA's liability in this case is to the client and any intended (ie, named) third-party beneficiaries.

- **Negligence** – The GAAS standard most often utilized is **due professional care**. Thus, the most common lawsuit against an auditor will charge negligence, which is an absence of due care. When negligent, the CPA's liability is to the client, any intended third-party beneficiary, and (in most states) any third party known or foreseen by the CPA.

- **Fraud or Gross Negligence** – A CPA who **intentionally or recklessly** departs from the standard of due care when performing an engagement faces liability for fraud or gross negligence. The CPA's liability under these circumstances is to the client, any intended third party, and any third party (known or unknown) who suffered financial loss.

There are **four key elements** that a **plaintiff must prove** in an action taken against an accountant:

- There is a misstatement or an omission of a **M**aterial fact.
- The plaintiff has reasonably *relied upon* the **I**nformation, or it was the *proximate cause* of harm.
- The plaintiff suffered a **L**oss.
- The accountant was in **E**rror.

Accountant's Common Law Liability			
	Contracts	Negligence	Fraud / Gross Negligence
Accountant's error	Breach of contract	Carelessness	Recklessness or intentional misconduct (scienter)
Who may sue	Client or intended user	Client or foreseen user	Anyone injured
Plaintiff must prove	All four elements		

Client Confidentiality

Accountants can also be sued for breach of **confidentiality** requirements if they share information or their **workpapers** without permission of the client.

Breach of Contract

An accountant who does not fulfill the terms of the contract or engagement will be held liable for breach of contract due to nonperformance. The accountant will be liable to the client (in privity) and any intended third-party beneficiaries for **compensatory damages**.

Who can sue?

- Anyone in privity → Anyone who hired you
- Intended 3rd party beneficiary (named in contract by client)

What do they have to prove?

Plaintiff (Purchaser) must prove (**MILE**):

- **M**aterial misstatement or omission – The financial statements (F/S) must contain material misstatements or omissions.
- **I**nfo in F/S was the *proximate cause* of harm to the plaintiff.
- **L**oss (damages) – Plaintiff must have suffered a financial loss (ie, injury).
- **E**rror
    - Caused by breach (nonperformance)

What are the defenses available?

- Didn't breach or fully performed under the contract terms.

Accountant Liability — REG 9

Negligence

An accountant has a duty in the performance of an engagement to exercise due professional care expected of an ordinarily prudent CPA. The accountant will be liable to the client or an intended 3rd party beneficiary named in the engagement (privity). In most states (those that follow the Second restatement of torts), liability extends to anyone (3rd party) who is **known or foreseen** by the CPA.

Who can sue?

- Anyone in *privity* (ie, client and intended 3rd party)
- Anyone *known and foreseen* by CPA (eg, a shareholder)
  - But not in the minority of states that follow the decision in *Ultramares v. Touche*

What do they have to prove?

Plaintiff must prove **(MILE + Privity)**:

- **M**aterial misstatement or omission – The F/S must contain material misstatements or omissions.
- **I**nfo in F/S was the *proximate cause* of harm to the plaintiff.
- **L**oss (damages) – Plaintiff must have suffered a financial loss (ie, injury).
- **E**rror
  - No due professional care / **Neg**ligent
  - **Absence of due care** – The auditor must have demonstrated carelessness in the audit.

(Same as above)

Nondisclosure of information to client (eg, I/C weaknesses)
Errors previously discovered not corrected
GAAS/GAAP not followed

The **privity** requirement is often the biggest obstacle in a negligence suit. The client that engaged the auditor to perform the work has privity of contract. Others normally must demonstrate the status of **intended third party beneficiary**, proving that a principal purpose of the audit was to provide them with audited F/S in connection with a loan or investment decision.

Parties that are not specifically cited as intended beneficiaries may attempt to prove they are **foreseen** beneficiaries. A **foreseen party** is a third party or a member of a limited class that the accountant *knew* would be relying on the F/S for a limited transaction.

- The accountant is generally liable to foreseen parties for negligence because most states have adopted the **Second Restatement of Torts**, which permits a user within a *class of people* known or foreseen by the auditor to be relying on the F/S to sue for negligence.
- Foreseen parties do not have privity to sue for negligence in a state that conforms to the *Ultramares* decision, however.

Foreseeable parties are any party the accountant could reasonably foresee would receive F/S and use them. The accountant is *not* usually liable for negligence to foreseeable parties.

In all states, an **unforeseeable third party** lacks proper standing to sue for negligence; thus, the auditor is never responsible for negligence to a third party that the auditor couldn't foresee would be relying on the F/S.

Summary of Privity Requirements			
3rd Party	Portion of States	Following:	Privity to sue?
Foreseen	Majority	2nd Restatement of Torts	Yes
Foreseen	Minority	*Ultramares*	No
Unforeseeable	All	Either	No

What are the defenses available?

- Followed GAAS (showing due professional care)
- Lack of privity (useless against client or intended 3rd party)
- Not the proximate cause of the loss

A CPA's **duty of due care** is guided by the following standards:

- State and federal statutes
- Court decisions
- Contract with the client
- GAAS and GAAP
- Customs of the profession

If the auditor cannot demonstrate that GAAS was followed, negligence cases make available the privity defense, since parties unknown to the auditor, and foreseen parties in a jurisdiction following *Ultramares*, lack the standing of privity required in a negligence case.

Fraud or Gross Negligence

A common law theory of liability that can be used by any party, including one who is unknown to the auditor, is fraud. Fraud refers to **intent to deceive**, and takes two basic forms:

- **Actual fraud** – Making false statements with **knowledge of their falsity** (ie, **scienter**). For example, an auditor issues an unmodified opinion on F/S knowing they contain material misstatements and should be receiving a qualified or adverse opinion, or recording a bribe in the F/S as a consulting fee.

- **Constructive fraud (Gross Negligence)** – Making false statements with a **reckless disregard for truth**, not knowing if the statements are true or false. For example, an auditor issues an unmodified opinion on F/S that have not been audited, and on which they should be disclaiming any opinion.

An audit meets the standards of constructive fraud if it is performed in a **grossly negligent** manner. Note that ordinary negligence does not meet this standard. It is sometimes difficult to evaluate the evidence to determine if the negligence in an audit is substantial enough to be considered gross negligence.

 Always assume on the CPA exam that negligence or carelessness is ordinary unless there is a clear statement in the problem that it constitutes gross or reckless behavior.

Who can sue?

- Anyone, including unforeseen parties

What do they have to prove?

Plaintiff must prove **(MILE)**:

- **M**aterial misstatement or omission – The F/S must contain material misstatements or omissions.
- **I**nfo in F/S was *relied* on. ← Different from above
- **L**oss (damages) – Plaintiff must have suffered a financial loss (ie, injury).
- **E**rror
    - Reckless or intentional misconduct
        - Actual fraud – Intent to deceive (scienter)
        - Constructive fraud – reckless disregard

What are the defenses available?

- Not gross negligent; followed GAAS (showing due professional care)
- Not material
- Good faith and no knowledge of falsity (lack of scienter)

There is a difference between the way an auditor will defend against a negligence and a fraud case.

- In either case, the best defense would be to prove that the audit was **conducted in accordance with GAAS**, since this would demonstrate that the audit was conducted with due professional care.
- Since **privity need not apply** in a fraud case, the privity defense wouldn't be useful in a case based on actual or constructive fraud, including gross negligence.
- Fraud cases make available the **good faith defense**, in which the auditor does not deny carelessness but claims a lack of knowledge of the falsity of the F/S (lack of scienter). This would not be sufficient to escape liability in a negligence case. Also keep in mind that the auditor must lack both actual and constructive knowledge of the falsity of the statements.

Keep in mind that the burden of proof is on the plaintiff to prove all the elements of the case, so exam questions in which all points have not been established should be decided in favor of the auditor-defendant. Also note that punitive damages are not levied under the common law principles discussed.

Summary

Common Law Liability

Breach of Contract	Negligence Law	Fraud / Gross Negligence
Who can sue:		
• Privity • Intended 3rd party beneficiary by client	• Privity • Known or Foreseen by CPA (*Ultramares* – only if in Privity)	• Anyone • Unforeseen
Plaintiff must prove:		

Material misrep/omission
Info caused harm
Lost money (damages)
Error caused injury
• Breach of contract
• Nonperformance
	M
	Info caused harm
	L
	Error
	• Lack of due diligence
	• Negligence (NEG)
	  o **N**ondisclosure of information to client (eg, I/C weaknesses)
	  o **E**rrors previously discovered not corrected
	  o **G**AAS/GAAP not followed
		M
		Info was relied upon
		L
		Error
		• Reckless or intentional misconduct
		  o **Actual Fraud** – Intent to deceive (*Scienter*)
		  o **Constructive Fraud** – Reckless Disregard

Defense:		
• Didn't breach	• Adhered to GAAS (not NEG) • Lack of Privity	• Adhered to GAAS (not negligent) • Not material • Good faith + no knowledge of falsity

Client Confidentiality

The accountant, not the client, owns the **workpapers** that an accountant creates during an engagement. Nevertheless, the accountant must maintain **confidentiality** and cannot provide the papers or information obtained during engagements to other parties without the permission of the client. Note that client confidentiality does not preclude a CPA from providing access to other members of their firm.

There are some **exceptions** to confidentiality, including:

- **Valid subpoena** - the accountant must honor a valid court order to turn over information.
- **IRS administrative subpoena**
- **Court order** (unless rare state with privilege statute).
- **Quality control peer review** - The accountant may allow other accountants and the PCAOB to see confidential information in connection with a valid program of peer review.
- Where disclosure is in compliance with **GAAP or GAAS**

Common law does not recognize the concept of **privilege**, which would allow the accountant to refuse to honor a court subpoena. A small number of states have enacted privilege statutes, and the federal government now recognizes working papers developed in connection with the preparation of a tax return to be privileged in certain circumstances.

Nevertheless, privilege may not be used if the accountant has already provided some of the information requested in the subpoena. The purpose of privilege is to protect the client, not the accountant, so the accountant may not assert privilege (even where privilege statutes exist) if the client waives the privilege.

9.02 Licensing & Disciplinary Systems

Role of State Boards of Accountancy

Each state has a State Board of Accountancy that issues CPA certificates as well as licenses to engage in the practice of public accounting. In some states, the CPA certificate is the license to practice but in others, both are required to practice. Each state has its own requirements, although there is a high degree of uniformity as many have adopted the basic requirements of the Uniform Accountancy Act.

In addition, each state establishes requirements that must be met to maintain the certificate and license. These include minimum requirements for *continuing professional education (CPE)* and adherence to the state's *code of professional conduct*. Most states have based their code of professional conduct on the AICPA code of conduct by adopting the major components and adding detail to some provisions, adding additional requirements that are unique to the state, or enhancing AICPA requirements.

A CPA who does not adhere to the AICPA Code of Professional Conduct (ET) will not be able to maintain membership in the AICPA. In addition, a violation of the AICPA code will likely result in a violation of each state's code and, as a result, may subject the CPA to sanctions. In some cases, a practitioner's *license will be suspended and it also may be revoked*.

Requirements of Regulatory Agencies

Internal Revenue Service (IRS)

The IRS is a bureau of the Department of the Treasury. The Secretary is authorized by the Internal Revenue Code (IRC) to administer and enforce internal revenue laws and created the IRS as the agency to accomplish that purpose. The Commissioner of the IRS, appointed by the Secretary, is charged with administering and supervising the execution and application of the IRC.

The mission of the IRS is to "Provide America's taxpayers top quality service" by helping them understand and meet their tax responsibilities and enforce the law with integrity and fairness to all.

This mission statement describes our role and the public's expectation about how we should perform that role.

- In the United States, Congress passes tax laws and requires taxpayers to comply.
- The taxpayer's role is to understand and meet his/her tax obligations.
- The IRS role is to help compliant taxpayers with the tax law, while ensuring that the minority who are unwilling to comply pay their fair share.

The domain of the IRS covers all federal taxes, including income taxes, excise taxes, payroll taxes, and gift and estate taxes. Violations may subject a taxpayer or a tax practitioner to disciplinary actions. Most infractions will result in **civil** liability, which may result in a tax practitioner losing their PTIN and a taxpayer in being fined. When fraud is involved, the result may be a **criminal** action, which could result in incarceration (Jail).

Securities and Exchange Commission (SEC)

The SEC was created by the Securities Exchange Act of 1934 to enforce the Securities Act of 1933. Since its formation, its jurisdiction has expanded to include enforcement of the Trust Indenture Act of 1939, the Investment Company Act of 1940, The Investment Advisers Act of 1940, and the Sarbanes-Oxley Act of 2002. "The mission of the U.S. Securities and Exchange Commission is to protect investors, maintain fair, orderly, and efficient markets, and facilitate capital formation."

The SEC designates the bodies authorized to establish standards for the performance of audits of entities that report to the SEC, and to establish accounting principles for those entities. The SEC has designated the Public Company Accounting Oversight Board (PCAOB) as having responsibility for auditing standards and the Financial Accounting Standards Board (FASB) as having responsibility for accounting principles.

Entities that do not report to the SEC basically follow the same accounting principles as those that do report. There are some accounting principles that have been designated as either not applying to nonpublic entities or applying with fewer specific requirements. In addition, the SEC staff has issued Staff Accounting Bulletins, which must also be taken into consideration by those who report to the SEC.

Auditing standards that apply to nonpublic entities are promulgated by the Auditing Standards Board (ASB) of the AICPA. Although these standards have minor differences from those of the PCAOB, the organizations cooperate with one another and differences are eliminated or reduced, when appropriate.

One significant difference between PCAOB (SEC) standards and those that apply to auditors of nonpublic entities (AICPA) relates to the area of auditor independence. Auditors of nonpublic entities are required to comply with the AICPA Code of Professional Conduct. Under this code of conduct, an auditor may perform nonattest services, such as bookkeeping or tax compliance services, for an audit client without impairing independence when certain requirements are adhered to. An auditor of a public company may not perform any nonattest services for an audit client without impairing independence.

There is an exception that allows the auditor to perform certain nonattest services for an audit client, such as certain tax services, provided the client's audit committee pre-approves the nonattest service after obtaining satisfaction that the nature of the service would not impair the auditor's independence. So, as you can see, the SEC (PCAOB) rules regarding independence are a bit **more restrictive** than those of the AICPA.

REG 10
Contracts

REG 10: Contracts

10.01 Common Law Contracts: Offer	1
10.02 Acceptance & Consideration	4
ACCEPTANCE	4
CONSIDERATION ("OF VALUE" AND "BARGAINED FOR")	7
10.03 Defenses	10
VOIDABLE CONTRACTS	10
VOID CONTRACTS	12
STATUTE OF FRAUDS	13
10.04 Other Contract Issues	15
PAROL EVIDENCE RULE	15
ASSIGNMENT OF RIGHTS AND DELEGATION OF DUTIES	16
THIRD PARTY RIGHTS	16
DISCHARGE OF CONTRACTS	17
REMEDIES FOR BREACH	18
STATUTE OF LIMITATIONS	19

10.01 Common Law Contracts: Offer

An agreement between parties that may involve either a promise being exchanged for a promise, or a promise being exchanged for an act.

- **Bilateral contract** – Two promises are made, so it is basically a promise for a promise (eg, I promise to pay you $50,000 if you promise to do my audit). A contract is formed when the promises are exchanged.
- **Unilateral contract** – One promise for an act (eg, I'll pay anyone $100 who will find my dog). A contract is formed when performance is completed.

There are two main sources of contract law, common law derived from courts (real estate and services) and the Uniform Commercial Code (UCC), derived from Statutory Law (Sales of goods). The UCC has adopted much of common law; so most of what we cover in this section will still apply for the sale of goods section.

Formation of a valid Common Law contract requires Offer, Acceptance, Consideration and a lack of Defenses.

The offeror expresses a willingness to enter into a contract with the offeree.

- **Definite terms** - may be implied.
    - Price to be paid
    - Parties
    - Nature of the subject matter
    - Quantity involved
    - Time for performance
- **Intent** to make offer or contract – We are concerned with Objective intent (what a reasonable person believes). An advertisement does not have such intent, so it is considered a mere invitation to offer (unless we limit the scope, for example, "offer valid to only the first 10 people in line," is a valid offer).
- **Communicated to offeree** – constructively received when available to offeree (mail delivered to offeree's home or fax printed at offeree's business).

The terms of an offer must be definite to permit the formation of a contract, including clear agreement as to subject matter (including quantity), price, and time of performance. This is called an *express contract* as it is formed by **express** language. This does **not** mean the terms must be explicitly stated by the offeror. The terms can be **implied-in-fact**, meaning that the behavior or conduct of the two parties makes clear what the terms of the agreement are.

For example, if an individual calls up a pizza parlor and orders a medium pepperoni pizza to go, it is not necessary for the parties to discuss the price on the phone. A **reasonable person** would presume that the caller intended to pay the posted prices in the restaurant or on the takeout menus.

In rare cases, a contract can also be **implied-in-law (Quasi-contract)**. This occurs when the courts decide that parties should be treated as if they had an agreement, even though they did not, to avoid one party being unjustly enriched at the expense of the other.

For example, if a person who appears to be destitute asks a doctor to provide substantial medical services for free, and the doctor does so, but later discovers the individual is extremely wealthy, the courts may invoke this principle to allow the doctor to bill the patient customary charges. The court-defined arrangement is known as a quasi-contract.

Offers must be intentional. A statement made in jest or anger is not an offer. Also, advertisements are considered invitations to negotiate deals and not offers.

Offers must be **received** by the offeree. If the offer is made to a specific person, a different person cannot accept it. If an offer is made to the public, such as a reward for information on a crime, it can be accepted by anyone who knows of the offer. A party who provides information without knowing of the reward is not entitled to receive it.

- An offer must be accepted before it **Terminates**. The following would terminate an offer:
  - **Expiration** – expires after reasonable time if no stated date.
  - **Revocation** – may revoke even if promised not to do so (unless **option contract**, consideration paid to keep offer open). Revocation must be received to be effective.
    - Direct – phone call
    - Indirect – knowing that the lost dog has been returned and the reward paid.
  - **Rejection** – refusal by offeree, must be received by offeror.
  - **Counteroffer** – a form of rejection by offeree (an inquiry is not a counteroffer).
  - Operation of law
    - Death or insanity of either party
    - Destruction of subject matter
    - Illegality of subject matter (an offer to commit a crime for compensation)

It is not a counteroffer for the offeree to make inquiries about possible changes in the original offer, so an inquiry doesn't terminate the original offer. Offers may not be assigned, but an option contract may be assigned.

Assume a homeowner offers to sell their house for $200,000, and the offeree responds by asking "Would you be willing to sell for $190,000?" This is simply an inquiry, and not a counteroffer to purchase at $190,000. As a result, if the offeror indicates they will not sell at $190,000, the offeree can still accept the original offer at $200,000.

On the other hand, acceptances that add or change conditions in the original offer **are** counteroffers.

For example, if the offeree responds to the offer at $200,000 by indicating that they accepted the price but wanted a termite inspection report and a 30-day escrow, they've actually rejected the offer and made a counteroffer with the two additional terms.

A contract is executory if certain duties still remain to be performed; however, a contract is considered executed when all contractual duties have been performed.

10.02 Acceptance & Consideration

Acceptance

Acceptance of an offer creates a contract. Two important rules:

- **Mirror image rule** – Must accept all terms and conditions of the offer without any alteration; otherwise, it's a counteroffer which would terminate the offer. An acceptance must be unequivocal and unqualified with respect to the precise terms specified by the offer.

- **Early acceptance rule** (mail-box rule) – Acceptance is effective when transmitted or *dispatched*. However, the maker is the master of his offer, so if the offer specifies the means of acceptance, the acceptance must conform to those specifications in the offer to be effective.

- Acceptance would be effective **when received** if:
    - States "only valid upon receipt" by offeror, so mailbox rule won't apply.
    - Acceptance is made by some unauthorized means.
    - Offer indicates that acceptance must be received by a specific date.
        - Note: If accept/reject, the early acceptance rule doesn't apply, and whatever is received first applies.
        - An acceptance received after an offer has terminated is considered a counteroffer.

For example, A sends offer on the 1st. B received the offer on the 4th. The offer expires on the 10th. B accepts on the 9th and B's acceptance is received by A on the 11th.

- If the early acceptance rule applies, then a contract is formed on the 9th.
- If A states "only valid upon receipt", there is no contract, but B has now made a counteroffer.

The trickiest responses are acceptances with **conditions precedent**. These are actually acceptances of the offer that cite events outside of the contract which must take place before the acceptance is effective.

For example, if the offeree responds to the $200,000 home sale offer by indicating they accepted as long as the bank approved the offeree's loan application, this would be a valid attempt to accept. The loan from the bank to the offeree is not a change that adds to the offeror's obligations or the offeree's rights under the home sale contract.

When a condition precedent is set, the offeree must make a good faith attempt to ensure the condition is satisfied. In this example, the offeree must submit a valid loan application and sincerely attempt to obtain loan approval from the bank.

In general, an acceptance must **mirror** the offer in all ways. If the offer requires the offeree to perform some action in order to accept, the offeree must perform the action and not merely promise to perform it. A contract that can be accepted by a promise is called a **bilateral contract,** and a contract that can only be accepted by actual performance is called a **unilateral contract.**

For example, if a firm partner offers to give a staff member a promotion to manager if they pass the CPA exam within a year, they've made an offer of a unilateral contract. The subordinate cannot accept merely by promising to the pass the exam, since that is an attempt to change a unilateral contract into a bilateral contract.

Of course, when an offer is in unilateral form, the offeree hasn't actually accepted until they've completed the required action, so there is the danger that the offeror will revoke the offer after the offeree has begun performance but before they've completed it. To prevent this, common law prohibits an offeror from revoking an offer if the offeree is in the process of performing such actions, although they can revoke if the offeree stops making reasonable efforts in the direction of completion.

For example, if the staff member in this example enrolls in a review course and pursues study, the partner cannot revoke the offer. If the staff member makes no efforts in the direction of study, or signs up for a course but then goes a month without studying with no special excuse, the partner may revoke the offer.

The mirror rule also requires the offeree to accept in a manner dictated by the offer. If the offeror indicated that acceptance must be by mail, any response other than by mail is a counteroffer. If the offeror sent the offer through the mail without indicating the manner of response, an acceptance by mail or any faster means is considered a valid acceptance.

Unlike offers, revocations, and rejections, which must be **received** by the other party to be effective, an acceptance is normally effective when transmitted, based on the early acceptance rule (sometimes called "the mailbox rule").

Assume an offer is mailed on the 1st and received on the 4th of the month. The offeror then mails a revocation on the 5th that is received on the 8th. The offeree mails a valid acceptance on the 6th that is received by the offeror on the 9th. A contract is formed in this case, since the offer is effective on the 4th, when received, the acceptance is effective on the 6th, when transmitted, but the revocation is not effective until the 8th, when received.

Action	Mailed	Received
Offer	1	4*
Revocation	5	8*
Acceptance	6*	9

*Effective date of the action

Note: the *early acceptance rule doesn't apply when the original offer explicitly requires acceptance to be received* by the offeror to be effective. The early acceptance rule does apply when the offeror indicates that the offeree must accept by a certain date, but doesn't indicate if acceptance refers to transmission or receipt.

For example, if the offer requires the offeree to accept by mail by 8/1, the acceptance only needs to be postmarked by 8/1 and not received. A valid early acceptance is effective even if the offeror never receives it due to an error by the delivery service.

The offeree cannot use the early acceptance rule if they send a contradictory rejection to the offeror.

Assume the offer is mailed on the 1st and received on the 4th, as before. This time, though, the offeree sends a rejection on the 5th that is received by the offeror on the 8th, and later mails an unconditional acceptance of the original offer on the 6th which is received by the offeror on the 9th.

Although rejections are normally effective when received and acceptances when transmitted, this would be unjust in the current situation, since the offeror receives a rejection on the 8th and doesn't know that an acceptance is in transit. As a result, the offeror might take action based on a belief that the offeree rejected the offer. Acceptance is not considered effective in this case until the 9th, when received, which is too late to accept, since rejection occurred the day before.

Action	Mailed	Received
Offer	1	4*
Rejection	5	8*
Acceptance	6	9*

*Effective date of action

It is possible, however, for acceptance to occur after a rejection has been transmitted, since the rejection is still not effective until received. The offeree must use a fast-enough means of acceptance so that it will be received by the offeror before the rejection is received.

If, in our example, the acceptance is sent by express mail on the 6th and is received on the 7th, the contract will be formed on the 7th, without needing the early acceptance rule.

Action	Mailed	Received
Offer	1	4*
Rejection	5	8*
Acceptance	6	7*

*Effective date of action

Consideration ("of value" and "bargained for")

Both parties to a contract must provide some consideration as a result of the contract. A contract in which only one side has obligations is not valid. The consideration offered must be **legally sufficient**, meaning it must represent a true value under law. It can take several different forms:

- Paying or lending money
- Transferring or lending property
- Rendering services
- Relinquishing the right to receive money, property, or services
- Waiving the right to take certain actions (forbearance to sue)

Examples of the last include:

- **Covenant not to compete** – A seller of a business agrees not to open a competing business. The agreement must be reasonable as to length of time, location, and type of business forbidden. It would be reasonable for a seller of a travel agency to agree not to start another travel agency business within 5 miles of the business being sold for the next 2 years. It would be unreasonable for the seller to be required not to open any business in the United States for the next 20 years.
- **Out-of-court settlement** – A plaintiff in a lawsuit agrees to drop all claims and refrain from any further legal action in exchange for a payment or promise from the defendant.

In order to be valid, the consideration in a contract must be the result of the contract. It *cannot be*:

- **Past consideration** – Actions taken before the contract was formed.
- **Pre-existing duty** – An obligation which the party already had before the contract was formed.

As an example of *past consideration,* assume that a corporation has a suggestion box to encourage employees to offer ideas that will benefit the company. Over the years, they've received only a handful of useful suggestions, including one that suggested they start paying for useful suggestions instead of expecting them for free!

The board of directors likes this idea, and proposes to pay 10% of the benefit to any employee who makes a suggestion that increases the corporation's net income. Letters are drafted and mailed to all employees about this decision. After the letters are mailed, one employee drops a suggestion in the box in the morning, then gets the letter in the mail when they return home in the evening and finds out about the new policy.

If the suggestion is helpful to the company, it does not have to pay the employee for it, since the offer was not made until it was received by the employee, and the employee had already made the suggestion before that time. Also, the company doesn't have to pay other employees who made suggestions in the past, including the one who suggested paying for suggestions.

It is not a case of past consideration for an offeree to respond to a unilateral contract offer by providing the consideration demanded in the offer.

> Assume a painter signs a contract with a homeowner on 11/1 to paint the house by 12/1 for $1,000. After signing the contract, the painter decides that the time estimates they gave the customer were unrealistic, and they inform the homeowner that the job cannot be completed by 12/1 unless the painter hires an assistant. The painter informs the homeowner that either the job cannot be completed as promised or the homeowner will have to pay $1,300 for a 12/1 completion to cover the painter's additional costs.
>
> The homeowner agrees to pay $1,300, and a new contract is signed by both parties on 11/4. The painter finishes the job by 12/1 with the help of the assistant. The homeowner is only obligated to pay $1,000. The additional $300 demanded by the painter was not supported by any consideration, since the facts make clear the assistant would have been needed to meet the original promise by the painter. On 11/4, the painter is only offering the same consideration they were already obligated to provide to fulfill the earlier agreement.

The pre-existing duty rule also applies to legal obligations that a party had from contracts with third parties or general law. A police officer cannot be offered a reward for catching a criminal, since their employment already implied an obligation to make their best efforts in this direction. A parent cannot charge their minor child for room and board, since the law mandates they provide it.

One exception that allows a modification of a contract without apparent consideration on one side is when there is a dispute, and an adjustment is made to settle it.

> For example, a client agrees to pay $2,000 to a financial planner for the development of a complete financial plan. The planner prepares a report which the client considers to be far less detailed and complete than was reasonable to expect, and refuses to pay the planner, charging that they didn't perform the work promised.
>
> The planner agrees to reduce the fee to $1,000 if the client agrees no further services are required from the planner. This is a valid modification, even though the client is receiving a fee reduction, since it settles a dispute over the level of services required of the planner.

A modification can, of course, be made when both sides have altered obligations, since the changes are mutual. A price increase offered in exchange for an increase in the services rendered, or a price decrease offered in exchange for a decrease in the services required, would be acceptable.

In all of the discussions, notice there is no evaluation of the size or fairness of the consideration offered. Under common law, it is generally assumed that the consideration is fair because it resulted from the bargaining of two parties. If, however, consideration is imposed without negotiation, the courts may refuse to enforce the agreement due to the absence of bargaining, unless it considers the agreement to be reasonable.

For example, if a motorist is stranded on an isolated highway, and a passerby agrees to give them a ride for a fee of $5,000, "take it or leave it," the motorist can accept the ride and the courts will not enforce the fee. The motorist clearly was not in a position to bargain and the passerby was imposing outrageous consideration without allowing negotiation.

Consideration

- **Of value** (legally sufficient)
    - Money, goods, services or the promise to perform
    - Giving up a legal right
    - No preexisting legal obligation
    - Need not be of equal value
- **Bargained for exchange**
    - What the parties intended to receive
    - A gift is not bargained for
    - Past consideration is no consideration
- **Modification** of contract requires **additional consideration** by both.
- Situations where no consideration is required to be binding
    - Promises to a charity (promissory estoppel) where a charity might rely upon that promise to its detriment.

10.03 Defenses

There are certain **defenses** available to parties seeking to escape a contract. They may claim the contract is invalid because it may either be void, or voidable.

Voidable Contracts

One or more of the parties may escape the contract.

- **Duress** – A party enters a contract as a result of an improper threat by the other party. Coerce someone into a contract through force or threats, but the threats are economic or social in nature ("sign or I will fire you").

> For example, a tax preparer refuses to turn over client records needed for an IRS audit until the client agrees to sign a contract engaging the preparer to do their tax returns for the next 5 years.

- **Undue Influence** – Violate or abuse a relationship of trust or confidence. A party has entered a contract because they trusted the other party as one who represented their interests.

> For example, a client enters a business partnership with their accountant based on the accountant's financial forecasts.

- **Misrepresentation of a Material Fact** – A contract is voidable if a party enters a contract after receiving inaccurate information about relevant matters from the other party.

> For example, a home buyer was told by the seller that the plumbing was in excellent shape when it was actually on the verge of failure.

    o To use this defense, the misinformed party must prove that the inaccurate statements were made with the expectation they'd be relied on, the information was the *proximate cause* of the harm to the plaintiff, and that this caused them some detriment or harm. This is known as **innocent misrepresentation**.

    o A contract is also voidable when there is **fraud in the inducement**. This is similar to innocent misrepresentation, except that the other party had actual or constructive knowledge that they were providing inaccurate information.

    o Both of these defenses permit the victim to elect to withdraw from the contract or to enforce it, as they prefer. Fraud in the inducement entitles the victim to damages as well.

- o **Innocent** misrepresentation allows contract to be rescinded – must prove **MILE**:
    - **M**aterial misrepresentation or Omission
    - **I**ntent to induce reliance by the party making the misrepresentations/Relied upon
    - **L**oss occurred (damages)
    - **E**rror caused by misrepresentation
- o **Fraudulent** misrepresentation (fraud is an intentional tort) allows suit for damages – must prove actual or constructive intent to deceive (scienter).
    - MIL & Error caused by Fraud (Scienter)
        - Scienter (constructive Fraud or Gross Negligence)
            - o Intent to mislead, deceive, manipulate, or defraud
                - Reckless disregard of truth or knowledge of falsity

- Mistake
  - o *Mutual mistake of fact* – both parties are mistaken
      - A mutual mistake of fact typically causes a contract to be unenforceable and allows it to be *rescinded*.
  - o *Unilateral* – one person is mistaken, usually offeror.
      - If the other party knew or should have known – Material
      - An immaterial unilateral mistake generally does not permit either party to void a contract.

- **Capacity** – One possible reason for the courts to refuse to enforce a contract is that a party to the contract lacked the **capacity** to make one.
  - o **Minor** – Someone under the age of 18 usually lacks capacity to enter a contract, unless they are for necessities, such as food, shelter, or clothing.
      - A contract between a minor and an adult is a valid contract, but is **voidable** by the minor, meaning the minor can withdraw from the contract (ie, *disaffirm* the contract) at any time prior to reaching adulthood, even if they have obtained substantial benefits from the contract so far. The other party to the contract cannot withdraw, however, so the contract is enforceable if the minor wishes it to be.
      - After reaching the necessary age, they may **ratify** the contract and become bound to it. In fact, a minor who reaches the age of majority is treated as having ratified it if they do not disaffirm the contract within a reasonable period of time after reaching adulthood.

 The age of majority varies between 18 and 21 in the various states, and will be provided in the CPA exam question, if necessary.

  - o **Intoxication** – can avoid if the other party knew of your impairment.

- o Similar capacity issues arise if a party to a contract was **legally intoxicated** at the time they made the contract. After becoming sober, they can ratify the contract if they wish to enforce it, or may withdraw from the contract once they understand what they have agreed to. Keep in mind that a person is not automatically intoxicated just because they've had a drink, and a person will have the capacity to make a contract even if they have consumed alcohol as long as they did not reach the point of being legally intoxicated.
- o **Incompetent Persons** – Contracts entered before adjudication of insanity, may be voidable by incompetent person, but once adjudicated insane by a court of law, they are considered void.

Void Contracts

Under certain circumstances, a contract is **void** and cannot be enforced by either party.

- **Extreme duress** – A party enters into a contract as a result of a physical threat of force, so great that it impairs any ability to exercise free will (eg, they sign the contract while a gun is being pointed at them).
- **Fraud in the Execution** – If a party enters into a contract without being aware of it, as a result of the other party getting them to sign an agreement without realizing they are signing a contract (deception), this is known as fraud in the execution.
  - o As in the case of fraud in the inducement, fraud in the execution refers to actual or constructive knowledge by the perpetrator that they are acting improperly, and entitles the victim to sue for damages.
- **Illegal subject matter** – contract to kill the CPA examiners.
  - o If violates licensing agreement, but it is merely for revenue generating purposes, still valid contract.
  - o Covenant not to compete is binding if not "too limiting."
- **Incompetent Persons** – Contracts entered into once adjudicated insane by a court of law are considered void.

The courts will not enforce any agreement to violate the law or public policy. Such contracts are **void** and cannot be enforced by either party.

Assume Smith agrees to pay $20,000 to Jones in exchange for Jones' promise to steal trade secrets from Jones' employer and pass them to Smith. Smith gives Jones a $5,000 deposit at the time the contract is formed. The courts will not help Jones collect the other $15,000 if they steal the secrets and will not help Smith recover the $5,000 deposit if Jones doesn't steal them. Of course, both persons are also subject to appropriate criminal prosecution.

Statute of Frauds

Under common law, there is no requirement that a contract be in writing. However, specific legislation known as the **statute of frauds** has been enacted to require written evidence supporting certain contracts.

- Requires written evidence signed by defendant to enforce certain contracts (**GROSS**):
  - Sale of **G**oods worth $500 or more
  - **R**eal estate sales
  - **O**ver one year required to perform contract (Bilateral contract)
  - **S**uretyship (Guarantee debt of another)
  - **S**tatements in consideration of marriage ("if you marry my daughter, I will make you VP of my co" – Marriage is the consideration, or my brother would always say, if you get married this week only, I will give you a washing machine!!).
- **Sales over the internet** – If a transaction over the internet falls under the Statute of Frauds, most states have passed laws allowing such contracts to be enforceable to facilitate commerce.
- Contract needs to be signed by person backing out (weasel).

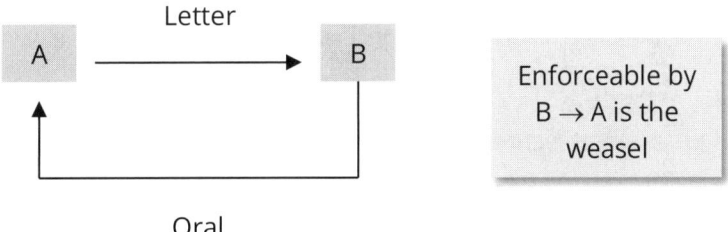

Note that a contract of **indefinite duration** does not fall within the over-one-year category, even if it is likely to take over one year to complete.

> For example, a contract hiring someone for a job may result in employment for several decades, but at the time the contract was made, it could have resulted in employment for a period shorter than a year. As a result, the statute of frauds doesn't apply, and such a contract does not have to written.

When the statute of frauds applies, the courts will generally not enforce a contract unless written evidence supporting the existence of the contract can be presented. This doesn't necessarily require a written contract, but requires some writing **signed by the defendant** that refers to the contract or otherwise indicates a contract was made. All the terms of the contract need not be in writing but, at a minimum, the subject matter of the contract must be mentioned. Must show that the contract was signed by the person trying to avoid the contract (the defendant).

For example, assume a buyer and seller orally agree on the sale of a home for $200,000. If the seller later denies in court that the contract was made, the buyer cannot enforce the sale, even if there were witnesses to the agreement willing to testify that the contract was made. If, however, the buyer can produce a letter signed by the seller and dated the day after the oral agreement, thanking the buyer for purchasing the home from them, the statute of frauds is satisfied and the contract is enforceable.

The statute of frauds provides for certain **exceptions** to the requirement of written evidence. A contract falling within the statute will still be enforced when:

- The contract has already been **performed** by both parties.

As an example of the latter, let's say an oral contract is made to sell a desk for $1,000. If the buyer pays the seller $1,000 and the seller delivers the desk to the buyer without any writing by either side, the courts will not allow either party to challenge the contract afterwards just because it was not written.

For contracts involving the sale of goods, there are additional **exceptions** (SPAM):

- A contract involving goods that are being **Specifically manufactured** by the seller can be enforced by the seller.
- A contract that has been **Partially performed** will be enforced to the extent of performance.
- The defendant **Admits in court** to having made the contract.
- If a written confirmation of a contract is sent to a merchant dealing in the goods in question, the confirmation can be used against the merchant if the **Merchant does not object within 10 days** of receiving the confirmation (Merchants bound by their silence).

10.04 Other Contract Issues

Parol Evidence Rule

The parol evidence rule prohibits the use of oral or written evidence that contradicts the terms of the written contract.

Even if a contract is *not* required to have written evidence under the statute of frauds, if the parties do choose to make a written contract, the **parol evidence rule** applies.

- This rule bars from court testimony any **prior or contemporaneous** oral or written contracts that contradict the written contract.

For example, if two parties make a written contract on August 20 to sell a house, and the contract includes a clause indicating that the seller makes no warranty as to the absence of termites, the buyer will not be allowed to introduce court evidence that the seller orally promised on August 15 to provide a warranty of freedom from termites in the sale. The buyer also would be prohibited from claiming in court that an oral discussion occurred at the same time the written contract was being signed, guaranteeing the absence of termites.

The parol evidence rule **does not prevent** the introduction of evidence about:

- Subsequent oral (or written) modifications of the contract.
- Fraud in the execution of the written contract.
- Oral discussions prior to the agreement that clarify ambiguous or missing terms in the written contract.

For example, if a written contract to sell a house is signed on August 20, and there are no clauses in the contract discussing the seller's responsibility for termites, the buyer is permitted in court to introduce testimony about oral promises made by the seller on August 15 regarding guarantees against termites.

A written contract sometimes includes an **entirety clause** claiming that there are no agreements other than those contained within the written contract. In this case, the absence of a promise involving termites is not considered an ambiguous or missing term, but a clear indication that there is no such promise. As a result, the buyer would not be allowed to contradict the entirety clause by claiming an oral promise had been made prior to the signing of the written contract. The entirety clause still doesn't prevent subsequent oral modifications, however, and these could be introduced.

Parol Evidence Rule

• Whenever a written contract exists, it bars from court:
   o Prior written or oral contracts on the same subject.
   o Concurrent oral contracts. (Contemporaneous)
• Rule doesn't bar (still admissible):
   o Subsequent oral modifications.
   o Evidence to prove fraud, duress, mistakes of written contract.
   o Subjects not addressed or ambiguous in written contract.

```
  o    o    o    o    Contract    o    o    o    o    o

   Not permissible in court      |   Subsequent oral evidence is permissible
```

Assignment of Rights and Delegation of Duties

Any right may be assigned and any duty may be delegated **unless**:

- Contract specifically prohibits it.
- The duty is personal in nature.
- Materially alters the rights and responsibilities of the other party.
- Involves specialized personal services.
    - Once assigned or delegated, both parties are now liable on the contract (assignor and assignee). The assignor makes certain **implied warranties**:
        - Assignor will not impair the assignment.
        - The assigned right actually exists.
        - The assignor has no knowledge of information that would impair the value of the assignment.
- The assignor is still liable on the contract, unless the other party to the contract accepts the assignee in place of the assignor, which is called a **novation.**

Third Party Rights

In general, contracts cannot be enforced by persons who are not participants in the formation of the contract. This is based on the concept of **privity**, which considers a contract to be a private matter not involving outsiders. There are several exceptions to this rule, however:

- **Assignment** – If a party transfers the rights they possess in a contract to a third party, the assignee will be able to enforce the rights transferred to them. The assignor loses the ability to enforce.

- **Intended third party beneficiary** – If a contract is specifically designed to benefit an outside party, that party has privity of contract and can enforce it.

There are two types of **intended beneficiaries:**

- A **donee beneficiary** who is receiving benefits as a gift may only enforce against the party owing them benefits, and not the party arranging them.

> For example, a customer purchases a car from a dealer to be delivered to the customer's child as a birthday present. If the car is not delivered, the child can sue the dealer but not their parent. The consideration paid by the parent binds the dealer to the contract.

- A **creditor beneficiary** who is receiving benefits to settle a debt owed them can sue either party.

> For example, a customer purchases a car from a dealer to be delivered to a person whose car was totaled by the customer in an auto accident. If the car is not delivered, the beneficiary can sue both the dealer and the car buyer.

Just because someone benefits from a contract doesn't make them an intended third-party beneficiary. An **incidental third-party beneficiary** obtains benefits that didn't represent the purpose of the contract, and cannot enforce against either party.

> For example, an auto mechanic is ordered by their customer to use replacement parts made by the car's original manufacturer because the customer believes them to be higher quality. If the mechanic fails to use the parts, the manufacturer cannot sue either party, since the purpose of the requirements in the contract was not to benefit the manufacturer.

Discharge of Contracts

- **By performance**
  - If fully performed, the parties are discharged.
  - Substantial performance – may not be discharged if used substandard materials.
- **By agreement**
  - Rescission – the parties are restored to their original position.
  - Accord and satisfaction – performance of the substituted duty is the "satisfaction" that discharges the original duty.
  - Novation – One party accepts the performance of a third party in place of the party obligated under the original contract.

- **By Operation of law**
  - Impossibility – the objective of the contract becomes impossible.
  - Death or incapacity of the party obligated to perform a personal service contract
  - Discharge in bankruptcy
  - Illegality of the services to be performed
- **By Breach**
  - Violation of contract terms
  - Anticipatory breach of contract – One party lets the other party to the contract know that performance will not occur.
    - Can cancel the contract.
    - Could sue for compensatory damages.
    - Doctrine of *anticipatory repudiation* allows a party to either sue at once or wait until after performance is due when the other party indicates performance will not occur.

Remedies for Breach

- Rescind (cancel) the contract and sue for restitution
- Affirm the contract and sue for damages

When a contract is breached, the victim of breach is normally only entitled to recover **actual damages**. This includes damages directly caused by the breach and incidental to it, but not unforeseen consequential damages. The courts also do **not** award **punitive damages** that are designed specifically to punish the defendant for the act of breach. The victim also cannot usually demand **specific performance** of the contract, unless it involves unique property.

To simplify enforcement, the parties to a contract sometimes place a **liquidated damages clause** in the contract, specifying an amount that will be awarded in the event of breach.

A student makes a 10% down payment to enroll in an upcoming course at a school, and the contract stipulates that the student forfeits the down payment if they do not pay the balance by the start date. Such a clause will be enforceable if the forfeited amount represents a reasonable estimate of the damages to the school. The clause will not be enforced if the payment is deemed a penalty, because of the prohibition against punitive damages for breach of contract.

Breach may occur when a party fails to perform a required term of a contract, or when a party indicates in advance that they will not perform a term required in the future. The latter is known as **anticipatory breach**. The victim of breach must take reasonable action to minimize the damages, and cannot recover damages they could have reasonably avoided.

- **Compensatory damages** – to compensate for direct losses and lost profits.
- **Consequential damages** – Indirect costs and anticipated losses.
- **Nominal damages** – no real, provable loss.

Contracts

- **Punitive damages** – to punish, usually for fraud, not for a breach of contract.
- **Specific performance** – available for *unique* property (patents), not for personal services.

For example, if a part needed for the functioning of a plant is not repaired when promised, the customer must attempt to obtain the necessary part as soon as possible, and cannot leave the plant idle and then attempt to collect all the lost revenues from the shutdown in production.

Statute of Limitations

- Time period in which a lawsuit must be initiated
- Enforcement is measured from the time the contract is made.
- An action for Breach of contract begins at the **date of breach.**
- Generally, 4 to 6 years

REG 11
Sales Contracts

REG 11: Sales Contracts

11.01 Sales of Goods Contracts Formation   1
    OVERVIEW   1
    OFFER (INTENT & COMMUNICATED)   1
    ACCEPTANCE   2
    CONSIDERATION   4
    STATUTE OF FRAUDS   4

11.02 Title & Risk of Loss Transfer   6

11.03 Sales Warranties & Breach of Contract   10
    WARRANTIES OVERVIEW   10
    EXPRESS WARRANTIES   10
    IMPLIED WARRANTIES   11
    PRODUCT LIABILITY   12
    BREACH OF CONTRACT   14

11.01 Sales of Goods Contracts Formation

Overview

Article 2 of the **UCC** (Uniform Commercial Code) deals with contracts for the sale of goods (**tangible personal property** that is moveable) derived from statutory law, not real property or services, which were covered in Common Law. When there are no specific provisions in the UCC, the rules of common law apply. The seller of the goods may be a *merchant or a nonmerchant*. A Merchant is a dealer in the goods involved in the transaction.

To have a binding sales contract, as with common law, we still need Offer, Acceptance, and Consideration. All rules of common law apply except as modified below.

Offer (Intent & Communicated)

- Terms can be **vague**. May be based on:
    - Standard trade practice
    - Past experience
        - Need not be definite as in Common Law.

Under the UCC, only the type and quantity of goods involved needs to be explicit. Price, delivery date, and other terms can be established by prior dealings between the parties or normal practices. Even the quantity need not be identified as a number, as long as there is a reasonable way to determine what is intended. Two typical examples are:

- **Output contract** – The buyer agrees to purchase as much as the seller is able to produce for a specific period of time, and the seller agrees to sell that entire output to the buyer.

- **Requirements contract** – The seller agrees to supply all of the needs of the buyer for a specified product for a specific period of time, and the buyer agrees to purchase whatever they need entirely from that seller.

Both contracts are subject to reasonable interpretation. If the buyer in a requirements contract acquires another business immediately after making the deal, and suddenly needs 20 times as much of the product as anticipated by the seller in making the agreement, the seller will not be considered in breach of contract if they're unable to supply all of the buyer's needs.

On the other hand, if the buyer in a requirements contract for heating oil needs much more of the product than expected due to a harsh winter, the seller **is** required to supply the additional amounts, since such a possible circumstance could have been reasonably anticipated when the contract was made.

Orders for specific quantities are not subject to such interpretations. If a buyer orders 3,000 gallons of heating oil for the winter, and then a very mild winter causes the buyer's needs to be much smaller, the buyer is still obligated to the contract for 3,000, since that is the clear agreement.

Under the UCC, however, there is an additional exception known as a **firm offer**, which cannot be revoked even if **no consideration** was provided by the offeree. A firm offer exists under the UCC when **all three (SUM)** of the following conditions are satisfied:

- **Signed** – The promise to keep the offer open must be in writing, and the offeror must specifically sign their name on the page containing the promise.
- **Up to 3 months** – The promise is enforceable for the time specified in the writing, or a reasonable period of time, up to a maximum of 3 months from the date of the writing.
- **Merchant** – The promise must be made by a merchant in the goods (remember that the UCC only applies to goods), referring to someone who deals in the goods on a regular basis or claims a special expertise in them. A merchant is one who either deals in the goods similar to the ones involved in the transaction or who, by occupation, represents that he has particular knowledge or skill relating to the practices or goods involved in the transaction. In the case of a merchant, "good faith" means honesty in fact and the observance of reasonable commercial standards of fair dealing in the trade. An example would be a *"rain check"* for advertised goods.

Under **common law,** an offer can be revoked at any time prior to acceptance, even if the offeror made a promise to keep the offer open for a certain period of time. The only exception is when the offeree has provided some **consideration** to keep the offer open, such as paying an option price of $100 to keep an offer on a house open for 30 days (**Option Contract**).

Acceptance

Can have *minor variations* from original offer unless prohibited in offer.

- Payment terms
- Change a warranty
  - **Major** change not ok:
    - Material Price increase
    - Quantity
    - Delivery date
- Do not need to Mirror the offer as in Common Law.
- Early acceptance rule (mail-box rule) still applies.
- An **auction** is an "invitation to offer," not an offer. A bid is an offer.
  - *With reserve* – right to withdraw the goods prior to acceptance (assumed unless otherwise stated).
  - *Without reserve* – the property will be sold to the highest bidder. Cannot be withdrawn unless no bid is made.

Another difference applicable only to the sale of goods by a merchant involves acceptance. Under common law, an acceptance must be unequivocal and unqualified with respect to the precise terms specified by the offer. The UCC allows the offeree to make minor changes in the process of acceptance, however.

For example, a party might order goods by requesting a prompt shipment. The offeree can accept by promising to ship the goods promptly. Had the contract involved real estate or services, where common law principles apply, the acceptance would not have been valid (it would have been treated as a counteroffer), since the offer was unilateral in form, requesting action (shipment), and the response was bilateral in form, making only a promise. The UCC doesn't make these distinctions.

In a sale of goods contract, the offeree can also add or adjust **minor** terms of a contract.

For example, the offer to buy goods could be accepted along with an indication by the seller that payment must be made by certified check at or before time of delivery. Although this identification of payment terms was not in the original offer, the offeror is assumed to have consented to the additional terms as long as the offeror is a **merchant** in the goods and **doesn't object** to the new term.

Minor changes in terms often occur in sale of goods contracts between merchants because of the use of standardized purchase order and sales order forms, which may have several terms pre-printed on the forms. The discrepancies would have invalidated the contract under common law, but the UCC treats them as a **battle of forms**, and enforces the contract as long as the parties are both acting as if they believe they have a contract.

Note that the assumption that the offeror has agreed to a change in terms contained in an acceptance only applies to merchants: a nonmerchant in the goods is only assumed to have consented to changes that they have explicitly agreed to make. A **merchant is bound by silence**, but a nonmerchant is not.

The consideration rule is extensively modified under the UCC. Essentially, as long as there is offer and acceptance, the contract will be enforceable. This includes **modification** of sales of goods contracts when **no consideration** at all is provided by one side.

Assume that Randi Retailer agrees on 11/1 to sell a chair to Carl Consumer at a price of $400, with a scheduled delivery to Carl's home on 11/30. After the contract is signed, Carl requests that the chair be delivered by 11/20, because Carl wishes to have it in time for a Thanksgiving party at the house.

If Randi agrees to change the terms of the contract to a delivery date of 11/20 at no additional charge, the change will be enforceable against Randi, even though Carl has provided no additional consideration for the change.

The same principle allows a seller and buyer to change the price on a bilateral contract after it is made but before it is performed. Of course, both parties must agree to the change in good faith.

In the example, if Randi notifies Carl on 11/5 that, due to a price increase from Randi's supplier, the cost of the chair once delivered will be $450, and Carl agrees to pay the increased price, Carl will owe $450 for the chair (notice that a similar agreement would not have been binding in a real estate or service contract under common law due to the absence of consideration).

If Carl had been a merchant buying the chair for his business, and he received a notice from Randi of the price increase, he would have been bound to the higher price as long as he didn't specifically object to the notice (for most purposes, a merchant has 10 days to object before their silence is treated as consent).

- **Acceptance by promise to ship**
  - Under the UCC, there is no distinction between unilateral and bilateral contracts, so can accept by prompt shipment or a prompt promise to ship.
  - If ship nonconforming goods, that constitutes both an acceptance and a breach by the seller.

If A (merchant) gives an offer to B (nonmerchant) and B accepts with a minor change, A has a reasonable period of time to respond, if no response is made, A is bound to the new changes. Hence, a Merchant is Bound by their silence. If A were a nonmerchant, it is just considered a proposal to change.

Consideration

Consideration is required to form a contract.
- For sale of goods, additional consideration is **not required** to make changes to a contract if it is a good faith price increase.
  - Common law, additional consideration is required.
- An **output or requirements contract** (I'll buy everything you produce) does satisfy the consideration requirement, even though the quantity is uncertain.

Statute of Frauds

Statute of frauds says that certain contracts need to be in writing in order to be enforceable by a court of law **(GROSS)**:
- **G**oods worth $500 or more
- **R**eal estate sales
- **O**ver one year required to perform contract (Bilateral contract)
- **S**uretyship
- **S**tatements in consideration of marriage

If the contract for the sale of goods is below $500, an oral agreement is binding. If the contract is changed, additional consideration is not required; however, if the new contract is now $500 or more, it must be in writing.

Exceptions

Exceptions to written requirement include (**SPAM**):

- **S**pecifically manufactured goods at request of buyer (eg, Roger CPA Review shirts).
- **P**erformance of contract already has occurred (partial performance binds to the extent of performance in sale of goods).
- **A**dmitted in court by defendant.
- **M**erchant in goods not objecting to written confirmation within 10 days, is treated as if they had signed it (merchants bound by their silence). All parties need not sign the contract, just the party against whom it is being enforced (the Weasel).

Parol evidence rule still applies, so subsequent oral evidence is admissible in court.

For example, if a written contract is orally changed from $700 to $450:

- New contract is oral – ok since <$500.
- No additional consideration required to make change.
- Admissible in court since not barred by parol evidence rule.

11.02 Title & Risk of Loss Transfer

Title to the goods means whose books the asset would be recorded in at year-end.

Risk of loss deals with who will bear the risk of loss if goods are damaged or lost.

- Neither may pass until **goods exist** and are **identified** to the contract.

Title and risk of loss transfer based upon:

1. **Contract terms** determine passage of title and risk of loss.
2. If no contract terms, then passage is determined by **shipping terms (Carrier case).**
   - Common carrier:
     - **Shipment contract** – title and risk of loss transfer when "placed with" the common carrier.
       - FAS – Free Along Side
       - CIF – Cost Insurance and Freight
       - FOB shipping point – Free On Board shipping point (seller's warehouse)
     - **Destination contract** – Title and risk of loss transfer when "Tendered" to the buyer.
       - FOB destination – Free On Board destination (buyer's warehouse)

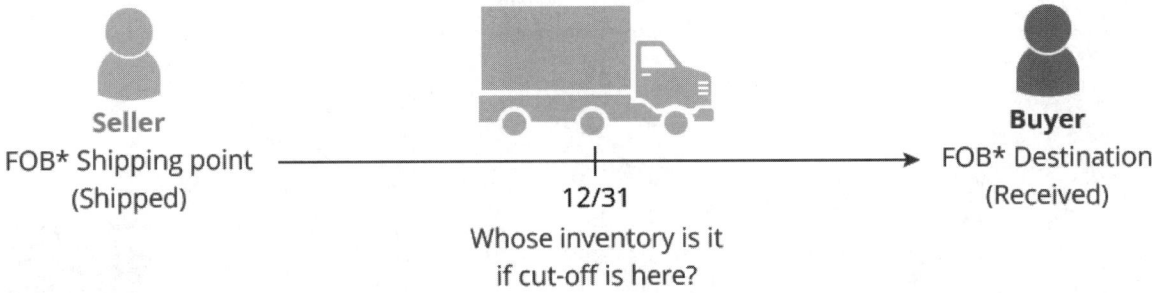

*FOB = Free on Board

3. If no contract terms and there are no carrier terms, then **not a common carrier**—buyer picks up the goods.
   - **Title** passes when contract formed.
   - **Risk** of loss
     - Merchant – Goods received by buyer (Sears)
     - Nonmerchant – Goods tendered to buyer (my garage sale)

Common carrier liability based on strict liability, whereby the carrier is liable for losses to property irrespective of negligence. Also, common carriers are not liable for losses due to causes deemed natural disasters and other "acts of God."

Under both the UCC and the United Nations Convention for the International Sale of Goods, the risk of loss of the goods will generally pass to the buyer when the seller delivers goods to the "first carrier" for transmission to the buyer.

Under common law, ownership of property confers all the rights and liabilities associated with the asset. The owner of a home is entitled to use it and receive the proceeds in the event of sale, but is also liable for injuries to people that occur in the home.

Under the Uniform Commercial Code (UCC), however, the rights to goods are distinguished from the liabilities in connection with the goods. It is possible for one person to have **title** to the goods and be entitled to the benefits while another person has **risk of loss** in the event the goods are damaged or destroyed. In fact, the UCC considers title irrelevant in determining the risk of loss.

One example of this situation is a **bailment**, in which the owner of goods (bailor) entrusts them to another party (bailee) temporarily. If the goods are damaged because of an absence of due care on the part of the bailee, they will generally bear the loss, even though the bailor has title to the goods. In this circumstance, the risk of loss is a result of the carelessness of the bailee.

In many situations, however, a party that has not been careless may still be liable on goods to which they have no title. If goods are sold as a result of the negligence of the bailee, a good faith purchaser will not be required to return the goods, and the bailor will not be able to retrieve the goods, but will be entitled to damages from the bailee.

The most common exam questions involve determining the point in time when title and risk of loss pass from the seller to the buyer in a transaction. Usually, this would be determined by the terms of the contract, but the following principles **override all other issues** in determining the time of passage:

- Neither title nor risk can pass on goods until the **goods exist**. For example, if a contract is signed for goods that have to be manufactured, the buyer cannot obtain the goods until they've actually been produced.

- Once they exist, they must also be **identified to the contract**. If, for example, the seller has a large inventory of the product being sold, the buyer cannot be provided with title or risk of loss if the seller hasn't determined which goods from the inventory will be transferred to the buyer.

Assuming these events have both occurred, the terms of the contract might still be overridden with regard to risk of loss if one of the parties commits a breach of contract. In such cases, **risk of loss is imposed on the party in breach**. This will not affect the issue of title, however.

Assuming goods exist and are identified to the contract, neither side has breached the contract, and the contract is silent as to the timing of the passage of title and risk of loss, these issues are settled by examining the terms of delivery of the goods:

- **Shipment contract** – The seller's rights (title) and responsibilities (risk of loss) end as soon as the goods have been properly transferred to the carrier (usually a trucking company) at the seller's location. Shipment contracts are identified by several different possible terms, including *FOB shipping point*, *FOB seller's place of business*, *FA vessel* (for items being sent by boat), *CIF* (cost, insurance, freight to be charged to the buyer), or *C & F* (cost and freight to be charged to the buyer). The references to *FOB* (free on board) and *FAS* (free alongside) are to indicate that the transfer of ownership occurs when the goods are loaded onto the truck or placed on the loading dock next to the boat, respectively.

- **Destination contract** – Title and risk of loss pass when the goods arrive at the buyer's location and are tendered (offered) to the buyer by the carrier. Destination contracts are identified by the terms *FOB destination point* or *FOB buyer's place of business*. Notice that the transfer of ownership occurs while the goods are still on board the truck, as soon as the carrier offers the goods to the buyer.

- **Not a common carrier, "Hold for pickup"** – In such contracts, the seller doesn't deliver the goods, but simply makes them available to the buyer for pickup. **Title passes** as soon as the contract is **formed** (assuming the goods exist and are identified to the contract, of course). **Risk** of loss, however, doesn't pass at that time. If the goods are being held by a **merchant seller**, risk of loss passes once the buyer has **received** the goods from the seller and removed them from the merchant's premises. If a **nonmerchant seller** is holding the goods, risk of loss passes as soon as the seller **tenders** the goods to the buyer.

Special situations often arise on the exam in determining the transfer of ownership. A common one involves **conditional sales**, in which the buyer is given the option to cancel the deal and return the goods. There are two possible situations:

- **Sale on approval** – This refers to a contract that permits the buyer to obtain the goods for use and make a decision as to whether or not to purchase them later. Normally, there is a time limit (typically 30 days) after which the buyer is presumed to have accepted the goods. In these contracts, title and risk of loss transfer to the buyer as soon as they've accepted the goods explicitly or the time period has elapsed.

- **Sale or return** – This refers to a contract in which the buyer is acquiring the goods for resale and is given the right to cancel the sale if they are unable to resell them to others. A sale or return contract is treated in the same fashion as normal sales, and the rules for passage of title and risk of loss are based on the shipping terms (shipment, destination, or pickup) discussed previously.

Also, there are times when a buyer attempts to cancel the contract. There are two different situations:

- **Buyer rejects delivery** – When the carrier arrives to tender delivery under either a shipment or destination contract, the buyer might refuse to accept delivery and order the carrier to return the goods to the buyer. Title, in such cases, immediately reverts to the seller. As for risk of loss, it depends on whether the buyer's rejection is proper. If so, then risk of loss reverts to the seller as well. If the buyer wrongfully rejects the goods, the overriding principle that holds the **party in breach** liable causes the buyer to continue to bear risk of loss.

- **Buyer revokes acceptance** – After accepting delivery of goods, the buyer might attempt to revoke acceptance. This commonly occurs when the buyer inspects goods after delivery and discovers they do not conform to the requirements of the contract. As long as the buyer's revocation is proper, title and risk of loss revert to the seller. A buyer's attempt to revoke acceptance without a valid reason has no effect, however, and the buyer retains both title and risk.

If there is a **document of title** representing goods held at a public warehouse, the transfer of the document to the buyer transfers title. Risk of loss also transfers to the buyer if the document of title is a negotiable instrument, but the warehouse must be notified of the transfer of a nonnegotiable document of title before the buyer can obtain them, so risk of loss doesn't transfer on nonnegotiable documents until such notice takes place.

Sales Contracts

If buyer rejects goods

1. **Title** reverts back to seller.
2. **Risk** of loss
    - **Rightful rejection** (nonconforming goods – seller breaches) – this is considered an acceptance and a breach; both title and risk of loss reverts back to seller.
    - **Wrongful rejection** (conforming goods – buyer breaches) – risk of loss stays with buyer.
        - Note: Risk of loss stays with party in breach.
        - If seller breaches, buyer may accept *all, some, or none* of the goods.

The following chart summarizes the time of transfer of title and risk of loss on goods that exist and are identified to the contract:

Situation	Passage of Title	Passage of Risk
Shipment contract	Placed with carrier	Placed with carrier
Destination contract	Tendered to buyer	Tendered to buyer
Pickup from merchant	Contract formed	Received by buyer
Pickup from nonmerchant	Contract formed	Tendered to buyer
Sale on approval	Accepted by buyer	Accepted by buyer
Sale or return	See normal sale rules	See normal sale rules
Buyer rejects goods	Reverts to seller	Reverts if proper
Buyer revokes acceptance	Reverts if proper	Reverts if proper
Negotiable document	Transfer of document	Transfer of document
Nonnegotiable document	Transfer of document	Transfer and notice

11.03 Sales Warranties & Breach of Contract

Warranties Overview

Warranties are an expectation the buyer has, that the seller is legally obligated to fulfill.

- **Implied Warranty of Title and Infringement** – Automatically exists in all sales. Seller warrants good title, transfer is rightful, no liens or encumbrances, and that transfer doesn't violate law or infringe on rights of third parties, such as patent or trademark rights.
    - Disclaimer must be explicit in the contract.
- **Express Warranty** – Any statements or claims that become a "basis of the bargain." This would include a description, sample, or model.
    - Cannot be disclaimed.
- Implied Warranties of:
    - **Merchantability** (ordinary purpose) – When seller is a merchant, seller warrants goods are in fair condition for their *ordinary purpose* and conform to all package claims.
        - Disclaimer may use language "as is" or "with all faults."
    - **Fitness for particular or ordinary purpose** – When buyer is relying on the seller's judgment in selecting the product, seller warrants the goods will fulfill the specific needs of the buyer.
        - Disclaimer must be in writing and use language such as "as is" or "with all faults."

When goods are sold, the seller makes certain promises to the buyer, and those that the buyer can legally enforce are known as warranties. Warranties come in two basic varieties:

- **Express warranties** refer to specific promises and claims about the goods made by the seller.
- **Implied warranties** refer to promises that are present without any specific statement by the seller.

Express Warranties

During the negotiation and formation of a contract, the seller usually makes certain claims about the product, and often demonstrates its use. These might become express warranties. The principle is that a statement or demonstration is an express warranty if it becomes a **basis of the bargain**, meaning it was one of the reasons the buyer made the purchase or it affected the price or other terms of the agreement in some way.

In contrast, there are certain claims that are clearly meant as "sales talk" and are not express warranties.

For example, if an auto dealer describes a specific car as "the sportiest car in America," this is not a warranty, since it has no specific meaning that could be claimed as a promise to the buyer. If the dealer says the car "goes from zero to 60 miles per hour in the blink of an eye," it is an obvious exaggeration. On the other hand, if the dealer says the car "goes from zero to 60 miles per hour in 8 seconds," this is a specific claim that is objective and might have been relied on by the buyer in deciding to make the purchase.

In general, claims and promises made by the seller after the contract is formed are not warranties, since the bargain has already been made. If the sale is conditional, however, and a promise is made to discourage the buyer from canceling the purchase, it may also become a basis of the bargain and an express warranty.

Express warranties made in the contract itself cannot be disclaimed, but express warranties that are created during the process of negotiation before sale can be disclaimed in the contract as long as the disclaimer is clear and understood by the buyer.

Implied Warranties

There are three possible implied warranties when a sale of goods takes place:

- **Title** – The seller claims to have good title to the product with no undisclosed liens or claims against it and also promises that the transfer of ownership to the buyer has been performed correctly and doesn't infringe on the rights of any other party. These rights may also include warranty against infringement, such as patent or trademark. This warranty is present in **all** sales of goods, unless specifically disclaimed by the seller in a manner that makes clear the seller is not promising clear title (general disclaimers of warranty or statements of "as is" or "with all faults" are not sufficient).

- **Merchantability** – The seller claims that the goods are fit for their normal uses and that they perform in accordance with any claims or descriptions on their packaging. This warranty is only implied when the goods are **sold by a merchant**. The merchant can disclaim this warranty by name or by selling the goods "as is" or "with all faults."

Fitness for particular or ordinary purpose – The seller promises that the goods will meet the specific needs of the buyer. This warranty is only implied when the **buyer relies on the seller's judgment** and skill in the selection of the product. The seller may disclaim this warranty by name or by selling the goods "as is" or "with all faults." Assume that a consumer enters a department store and asks a clerk in the tools section for a recommendation of a saw to cut down a tree in the consumer's backyard. The clerk recommends a particular power chainsaw and the consumer purchases it. Even if no promises are expressly made by the clerk, the consumer has an automatic warranty of title, a warranty of merchantability since the store selling the saw is a merchant, and a warranty of fitness for particular purpose because the consumer relied on the store employee's judgment and skill in selecting the saw.

Disclaimers

In general, disclaimers may be either written or oral, as long as they are clearly understood by the buyer. An attempt to disclaim the fitness for particular purpose by name must be written, however.

Product Liability

No Privity Defense

When a user of a product suffers an injury or illness in connection with it, the UCC permits claims based on **product liability law**. In such cases, the defendant in the case is not permitted to use the **privity** defense, meaning that the plaintiff need not have purchased the product from the defendant. As a result, a manufacturer can be held liable by a consumer, even though the consumer actually purchased the product from a retail store, and the plaintiff need not have been a purchaser at all, but could have been a relative or friend of the purchaser.

> Assume, for example, that the purchaser of the chainsaw in the previous example was buying it as a gift for a friend, and the friend suffers an injury in its use because of a defective part. The friend may be able to sue the department store, the distributor, and the saw manufacturer, and none of them can use the privity defense.

Breach of Warranty

The use of breach of warranty as a theory of liability in such cases requires the plaintiff to demonstrate all the following:

- An express or implied warranty that wasn't effectively disclaimed.
- An injury or illness that resulted from the breach.

Negligence

A common theory of liability is **negligence** law, which holds a person responsible for careless acts causing harm to others. In a product liability case, the **plaintiff must prove** all the following:

- An **Absence of due care** by the defendant in connection with the product.
- A **Defect** in the product caused by the carelessness.
- **Damages** to the plaintiff resulting from the defect.

Negligence cases can be difficult for plaintiffs because they must prove the existence of a defect that is the fault of the defendant. Often, a product is dangerous, but all manufacturers produce the item in a manner that contains that danger, so it is not considered a defect. Also, the party that caused the defect can be difficult to identify.

Sales Contracts

A customer in a store who is injured when clothing is caught in an escalator might sue the store, which may claim the escalator was defectively designed so that the store is not at fault. The customer then sues the manufacturer, who claims the cause of the injury was not the design but improper maintenance by the store. Even though both defendants concede the product has a defect, the difficulty of identifying the cause of the defect makes it difficult for the customer to win either case.

Additionally, a defense against negligence is **contributory negligence** on the part of the plaintiff. In some states, any evidence that the plaintiff was also careless is a total bar to recovery, and in all other states, such evidence reduces the liability based on the doctrine of comparative negligence.

Strict Liability

The easiest cases for plaintiffs to win are based on **strict liability** law. In such cases, the plaintiff must prove:

- A defect or unreasonable danger in the product.
- **Damages** caused by this danger.
- The danger existed when the product left the defendant's control.
- The defendant is in the **business of selling** the product.

Notice that there is no need to prove that the product contained a defect in the traditional sense: any danger in the product that wasn't a necessary part of it could be sufficient. Also notice that the plaintiff doesn't need to prove that the defendant caused the danger. If a dangerously manufactured product is sold to a distributor, who sells it to a retail store, who sells it to a customer, the customer can collect for damages from any of the three parties in the chain of sale under the theory of strict liability.

Contributory negligence cannot be used as a defense in a strict liability case. Intentional misuse of the product by the plaintiff or reasonable danger may be used.

For example, a kitchen knife must be capable of cutting easily in order to be useful, and a cook who is injured by a cut while chopping vegetables cannot sue for the injury, since a knife not capable of cutting, is not functional.

If a defective product injures someone, the manufacturer and seller may be liable under the theory of **Strict Liability in Tort** (liable without fault). The Injured party must prove:

- Suffered an **injury**.
- Seller was in the business of selling that product.
- Product was sold in a **defective** condition (unreasonably dangerous condition).
- The defect made the product **unreasonably dangerous**.
    - Seller is liable regardless of:
        - Unaware of the defect and were not negligent.

- Injured party didn't exercise due care in the use of the product.
- *Not in privity* with the injured party.
  - Cannot disclaim product liability.
- Under the UCC, limitation of damages for personal injury in the case of consumer goods is considered to be unconscionable and, thus, not allowed.

Breach of Contract

When it doesn't appear that one party to the contract will perform (**anticipatory breach** of contract), reasonable and/or adequate assurance of their ability to perform can be requested. If they refuse, the wronged party can cancel the contract and be released of all obligations.

Anticipatory repudiation occurs when a party renounces the duty to perform the contract before the party's obligation to perform arises. The seller may then resell the goods to another party and recover damages.

Both parties are expected to act in good faith; if this doesn't occur, there are remedies available to the seller and the buyer.

Seller's Remedies

- Right to resell the goods
- Right to stop the carrier from delivering the goods (Rescind contract)
- Cancel the contract
- Recover damages
  - Incidental damages
  - Consequential damages
  - *Not* punitive damages
- **Cure** – Seller has time to cure nonconforming goods before the contract due date.

The UCC provides a victim of breach of contract with several options. The victim may cancel the contract while retaining the right to sue for damages (under common law, such cancellation normally cancels the right to damages).

If the seller has not yet completed the manufacture of goods when the buyer notifies them that they intend to dishonor the contract (**anticipatory breach**), the seller may sell the uncompleted goods for scrap or complete them and attempt to sell them elsewhere, whichever seems more commercially feasible. The seller has the right to recover from the buyer whatever losses cannot be avoided by such actions. If the seller learns that the buyer is insolvent, they may stop delivery on goods or reclaim them within 10 days after delivery. The seller must honor the contract, however, if the insolvent buyer pays cash for the goods.

Buyer's Remedies (Nonconforming Goods)

- **Accept** all, some or none of the goods.
- **Cover** – Purchase goods elsewhere and recover the excess paid from the seller.
- **Specific performance** – very unique goods only.
- Recover **damages**
    - Incidental damages
    - Consequential damages
    - *Not* punitive damages
- **Rescission** of contract
- If a **strike** happens and delivery cannot occur by the agreed-upon means, if a valid substituted performance occurs, both parties are still liable.
- A **liquidated damages** clause is valid as long as the amount is reasonable in light of the anticipated loss. When no provision is stated, the seller may keep the lesser of $500 or 20% of the contract price.
- If the goods are in the possession of the seller, the buyer may exercise the right of **replevin** and claim ownership of the goods, if the buyer has paid the seller for them.
- If goods are destroyed before risk of loss passes, the contract is voided and the seller is released from obligation to perform.
- If the buyer receives nonconforming goods, they should inform the seller, who has the right to **cure** by sending conforming goods by the original contract date or within a reasonable time after learning the goods do not conform to the contract.

Statute of Limitations

There is a statute of limitations on sales contracts of four years, starting from the date of breach (technically, the statute starts running the day after breach). The parties can mutually agree to shorten the statute of limitations to as little as one year but cannot agree to lengthen it. Once the statute of limitations has expired, no claims can be filed in court charging breach of contract.

REG 12
Business Structures

REG 12: Business Structures

12.01 General Partnerships   1
    OVERVIEW   1
    THREE BASIC PARTNER RIGHTS   1
    FORMATION (INFORMAL)   2

12.02 Fiduciary Duties of Partners   5
    LIABILITY   5
    ADMITTING OR RETIRING A PARTNER   5
    DISSOLUTION & TERMINATION   7
    LIMITED PARTNERSHIPS (LP) (FORMAL)   9

12.03 Limited Partnerships, LLC, LLP   9
    OTHER BUSINESS STRUCTURES   12

12.04 Corporations   19
    CLOSELY HELD CORPORATION   20

12.05 Board of Directors   22
    OVERVIEW   22
    ROLE OF THE BOD   22
    FIDUCIARY DUTY   25

12.06 Shareholders' Rights   27
    VOTING RIGHTS   27
    RIGHT TO DIVIDENDS   28
    INSPECTION RIGHTS   28
    OTHER SHAREHOLDER RIGHTS   29
    SHAREHOLDER LIABILITY   29
    CONCENTRATIONS OF VOTING POWER   30

12.01 General Partnerships

Overview

A partnership (General Partnership) is an association between two or more persons to operate a business as co-owners *for profit*. Nonprofit associations such as charitable organizations, labor unions or clubs do not qualify. **Informally created** since the partners have **unlimited** liability. The partners are **agents** of the partnership.

- Limited duration.
- Transfer of ownership requires agreement.
- Under RUPA (Revised Uniform P/S Act), partnerships are *separate legal entities*.
    - May sue and be sued.
    - May own property in partnership name.
- Unlimited liability of partners for partnership debts.
- Ease of formation—can be very informal.
- Not a taxable entity, flow-through entity (1065).

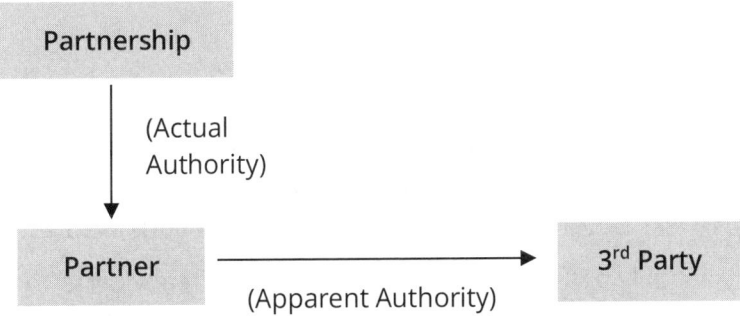

Three Basic Partner Rights

- **Profits (Interest)** – Each partner generally has a right to a proportionate share of (1) the profits generated by the business and (2) a return of the net assets in the partnership in the event the partnership terminates. This is known as the **partnership interest**. The right is personal and **transferable/assignable** without the need for approval by the other partners. As a result, a partner can transfer their interest in the partnership to a personal creditor, or the courts may permit a personal creditor to seize that interest to satisfy an unpaid personal debt of the partner. When that occurs, the creditor is entitled to receive that partner's share of profits and distributions.

- **Property** – All property acquired by a partnership becomes partnership property and belongs to the partnership as an entity, rather than to the individual partners. Each partner has a right to use partnership property for partnership purposes. Under RUPA, partnership property not only includes property purchased in the partnership name but also includes property purchased by a partner, who is an agent of the partnership, with partnership funds. This right is **not transferable/assignable**, so a personal creditor of a partner cannot obtain a right to any specific partnership property as a result of an assignment of interest by that partner.

- **Participation (Management Right – vote/make contracts/debts)** – Each partner has a right to participate in the management of the business, including a right to inspect the books and records of the business at any time, make contracts, and vote on partnership actions. This right is also **not transferable/assignable**.

Formation (Informal)

The establishment of a partnership can result from an agreement that is:

- **Written** – This is required only when the *statute of frauds* applies, such as a partnership with a specific term exceeding one year. Requires written evidence signed by defendant to enforce certain contracts (**GROSS**):
    - Sale of **G**oods worth $500 or more
    - **R**eal estate sales
    - **O**ver one year required to perform contract (Bilateral contract)
    - **S**uretyship (Guarantee debt of another)
    - **S**tatements in consideration of marriage ("if you marry my daughter, I will make you VP of my co" - Marriage is the consideration).
- **Oral** – This is acceptable when the statute of frauds doesn't apply.
- **Implied** – Whenever two or more persons are **sharing profits from a venture**, they are presumed to be partners, unless they can prove otherwise (a person proves they're not a partner by showing they do not use partnership property and do not participate in the management of the business). This is known as a partnership by rebuttable presumption.
    - Partners' capital may not only be in cash, property, or services already performed, but also may be in the form of promises to give or perform these at a future date.

No government approval is needed for the creation of a partnership (**informal**), and there are no special filings required. A partnership may use the names of current or former partners without approval. A partnership that wishes to have a business name with other information may need to file a fictitious name statement with the appropriate government agency.

Types of Authority

- **Actual** – Partnership intends to give the partner power to contract.
  - **Express** – Partnership explicitly states partner has authority.
  - **Implied** – Partnership assigns task, which requires authority to carry out duties. Reasonable and necessary to get job done.
- **Apparent** – Partnership creates impression that partner has authority.
  - **Good faith 3rd party** reasonably assumes you have.
- **Unauthorized action** – not liable unless ratify.
  - **Ratification** – Partnership gives partner authority after contract is made.
    - Principal (Partnership) must be fully or partially disclosed.
    - Must know details of contract made by partner on behalf of Partnership.
    - Must ratify before 3rd party withdraws.

The right of a partner to participate in management includes broad agency authority: the partners are, in effect, mutual agents and principals with the power to make contracts binding each other. The actual authority of a partner is based on agreement, but a partner has the **apparent authority** to make virtually any contract that involves the business of the partnership, with the following exceptions:

- **Admitting a new partner** – No partner may admit a new partner to the business without the unanimous consent of all partners. This is because each new partner has agency power and is entitled to a share of the profits, and such rights must be clearly agreed to by all affected parties.

- **Selling or pledging property (Can't sell Goodwill of P/S)** – The sale of property or pledging as collateral for a loan requires consent of all partners; although, partners have the right to use partnership property. A partner *does*, however, have the apparent authority to sell *inventory* in the ordinary course of business.

- **Admitting or submitting a legal claim** – No partner may waive the legal rights of the other partners by admitting responsibility in *court* or by agreeing to submit disputes with others to binding *arbitration* without all partners consenting to the arrangement.

- **Promising to pay the debts of another** – No partner can make the partnership a surety or guarantor of the debts of another party. Furthermore, surety arrangements fall within the statute of frauds, so each partner who is to act as a *surety* must individually sign the agreement.

In addition to these four limits on the apparent authority of a partner, the doctrine of apparent authority does not apply when the partners **agree to limits on the actual authority** of a partner **and notify third parties of the limits**.

For example, assume the partners are negotiating the purchase of machinery, a transaction that normally can be approved by any one of them and be binding on the entire partnership. If the partners privately agree that the purchase decision will require the unanimous consent of the partners, this will not change the apparent authority of a partner to make the deal *without* such consent. If, however, the owner of the machinery is informed of the private agreement, apparent authority is eliminated, and the deal *will* require unanimous consent.

- Unanimous consent required for the following (**AGAST**):
    - **A**dmitting a new partner.
    - **G**uaranteeing the debts of a third party (suretyship).
    - **A**dmitting or submitting a legal claim in court or to arbitration.
    - **S**ale or pledge of partnership property (sell goodwill).
    - **T**hird parties are notified (aware) of a limit to the partner's actual authority.

12.02 Fiduciary Duties of Partners

- Duty of *loyalty*
- Duty of *care* – Partners must refrain from engaging in grossly negligent or reckless conduct, intentional misconduct, or knowingly violate the law.
- Partners must *refrain from competing* with the partnership.
- Partners also have a duty of *good faith and fair dealing* in the discharge of all their duties.

Liability

Partners have **joint & several** liability on the **contracts & debts** (voluntary) made by the partnership with third parties. If the partnership breaches a contract, the third party must attempt to recover damages out of partnership assets first, then may access the personal assets of the partners for remaining amounts owed. If one partner is personally bankrupt, the third party may access sufficient assets of the solvent partners to satisfy the claim.

Partners are **jointly and severally** liable on the **torts** (involuntary) committed by any of the partners within the scope of the partnership. Third parties may access partnership and personal assets of the partners in any order. A tort is a wrongful act, whether intentional or negligent, not arising out of contractual obligations, which causes an injury and can be remedied at civil law, usually through awarding damages.

Partners are normally not liable for **crimes** committed by other partners, but recent legislation has expanded liability in some cases, and the CPA exam generally avoids areas of law that are not consistent on a nationwide basis.

- RUPA requires creditors to first attempt collection from the partnership before partners, unless the partnership is bankrupt.
- A *silent partner* in a general partnership does not participate in the management of the partnership, but nonetheless has unlimited liability.

Admitting or Retiring a Partner

When a new partner enters a partnership, the partner will be liable for contracts and torts that arise after the date of admission in accordance with the principles just discussed.

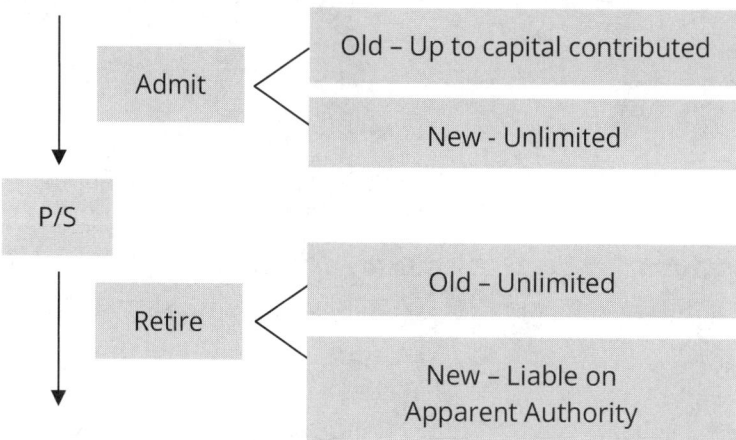

Unless they make a specific agreement to become so, a new partner is **not personally liable** for actions taken **before admission**. Any capital contributions made by the partner, however, can be accessed by partnership creditors with claims arising before that partner's admission.

When an existing partner retires from the partnership, the partner will continue to be liable for debts created before retirement, unless the **creditors** agree to perform a **novation** to release the retiree. An agreement by the **other partners** to hold the retiring partner harmless for all debts will **not** release them, since the debts are not owed to the other partners. Such an agreement will, however, serve as an indemnification agreement requiring the remaining partners to reimburse the retiree for any amounts they are forced to pay creditors.

A retiree may continue to be held **liable** for debts created **after retirement** if proper notice of retirement isn't given. Parties that dealt with the retiree in the past must be given **actual notice**, while others who might have become aware of the partner are considered notified if the partnership provides **constructive notice** of the retirement through the publication of an announcement of the change. Notice is not required upon the death of a partner, since the termination of that partner's participation is by operation of law. Note that a retiring partner can enter contracts that are binding on the remaining partners if proper notice of retirement hasn't been made.

- **Actual notice** – Third parties are directly informed (personal notice).
- **Constructive notice** – An announcement of the termination is made in publications that third parties are likely to read (public notice).

The allocation of losses to the partners is based on their agreement. In the absence of an explicit agreement, partners share losses in the same proportion that they share profits. If there is no agreement on the sharing of profits either, then profits and losses are **shared equally based on the number of partners,** except in unusual circumstances. If a partner's losses reduce the partner's capital account below zero, the partner is personally liable for the deficit.

When a partner **transfers their interest** in the partnership to another party (eg, a personal creditor in settlement of a claim), the transferor remains the partner and continues to have liability for losses and claims against the partnership. The transferee is entitled to that partner's share of profits and surplus, but has no other rights or obligations in connection with the partnership, and is *not* considered a partner.

Dissolution & Termination

Dissolution is the result of the change in the relation of the partners when a partner ceases to be associated with the carrying on of the business. The partnership does not terminate on dissolution, but continues until the winding up of the partnership is complete. Dissolution may be accomplished either without violation of the partnership agreement or in violation of the partnership agreement. The **entity theory** of partnership provides a conceptual basis for continuing the firm itself, despite a partner's withdrawal from the firm.

Under RUPA, a **change in the makeup of the partnership does not dissolve** it, unless the partners agree to do so (a withdrawal leaving only one partner, however, does cause dissolution, since one person alone cannot be considered a partnership). Dissolution does not mean that the partnership must liquidate all assets and cease business, but simply that the legal entity that exists after the change in partners is not considered a continuation of the previous partnership. As a result, various legal arrangements and claims may need to be modified or refiled in court.

Because of the inconvenience dissolution causes, partners normally will make an agreement not to dissolve upon a change in partners. A "**partnership at will**" is used to describe a partnership without a specified duration.

Tax law treats a partnership as a separate legal entity for the purpose of collection and payment of payroll taxes. A partnership is not obligated to pay income taxes but must file annual information returns (Form 1065), allocating the income of the partnership to the partners, who are personally responsible for all income tax obligations.

Dissolution of a partnership is generally the first step in terminating it. A partnership may be dissolved without being terminated but, if it is to be terminated, dissolution will be followed by a winding up of partnership affairs and the distribution of partnership property. During the period of dissolution and winding up, the partners continue to have the authority to bind the partnership, which continues until such time as the partnership is terminated.

A partnership agreement may specify the length of time it is intended to remain in operation and dissolution will occur when its term expires. When a term is specified, a partner may dissolve the partnership only with the consent of the other partners. If there is no term specified, however, any partner may dissolve the partnership at any time. A partnership may also be dissolved as a result of:

- *A court decree*, which will likely be granted if a partner becomes insane or incapacitated
- A *violation* of the partnership agreement

Since RUPA considers a partnership to be a legal entity, it is **not automatically dissolved** as a result of the **withdrawal, death, or bankruptcy** of a partner. When one of those circumstances does occur, remaining partners with a majority share of the partnership may continue the partnership

- A partnership may *not* continue if only one partner remains, since a partnership requires two or more partners.
- Any partner has the power to withdraw from the partnership.
- A withdrawing partner who had agreed not to withdraw may be in breach of contract.

When a partnership is terminated, there is a **winding up** of the partnership's affairs. All assets will be sold, liabilities will be paid, and any surplus will be distributed to the partners. Gains or losses will be allocated among the partners according to their profit and loss percentages.

A partner with a **deficit balance** is generally required to make a contribution to the partnership to eliminate the deficit. If the partner is bankrupt, however, the partner's deficit balance will be allocated among the remaining partners according to their profit and loss percentages.

In determining the amount that will be distributed to a partner upon **termination** of the partnership:

- First, upon the sale of assets, allocate all gains and losses to the partners in accordance with their profit and loss percentages.
- If any partner has a deficit balance and is bankrupt and unable to contribute the amount of the deficit, any remaining deficit, after what contributions the partner does make, is allocated to the remaining partners in accordance with their profit and loss percentages.
- When all assets are sold, profits and losses are allocated, and liabilities are paid, the remaining cash will be equal to the total of the partners' capital balances.
- The cash will then be distributed to the partners.

Distributions to partners will be made in the following order:

- Amounts owed to partners for loans to the partnership
- Partners' capital accounts
- Amounts owed to partners for profits

12.03 Limited Partnerships, LLC, LLP

Limited Partnerships (LP) (Formal)

In some circumstances, individuals will want to achieve the benefits of the corporate structure—limited liability in particular—with the benefits of a partnership that include the ease of formation and being treated as a pass-through entity for tax purposes. The solution is the limited partnership (LP), which has many of the characteristics of a partnership, while providing limited liability to some of its partners.

Formation

Not all states allow the formation of an LP and one cannot be formed in a state without an enabling statute. Most states that allow LPs have adopted the Revised Uniform Limited Partnership Act (RULPA), although a few states have adopted the newer Uniform Limited Partnership Act (New ULPA).

To be formed, an LP requires at least one general partner and at least one limited partner. As a general rule, the **general partner** is responsible for the management and operations of the partnership and has unlimited liability while a **limited partner** is a passive investor with limited authority and liability that, in most cases, is limited to the amount invested. A limited partner generally has no personal liability for the obligations of the partnership, including those resulting from contracts or torts.

Because of the limited liability provided to some partners, forming a limited partnership requires a more formal process than forming a partnership, including the filing of **a certificate of limited partnership** (Formal) with the Secretary of State, which generally includes:

- The names and signatures of all general partners
- The name and address of the LP, which may not include the name of a limited partner who is not also a general partner and must include the words "limited partnership" or the abbreviation
- The name and address of its agent
- The latest date on which the LP is expected to terminate

The certificate, which does not require the names of the limited partners, must be amended for the addition or deletion of general partners. If the certificate is not properly filed, the LP will be treated as a general partnership.

Both general and limited partners may obtain their partnership interests in exchange for cash or other monetary or nonmonetary assets, the performance of services, or the promises to deliver cash or other assets or perform services.

Rights & Obligations

General partners, as indicated, are responsible for the management of the entity, have a fiduciary responsibility to the LP and its partners, and have unlimited personal liability for the obligations of the partnership. A general partner may, however, be a corporation providing its limited liability protections.

A person can become a **general partner** by being so indicated in the limited partnership agreement, as a replacement for a general partner that is dissociated from the partnership, as a result of a conversion or merger, or with the consent of all partners.

- A general partner is an **agent** of the limited partnership with all the rights and obligations associated with agency.
- A limited partnership is liable for the actions of the general partner that are in the ordinary course of the partnership's business or are with the authority of the partnership.
- All general partners are *jointly and severally liable* for the *obligations* of the limited partnership.
    - A person becoming a general partner is not liable for partnership obligations *before* they became a general partner.
    - Obligations incurred by a limited partnership during a time that it is an LLLP are solely the obligation of the limited partnership, not the general partners.
- General partners have equal *rights of management.*
- General partners have a *fiduciary duty* to the limited partnership and the partners that is limited to the duties of loyalty and care.
    - Refrain from dealing with parties whose interests are adverse to the partnership
    - Refrain from competing with the partnership
    - Refrain from grossly negligent or reckless conduct, intentional misconduct, or knowingly violating the law

A **general partner** may **withdraw** from the partnership upon:

- Providing notice of an express will to withdraw to the partnership.
- Occurrence of an event specified in the partnership agreement.
- Expulsion either in accordance with the terms of the partnership agreement, or by the unanimous consent of the other partners.

Limited partners also may be general partners, in which case they will have the same liability as general partners. One that is not, however, may not participate in management, and doing so will generally eliminate that partner's limited liability protection.

A limited partner does *not have a fiduciary duty* to the LP, or to the other partners, and may conduct business with the LP in the same manner as a third party, and may have a competing interest. A limited partner may act as an agent or surety for the LP, may be a creditor (secured or unsecured), or act as a consultant to the LP without impairing the protection of limited liability.

In addition, a limited partner may bring a **derivative suit** on behalf of the LP and may participate in (ie, **vote on**) decisions related to:

- Amendments the LP agreement
- Dissolution or winding up
- Changes to the nature of the LP's business
- Loans
- General partner changes

Profits and losses of an LP are distributed in accordance with the provisions of the LP agreement. When there is no agreement, unlike a general partnership, which calls for the equal distribution of profits and losses, profits and losses in an LP are distributed in proportion to LPs' capital investments.

A limited partner has certain **rights** that include the right to inspect the partnership's books and records. Although the admission of a new partner requires the approval in writing of all partners,

unless otherwise specified in the LP agreement, an LP interest may be assigned without the approval of other partners. The acquirer, however, obtains only the limited partner's rights to profits and is considered a creditor of the LP.

A **limited partner** does not have the **right to withdraw** from the limited partnership but may do so:

- By giving notice to the limited partnership of the express will to withdraw
- Upon occurrence of an event or condition cited in the partnership agreement
- Upon expulsion either in accordance with the partnership agreement or by the unanimous vote of the other partners

Distributions by a limited partnership are required to be made to all partners in proportion to the value of contributions the partner has made to the limited partnership. The value is required to be stated in the records of the limited partnership. A distribution **may not be made**:

- In violation of the partnership agreement.
- Such that the limited partnership will be unable to pay its debts as they come due.

Dissolution & Termination

An LP agreement will generally specify the term of the partnership, or the date on which it is to be dissolved, or the event or transaction that the LP was formed to enter into, after which the LP would terminate. In addition, an LP may be **dissolved** as a result of:

- The written consent of all partners
- Court decree
- The illegality of the LP's business

In addition, the **withdrawal of the general partner**, other than as a result of insolvency, will generally dissolve an LP. It will continue, however, if allowed to by the LP agreement or all remaining partners agree to do so in writing. The death or withdrawal of a limited partner does not result in dissolution.

When an LP will not continue, **distributions upon winding up** will first be made to creditors, followed by unpaid distributions to partners and ex-partners. All partners will next receive a return of capital, after which any remaining partnership assets will be distributed in proportion to the partners' profit percentages (unless otherwise agreed-upon).

Other Business Structures

There are a variety of business structures that may be used in addition to partnerships, each of which has different characteristics and each of which would be used for a different purpose. These include limited partnerships (LPs), limited liability partnerships (LLPs), limited liability companies (LLCs), and limited liability limited partnerships (LLLPs).

- **LPs** (just discussed) are most applicable in arrangements like real estate deals where one group of partners, the limited partners, provide most of the capital and benefit from limited liability; and another group, the general partners, do the work and make the decisions and do not have limited liability.
- **LLPs** are popular among professionals, such as accountants, and many states allow LLPs only for such groups. They are designed to provide protection to innocent partners against the actions of other partners.
- **LLCs** are used by other entities to provide characteristics of a corporation in the form of limited liability to its owners with the tax characteristics of a sole proprietorship, in the case of a single member LLC (Schedule C), or a partnership (Schedule E), in a multi-member LLC. In many cases, an LLC is the general partner in an LP for the purpose of providing the general partners with the same limited liability as limited partners.

As indicated above, some states have adopted a newer version of the **ULPA,** which is designed to **replace** the **Revised Uniform Limited Partnership Act (RULPA).** Under the new ULPA, the basic structure of a limited partnership remains the same. The ULPA, however, allows for the formation of a **limited liability limited partnership (LLLP)** under which neither general partners nor limited partners are personally liable for the obligations of the partnership.

In an LLLP, both limited partners and general partners are free of liability for the limited partnership's obligations similarly to corporate shareholders, members of an LLC, or partners in an LLP. A general partner is only responsible for the debts incurred by the LLLP by agreeing to be held liable. A limited partnership does not obtain LLLP status automatically, but does so by including a statement to that effect in the **certificate of limited partnership**.

Some of the **additional differences** between the RULPA and the ULPA include:

- **Term**
    - RULPA – specific term identified in certificate of limited partnership
    - ULPA – perpetual
- **Inclusion of name** of limited partner in partnership name
    - RULPA – prohibited
    - ULPA – permitted

- Personal liability of **limited partners** for **debts and obligations** of limited partnership
  - RULPA – none, unless limited partner participates in management
  - ULPA – none, even if limited partner participates in management
- Personal liability of **general partners** for **debts and obligations** of limited partnership
  - RULPA – unlimited liability, subject to its own protection, such as if the general partner is a corporation
  - ULPA – may be avoided through LLLP status by including a statement to that effect in the certificate of limited partnership
- **Withdrawal** of limited partner
  - RULPA - May withdraw with 6 months' notice unless otherwise specified in limited partnership agreement
  - ULPA – no right to withdraw from the partnership before termination of limited partner

Limited Liability Companies (LLC)

Some states, most of which follow the Revised Uniform Limited Liability Company Act (RULLCA), have an enabling statute that allows for the formation of **Limited Liability Companies** (**LLC**s). LLCs have characteristics of both partnerships and corporations; they are pass-through entities from a tax standpoint, while they provide their owners, referred to as members, with the limited liability protection of a corporation. Also, like a corporation, members have no interest in the LLC's assets but only in the LLC itself.

For **tax purposes**, a single-member LLC is generally referred to as a "disregarded entity." It is treated like a sole proprietorship, and its information is reported to the IRS on a Schedule C, accompanying the single owner's tax return. An LLC with multiple owners is generally treated as a partnership for tax purposes. The LLC files a Form 1065 information return and each member of the LLC will receive a Schedule K-1 that flows to their Schedule E (similar to an S corporation).

An LLC is a legal entity that can only be formed in a state that allows their formation and, as a result, can be sued or file suit in its own name. Like limited partnerships, they file a **certificate with the Secretary of State**. The certificate must include the entity's name, which must include the words limited liability company, limited company, or appropriate abbreviations.

Members may participate in management (agents) without restriction and owe the same duties of loyalty and care to the LLC as owed to a limited partnership by the general partner. Also, similar to a general partner in a limited partnership, a member cannot freely transfer an interest, and a new member must be admitted upon the consent of the other members.

An LLC may be member-managed or manager-managed. A member-managed LLC will be bound by the actions of any of its members, who are considered agents of the LLC. A manager-managed LLC is only bound by the actions of the manager that are either authorized or in the ordinary course of business. In either case, a member or manager able to bind the LLC owes it both a duty of loyalty and of care. A member of a manager-managed LLC, however, owes no fiduciary duty to the LLC.

Allocations of profits and losses of an LLC will generally be made in accordance with the LLC agreement. In its absence, profits and losses in states that have adopted the RULLCA will be allocated to the members equally. In those states that have not adopted the RULLCA, allocations are generally in proportion to members' capital contributions.

Like an LP, many LLCs will terminate upon expiration of the term specified in the LLC agreement or upon the occurrence of an event or transaction. It may also be **dissolved** as a result of:

- The written agreement of all members
- Withdrawal, death, bankruptcy, or incompetency of a member
- Court order

Upon dissolution, after settlement with creditors, including amounts owed to members for loans but not for profits, distributions are made first for unpaid distributions and then capital contributions. Remaining distributions are allocated similarly to profits.

Businesses such as doctors' offices and CPA firms that are required to obtain a license in order to perform services are not allowed to form LLCs in many states and may instead form Professional Limited Liability Companies.

Limited Liability Partnership (LLP)

Another form of entity that is allowed by most states and that provides some or all of its owners limited liability is the **Limited Liability Partnership (LLP)**. In most circumstances, a partnership will qualify as an LLP by registering with the Secretary of State. Some require proof of adequate insurance or proof that assets are adequate to satisfy claims against the LLP.

Most states require an LLP to file articles with the Secretary of State and have a name that includes the words limited liability partnership or registered limited liability partnership, or appropriate initials.

Like an LLC, an LLP has characteristics of partnerships and of corporations. For tax purposes, LLPs are pass-through entities but, as indicated, both general and limited partners may be afforded limited liability. Partners are personally liable for their own torts and, in many cases, the torts of those under their supervision.

The degree of protection (from **Liability**) available to partners in an LLP depends largely on the jurisdiction in which it is formed. In general:

- Partners are not liable for the actions of other partners, including negligence, incompetence, error, omission, or malfeasance.
- Some jurisdictions provide very broad protection, but many hold partners liable for their own negligence or misconduct.
- Others hold partners personally liable for the contracts and debts of the LLP without limit.
- LLPs are taxed as a partnership, so the income is passed through to the individual taxpayer's tax return on Schedule E.

Similarities & Differences between LLPs & LLCs

- **Formation**
    - Both require an enabling statute in the state of formation.
    - Both are easier to form than a corporation.

- Both require filing a certificate with an appropriate state authority, such as the Secretary of State.
- An LLC may be formed with one or more owners, referred to as members, while an LLP requires 2 or more partners.

- **Taxation**
  - Both are pass-through entities.
  - Both may report their operations by filing Form 1065 and distributing K-1s to its members or partners.
    - An LLP is always treated as a partnership.
    - An LLC with more than one member is treated as a partnership, and those with one member are treated as sole proprietorships (Schedule C). These are the default tax classifications; an LLC also can elect to be treated as a corporation by filing Form 8832, *Entity Classification Election*.

- **Liability**
  - Both provide owners with some degree of protection.
    - LLCs generally limit the liability of members to their investments, plus the costs resulting from their own negligence or malpractice.
    - Partners of LLPs are generally not liable for the actions of co-partners, but are generally liable for the obligations and debts of the LLP.

Joint Ventures

A *joint venture* is an informal arrangement between two or more parties to conduct business with one another. A joint venture is not a legal entity, although it has *many characteristics of a partnership*. It generally has a finite life and is established for a specific period of time, or to accomplish a particular objective.

All joint venturers have access to the property that is the subject to the joint venture, have the right to participate in management, are jointly and severally liable for the obligations of the joint venture, and owe a fiduciary duty to the other venturers. The death of a joint venturer does *not* dissolve the joint venture.

Sole Proprietorships

A sole proprietorship is the most common form of business in the U.S. and is not a legal entity that is separated from its owner. One can be established by an individual (one owner), who will have exclusive right to manage the business, will have access to all assets, and will have *unlimited personal liability* for all obligations of the sole proprietorship. A fictitious name statement must be filed with the government if operating under a name other than that of the sole proprietor.

A sole proprietorship is *not a taxable entity*. The single owner includes its operations on a Schedule C, filed with the owner's individual tax return, and the income is taxable directly to the owner.

LLC	LLP (Accounting Firms)	LLLP
Formal creation	Formal	Formal
1 Person	2+ people	2+ people
• Limited Liability for Contracts & debts • Unlimited Liability for Malpractice or Negligence	• Limited Liability for Malpractice or Negligence • Unlimited Liability for Contracts/Debts	• Limited Liability for ALL Partners (General & Limited)
Agents/Member	Agents	Agents
Taxed as a P/S	Taxed as a P/S	Taxed as a P/S

Partnership	Limited Partnership		C Corporation
Informal creation	Formal		Formal
Unlimited liability	**(General)** Unlimited	**(Limited)** Limited	Limited Liability
Partnership **Interest** (Profit/Losses)	→	Interest	→
Partnership **Property**	→	NO Property	→
Partnership **Management**	→	NO Management – EXCEPT can look at the **books** and **vote**	→
Agents	→	NOT automatically Agent	→

↳ Survivorship

Comparison of Business Structures

	General P/S	Limited P/S	LLP	LLC	LLLP	Corporation
Governed by:	RUPA	RULPA	Individual Secretary of State LLP Act	RULLCA	ULPA	MBCA
Required to Formally File w/ State?	No	Yes	Yes	Yes	Yes	Yes
Owners referred to as:	Partners	General Partners & Limited Partners	Partners	Members	Partners	Shareholders
Authority to Bind to Contracts	Partners	General Partners	Partners	Managers	Partners	Officers/Directors
Formal Creation?	P/S Agreement	Certificate & Partnership Agreement	P/S Agreement & Application for LLP	Articles of Organization & Operating Agreement	Certificate of Limited P/S	Articles of Incorporation & Bylaws, Shareholder Agreements
Limited Liability	No	**No** for general Partners, **Yes** for Limited Partners	Yes, if election made	Yes	Yes	Yes

Comparison of Business Structures

	General P/S	Limited P/S	LLP	LLC	LLLP	Corporation
Ownership Interest Considered a Security under 1933 Fed Sec Reg's	Generally No	*General* P/S interests – NO **Limited** P/S Interests - Yes	Generally No	Generally No	Generally No	Generally Yes
Taxation	Income passed through to partners on K-1 then to Sch. E	Income passed through to partners on K-1 then to Sch. E	Income passed through to partners on K-1 then to Sch. E	Income passed through to members. If single member, Sch. C, if multiple, Sch. E	Income passed through to partners on K-1 then to Sch. E	**S Corp** – Income passed through to shareholders on K-1 then Sch. E. **C Corp** – Taxed directly on 1120 & distributions taxed to shareholders on Sch. B

12.04 Corporations

C Corporations

A C corporation is an artificial person created by statute and governed by the Model Business Corporation Act (MBCA). It is considered to be separate from the owners (ie, shareholders), giving it several characteristics not present in other forms of business organization (such as partnerships and proprietorships).

Under the federal Subchapter S Revision Act, all corporations are designated as either a Subchapter S corporation or a Subchapter C corporation, and any corporation that does not meet all the criteria of a Subchapter S corporation is categorized as a Subchapter C corporation.

Among the *characteristics* (with certain minor exceptions) that distinguish C corporations are:

- **Limited liability** – Shareholders are not responsible for the debts of the corporation.
- **Independent life** – The death of a shareholder doesn't cause the corporation to dissolve (Perpetuity).
- **Ease of transfer** – Changes in ownership are effected simply by a transfer of shares (intangible personal property) and require no approval from others in the business or novations by creditors of business.
- **Taxation** – The corporation must file and pay its own income taxes (Form 1120). Since dividends paid to shareholders by C corporations are not deductible for tax purposes, the earnings of such corporations are said to be subject to double taxation to the extent that they are paid out as dividends.
- **Centralized management** – The corporation is effectively controlled by an internal group known as the board of directors (BOD), and not by the shareholders.

S Corporations

An S corporation is a special type of corporation that avoids taxes at the corporate level since they flow through to the individual shareholder's tax return (**K-1**). The requirements that must be met to qualify are (**Simple & Small**):

- Formal creation as shareholders generally have limited liability.
- There can be no more than 100 shareholders (family members with a common ancestor no more than six generations above and their spouses may be treated as a single shareholder for purposes of this rule).
- All shareholders must be individuals (or certain estates or trusts for the benefit of individuals).
    - Husband and wife count as one until divorce is final.
    - No corporations, partnerships or big trusts.
- All shareholders must be either **residents or citizens** of the United States.
- The corporation must be a **domestic** corporation.

- There can be only **one class** of stock. No preferred stock.
- Once an S corporation's status has been revoked, it cannot reelect such status for **5 years.**

Closely Held Corporation

Closely held corporation (also called "close corporation" or "closed corporation") is one whose stock is NOT offered to the public on a securities exchange and is owned by a limited number of persons (< 50 shareholders) usually with restrictions on the transfer of stock to keep it out of the hands of outsiders. Many of the shareholders participate in the management of the business.

A corporation receives its charter from the state in which it incorporates, and is considered a **domestic** corporation in that state. A corporation that attempts to operate in a state other than the state that provided the charter is considered a **foreign** corporation, and must meet the operating requirements (file a certificate of Authority) of that state if it wishes court protection.

For example, let's say a company with a charter in California starts doing business in Texas, but fails to obtain regulatory licenses required by the Texas government to protect the public. If it is a victim of breach of contract in Texas, the corporation will not be able to sue in Texas court and cannot recover its loss. This prohibition doesn't apply if the company has violated non-substantive rules, such as licenses that are only for the purpose of raising revenue for the state.

Prior to the formation of a corporation, **promoters** might enter contracts on its behalf. A promoter is not an agent of the corporation, since the promoter performs work before the corporation itself exists. As a result, a contract by a promoter is not binding on the corporation unless the BOD elects to **adopt** the contract.

The promoter is personally liable on the contract prior to adoption, and remains liable afterwards unless the other party to the contract releases the promoter and gives them a **novation** (substitution of promoter for the new corporation).

The BOD cannot ratify the contract (giving it retroactive authority to the date it was made), since it cannot go back to a time prior to the corporation's birth. Promoters have a **fiduciary duty** to act loyally toward the future corporation, but aren't entitled to compensation. The BOD also adopts the corporation's initial bylaws.

The corporation is **formed (formal)** once the state receives and accepts the **articles of incorporation** filed on its behalf. The Articles can subsequently be amended by a shareholder vote. Some of the items that are included in the articles are:

- **Name** – The proposed name of the corporation.
- **Nature & Purpose** – An indication of the powers sought and restrictions on the charter. For example, a corporation may be established for strictly charitable purposes as a nonprofit organization, or as a business with broad powers to enter into any types of for-profit ventures.
- **Term** – The life of the corporation. Most articles request an indefinite duration (Perpetuity).
- **Name and address** – of each Incorporator.

- **Capitalization** – The amount and types of shares of stock that the corporation wants to be authorized to issue. It is no longer necessary for the corporation to assign a par value to shares.
- **Initial Board** – The names of the people who will serve as the members of the BOD until the first shareholder meeting.
- **Registered Agent** – The place where the state may serve a court order if the corporation is being sued or needs to be legally notified of actions involving it. The registered agent is often an attorney. The corporation need not identify the places of business, and may not even do business within the state of incorporation, but the registered agent must be located within the state.
    - When complete, the articles of incorporation are filed with the state which issues a certificate of incorporation or corporate **Charter**.

By-Laws – Rules and regulations that govern and help to guide the internal management in performing its duties. Either the incorporators or the BOD adopts them.

12.05 Board of Directors

Overview

The principal agent of the corporation is the board of directors (BOD), a small group that meets 1 to 12 times per year to set policy and make broad decisions. They are in charge of the *general operations* of the corporation.

> **Board of Directors**
>
> - Act as a board (act as a group)
> - Not agents
> - In charge of general operations
> - Adopt the bylaws
>   - Select the **officers** (eg, president)
>   - In charge of day-to-day operations
>   - Agents of Corporation
>   - Right to be Indemnified (right to reimbursement)
>   - **Reacquire** treasury stock unless insolvent or makes them insolvent (stock that is authorized, issued but not outstanding)
>   - **Declare** dividends

Role of the BOD

The role of the BOD, including some of its operating characteristics, its areas of authority, and its responsibilities include the following:

- **Collective** – The power rests with the board, and not individual directors. A director has a vote at official board meetings the director attends. Directors may not enter into contracts on behalf of the corporation individually (**Not agents of corporation**), and *must be present* at board meetings in order to vote (they cannot vote by proxy).

- **Issuing Stock** – The BOD is the authority that issues stock. It may issue stock at any price that is mutually agreeable to the board and the purchaser, but some real consideration, in the form of cash, property, or services, must be provided. Valid consideration for the purchase of stock can be any benefit to the corporation, including any services contracted for that are yet to be performed.

- **Repurchasing Stock** – The BOD has the implied authority to reverse issuances by repurchasing stock on the open market or in a private arrangement with specific shareholders, at any mutually agreeable price. Once repurchased, the stock is either retired (canceled) or held as **treasury stock.** Treasury stock cannot be voted or receive a cash dividend, since it has no formal owner. The BOD can resell it below par. *Treasury stock is stock that is authorized, issued, but no longer outstanding. Canceled stock* is stock that is no longer issued nor outstanding.

- **Officers** – The BOD hires, fires, and sets salaries of officers, who are responsible for the *day-to-day management* of the business. The authority of an officer is based on the delegation of the BOD's authority, so the BOD may adjust it as it chooses. The BOD has the right to fire an officer, even in breach of contract, if it believes this is in the best interests of the corporation and its shareholders. Officers are considered **agents** of the corporation. Officers and managers of the corporation may be, but need not be, shareholders of the corporation. Officers have the rights of Participation and inspection, may be compensated and indemnified (Reimbursement).

- **Borrowing** – As part of their responsibility for the day-to-day management of the businesses, officers may issue corporate debt securities as permitted by the corporate bylaws. Such securities include registered bonds, bearer bonds, debenture bonds, mortgage bonds, redeemable bonds, convertible bonds, etc. A warrant is not a corporate debt security, but rather written evidence of a stock option which grants its owner the right to purchase a specified number of shares of stock at a fixed price within a specified period of time.

- **Dividend Policy** – The BOD determines if and when dividends will be declared and paid to common and preferred shareholders. Until declaration, the corporation has no liability to the shareholders. The BOD may not declare a dividend if the company is insolvent or the dividend will render it insolvent, since creditors have priority over shareholders. If the corporation is solvent, the BOD may declare any dividend amount up to the higher of the company's retained earnings or current period earnings.

- If the BOD wishes to declare a dividend that exceeds these amounts, the shareholders must approve the portion that is a return of capital (liquidating dividend). If a corporation improperly pays a dividend, the shareholder may keep it as long as the shareholder was unaware that it was illegal and the corporation was solvent. Shareholders must repay illegal distributions that they receive when the corporation is insolvent.

- **Common Stock** –A corporation begins operations by issuing stock in order to raise funds. It will obtain the authority to issue shares from the state of incorporation. All corporations will issue some form of common stock, which normally has a **par value (Certificate of Incorporation)** or **stated value (BOD)** assigned to it. Common shareholders vote in the BOD.

- **Preferred stock** refers to stock similar to debt instruments, with two advantages over common stock:
    - **Dividends** – Preferred shareholders must be paid a dividend before the company is allowed to pay the common shareholders a dividend.
    - **Liquidation** – If the corporation liquidates, preferred shareholders must be paid before the common shareholders.

Along with the stated annual preference, preferred shareholders may be paid additional amounts if the shares are:
- **Cumulative** – Dividends missed in earlier years also must be paid before the common shareholders receive anything (*arrears*).

- o **Participating** – If the common shareholders get a dividend that is a higher rate on its par value than the stated rate on the preferred shares, the preferred shareholders must get the same higher rate.

Three Important Dates for Dividends

- **Declaration** = Not a liability until declared

Retained Earnings	XXX	
Dividend Payable		XXX

- **Date of Record** = No journal entry → who gets the money (determined as of the *ex-dividend date*, which is generally two days prior to the date of record)
- Date of Distribution

Dividend Payable	XXX	
Cash		XXX

- o Types of Dividends (BOD – declares)
    - Cash
    - Property (FMV @ date of declaration)
    - Scrip
    - Liquidating
    - Stock – Small (FMV) / Large (Par)
    - Stock split

Cash Dividend	Scrip—Give dividend but no money	Stock Dividend

RE   25
     Cash   25
	RE 25
	     Note payable 25
		Small < 20–25% – FMV
		 RE 25
		     CS 20
		     APIC 5

	Partial Liquidating Dividend
	 RE 15
	 APIC 10
	     Cash 25
		Large > 20–25% – Par
		 RE 20
		     CS 20

Property (FMV)
 RE   25
     Asset   20
     Gain   5
	Person receiving Liq Div
	 Cash 25
	     Div income 15
	     Investment 10
		Stock Splits: Double shares, half par
		 CS (10(10)) 100
		     CS (20(5)) 100

Net effect on Stockholders' Equity = 20

Note: All dividends reduce Stockholders' Equity except for stock dividends and stock splits.

The members of the BOD are bound by a **fiduciary duty** to act loyally in the best interests of the corporation and its shareholders. The directors are not liable for honest errors of judgment, but can be held **individually** liable for acts of bad faith or negligence.

> For example, if the BOD or its management takes an action that exceeds the powers granted to it under the corporate charter (this is known as an **ultra vires** act, eg, making the corporation a Surety, when the Articles do not allow it), the directors who voted to take the action can be sued individually. The directors who voted not to take the action aren't held liable for the misbehavior of the majority.

The doctrine of **respondeat superior** provides that an employer is responsible for the torts committed by employees in the normal scope of duties.

Fiduciary Duty

Officers of a corporation also have a fiduciary duty to the corporation and shareholders. The BOD, however, may vote to *indemnify* the officers against personal liability for negligent or illegal acts if the BOD believes this is in the best interests of the corporation and the court does not hold such a reimbursement agreement to be a violation of public policy. The doctrine of *respondeat superior* provides that an employer (the corporation) is responsible for the torts committed by its employees in the normal scope of their duties.

Directors and officers must act with a duty of care (honestly and prudently) and with a duty of loyalty. They **may not**:

- Compete with the corporation
- Take advantage of a corporate opportunity for personal gain
- Have an interest that conflicts with the interests of the corporation
- Engage in insider trading
- Authorize transactions that are detrimental to minority shareholders
- Sell control over the corporation

The **"Business Judgment Rule"** is a principle that protects directors, officers, and managers from personal liability for acts performed in good faith (not liable for *errors of judgment*) on behalf of a corporation that are within the scope of their authority. They are still liable for their own negligence.

12.06 Shareholders' Rights

Voting Rights

Shareholders with common stock normally have a **right to vote** at shareholder meetings on certain significant matters affecting the company. A shareholder need not attend the meeting in order to vote, but may sign a proxy, authorizing others to vote their shares on their behalf at the meeting.

Shareholders' Rights

- Right to **vote** for the following:
  - Board of Directors
  - Liquidating dividends
  - Dissolve Corporation
  - Mergers/Consolidations
  - Amend the Articles of Incorporation
  - Loans to Directors
- They are Not considered an *Agent*.
- *Transfer shares* without approval (freely transferable)
- Right to declared dividends (unsecured creditor)
- Right to inspect books and records (*Inspection Rights*)
- **Appraisal Right** – Right to get stock appraised if disagree with merger
- Right to bring a **derivative lawsuit** → sue in name of corporation (on behalf of the corporate name)
- **Preemptive right** – prevent dilution of ownership with newly authorized stock only
- Limited liability unless **pierce the corporate veil** (do something illegal) → will do if fraudulent corporation, commingled funds, undercapitalized

Examples of matters that may be voted on at shareholder meetings include:

- **Board of directors** – At least once a year, the shareholders must vote on the members who will constitute the BOD. The shareholder has one vote for each available position on the board. Thus, if there are nine directors on the board, each shareholder is given nine votes. In some states, voting for directors is **cumulative**, which allows a shareholder to place all the votes available for the same person. This prevents significant minority shareholders from being locked out of representation on the board by a majority block of shareholders that all vote for the same slate of people and would be able to get unanimous control of the board without cumulative voting.

- **Liquidating dividends** – The BOD may declare dividends out of the earnings of the company without shareholder approval, but dividends that are to come out of contributed capital must be declared by the BOD and then approved by the shareholders.
- **Changes in the corporate structure** – Amendments to the bylaws, Articles of Incorporation and changes in the charter of the corporation require shareholder approval.
- **Business combinations** – Mergers (one company absorbing another and becoming liable for all obligations of the acquired corporation) and consolidations (two companies forming a new entity) require support of a majority of both boards and both sets of shareholders (unless the change in ownership isn't significant, such as the merger of a subsidiary that is already 90%-owned by the parent). Any shareholder that dissents from the combination is entitled to make a written demand for **appraisal** of their shares, which the BOD must then repurchase at the appraised amount.
- **Dissolution** – A corporation may be dissolved:
  - *Voluntary* – by a board resolution to dissolve that is approved by a majority of shareholders.
  - *Involuntary* – by shareholder action (if BOD has committed fraud or is deadlocked), by state action if corp. exceeds its authority, by merger, consolidation or expiration of time period set out in the charter.

Right to Dividends

Although shareholders have the right to dividends out of available profits and surplus of the corporations, the decision to declare them must be made by the BOD. Once a dividend is declared, the shareholders are considered **unsecured creditors** for that amount. Preferred shareholders with a dividend preference are entitled to be paid prior to common shareholders, but have no creditor claim for dividends until they are declared, even on cumulative stock.

Inspection Rights

Shareholders have the right to **inspect the books and records** of the corporation at a reasonable time and place for a reasonable purpose. Examples of reasonable purposes are inspection of books to determine that they agree with financial reports and obtaining shareholder lists to send proxy solicitations to replace the existing BOD. Generally, a shareholder is presumed to have a reasonable purpose if they own at least 5% of the stock or have owned stock for at least 6 months. Otherwise, they may be required to prove a reasonable purpose before being allowed to inspect.

Any misuse of information by a shareholder bars them for **2 years** from access to records. Examples of misuse include inspection of books to help establish a competing firm and obtaining shareholder lists in order to send them advertising literature for a personal business of the shareholder.

Other Shareholder Rights

Various other **Shareholder rights** that are occasionally tested on the exam include:

- **Transfer of shares** – A shareholder can transfer ownership of shares without requiring the approval of the BOD or other shareholders. Limited restrictions are permitted for *closely held corporations* (in which shareholders wishing to sell are expected to offer their stock to the other existing shareholders before selling to outsiders), but must be printed directly on the certificates to be enforceable.

- **Preemptive rights** – Existing shareholders have the right to subscribe to new issuances of shares up to the percentage they own of existing shares, to prevent dilution of their interests.

- **Derivative lawsuits** – A shareholder may sue on behalf of the corporation if harmful actions against the company are not countered by the BOD (or if the board itself has committed the acts). The corporation, not the shareholder, receives the damages awarded if the action is successful.

- **Loans to directors** – Generally, shareholder approval is required for corporate loans to directors; however, shareholder approval is not generally required for charitable contributions made by the corporation.

Shareholder Liability

Shareholder liability is not always limited to the amount of their investment. If stock is issued for less than its par value, it is considered **watered stock**, and the shareholder acquiring such shares (as well as a subsequent shareholder who knew the stock was watered when they acquired it) has a contingent liability for the difference between the issue price and par value. The watered stock rule doesn't apply to treasury shares or to subsequent resale by a shareholder at below par value.

If 1,000 shares of $10 par value common stock are issued for $8 per share to Fred. First, Fred is liable for an additional $2,000 if the corporation becomes insolvent and creditors of the corporation demand these funds be contributed to the corporation.

Let's say Fred sells 500 shares to Irv Ignorant, who doesn't know the shares were originally issued below par value, and the other 500 shares to Alice Aware, who knows Fred originally paid only $8 when the shares were issued.

The creditors of the corporation cannot demand payment from Irv, but Alice is liable for $1,000 as well (unless Fred pays the full $2,000 into the corporation). The prices paid by Irv and Alice to Fred are irrelevant, since those amounts did not benefit the corporation.

Sometimes, the courts will **pierce the corporate veil** and hold shareholders personally liable for all the corporation's debts. Circumstances that may cause the court to act in this manner include:

- **Undercapitalized** – The courts examine the amount of capital present at the formation of the corporation. If that amount is inadequate to meet the reasonable foreseeable financial needs, it is undercapitalized and shareholders may be held personally liable upon the insolvency of the corporation.

- **Shareholder fraud** – The shareholders are intentionally using the corporation for illegal activities (do not confuse this with ultra vires acts by directors or officers, which do not result in shareholder liability).

- **Direct action** – The shareholders are running the business directly, without electing a BOD, or without the board meeting at least once a year.

- **Commingling assets** – The shareholders are treating corporate assets as if they were personal assets, regularly using them for personal purposes, such as home mortgage payments or grocery purchases for their family.

Concentrations of Voting Power

Certain devices enable groups of shareholders to combine their voting power for purposes such as obtaining or maintaining control or maximizing the impact of cumulative voting. The most important methods of concentrating voting power are proxies, voting trusts and shareholder agreements.

- **Proxies** – A proxy is the authorization by a shareholder to an agent to vote his shares at a particular meeting. Proxies must be in writing to be effective and are revocable. The duration is limited by statute to no more than 11 months, unless the proxy specifically provides otherwise. The solicitation of proxies by publicly held corporations is also regulated by the Securities Exchange Act of 1934.

- **Voting Trusts** – A device by which one or more shareholders separate the voting rights of their shares from the ownership of them. Under a voting trust, all or part of the stock of a corporation may, by written agreement among the shareholders, be issued to a trustee who then holds legal title to the stock and has all of the voting rights possessed by the stock. They are usually limited in duration to 10 years.

- **Shareholder Agreements** – Shareholders may agree in advance to vote in a specified manner for the election or removal of directors or any matter subject to shareholder approval. Unlike voting trusts, shareholder agreements are NOT limited in duration. They are frequently used in closely held corporations, especially in conjunction with restriction on the transfer of shares.

Other circumstances occasionally tested that may result in shareholder liability include:

- **Majority ownership** – A shareholder holding a majority of the voting stock of a company is in a position to effectively control the activities of the corporation. As a result, the law imposes a *fiduciary obligation* on the majority shareholder to act loyally to protect the interests of the minority shareholders.

- **Subscriptions** – If a person signs a contract agreeing to purchase shares of a corporation once they become available, they are bound to this contract and cannot revoke it under the Model Business Corporation Act if the shares are made available to them within 6 months of the subscription.

- **Professional corporation** – The shareholders in a professional corporation are licensed members of the specified profession, and are held personally liable for acts of malpractice in accordance with the licensing laws. Normally, only licensed professionals can be shareholders in such corporations. They still have normal protection for corporate debts not associated with the practice of their professional responsibilities.

Partnership	Limited Partnership		C Corporation
Informal creation	Formal		Formal
Unlimited liability	(General) Unlimited	(Limited) Limited	Limited Liability
Partnership **Interest** (Profit/Losses) →		Interest	→
Partnership **Property** →		NO Property	→
Partnership **Management** →		NO Management – EXCEPT can look at the **books** and **vote**	→
Agents →		NOT automatically Agent	→
Survivorship			

REG 13
Property & Regulation of Business

REG 13: Property & Regulation of Business

13.01 Property Law — 1
- Ownership of Property — 1
- Transfer of Ownership — 1
- Ownership of Personal Property — 2
- Ownership of Real Property — 2

13.02 Different Forms of Concurrent Ownership — 5
- Mortgages – A Security Interest in Real Property — 6
- Leases — 7

13.03 Intellectual Property & Computer Technology Rights — 9
- Overview — 9
- Copyrights (©) — 9
- Patents — 10
- Trademarks (® and TM) — 10
- Trade Secrets — 10
- Semiconductor Chip Protection Act — 11
- Money Laundering Control Act (MLCA) — 11

13.04 Regulation of Employment, Environment & Antitrust — 12
- Federal Unemployment Tax Act (FUTA) — 12
- Federal Insurance Contributions Act (FICA) — 12
- Regulation of Employee Benefits & Compensation — 13
- Telephone Consumer Protection Act - TCPA (Do Not Call List) — 13
- Other Employment Regulations — 14
- Antitrust Laws — 16
- Environmental Regulation — 17

13.01 Property Law

Ownership of Property

Property is classified in one of two categories:

- **Real** – Property that is fixed to one specific location. Examples include land and buildings that are permanently attached to the land.
- **Personal** – All other property. Examples include tangible property that is movable, such as furniture, equipment, and automobiles, and intangible assets such as patents, receivables, stock, and royalty rights.

Fixtures are assets that start out as personal property but are attached (**affixed**) to real property. Sometimes, personal property is attached in a manner that makes it become a part of the real property (eg, cementing a chalkboard to a wall), and at other times it remains personal property (eg, the same chalkboard attached to the wall using screws instead of cement).

Personal property is subject to many of the legal sections of the Uniform Commercial Code, including the sales, secured transactions, and negotiables sections. Real estate is specifically exempt from the UCC. As a result, the determination as to whether property is real or personal affects the methods of transfer, rights of creditors, and negotiability of documents of ownership to the property.

Crops under cultivation are part of the land and are generally considered real property. Since crops can be sold separately from land, however, they can be considered personal property under the UCC.

Determining whether a fixture has become part of the real estate can be especially important in the case of leased property, since it may determine what the lessee is permitted to remove from the property at termination of the lease. In general, the determination is based on the **intentions of the parties**, but in the absence of an explicit contractual agreement, the courts can evaluate the intentions of the parties by the manner of attachment and the damage that would be caused by removal of the fixture.

Based upon:

- Use
- Intention of parties
- How attached
  - **Not** – price or depreciable life.

Transfer of Ownership

There are a variety of ways in which property can be transferred from one party to another. The rights of the party obtaining ownership, and any rights retained by the party transferring the property will depend on the how the transfer of ownership is accomplished. Different methods of transferring ownership are used for personal property and real property.

Ownership of Personal Property

Ownership of personal property can be acquired in numerous ways. When personal property is not acquired by purchase, ownership may be acquired by:

- Taking **possession** of property that is not owned by another party, such as the capture of a wild animal
- **Production** of property through the use of the party's own efforts
- Receiving the property as a **gift**
- Obtaining the property through a **will** or by **inheritance**
- **Accession**, where property is improved or added to, generally making the owner of the original property the owner of the addition
- **Confusion**, such as when identical goods are commingled

A party finding personal property may take title to it, depending on the circumstances. When property is **mislaid**, such as someone leaving their glasses at the theater, the finder does not obtain title but becomes the caretaker of the property. When property is **lost**, the finder takes title to the property that is effective against anyone but the true owner of the property. When property is **abandoned** (discarded), the finder takes title to it that is effective against all parties, including the original owner.

Adverse possession: A possessor of land who is not the lawful owner may acquire title if they hold it for the statutory period, which varies by state. The true owner must begin legal action before statute runs or the adverse possessor obtains title. The necessary elements for adverse possession are as follows:

- Open possession, such that the lawful owner is deemed to have reasonable notice.
- Hostile possession - the possessor must indicate intention of ownership.
- Actual possession - possession consistent with normal use (cultivation of farmland, use of a warehouse, etc.)
- Continuous and exclusive possession.

Easements (such as a right-of-way) are established in the same fashion as adverse possession.

Ownership of Real Property

Transferring the ownership of real estate is accomplished through the use of a document of title, known as a deed. The deed must identify the property and be signed by the transferor of the property. It does not need to be recorded in order to be valid between the transferor and transferee.

Deed – To transfer ownership (to be **effective**) / (**Statute of frauds**)

- Names of Grantor (transferor) and Grantee (transferee)
- Intent
- Description
- The deed must be delivered to the purchaser.

- Grantor's signature
  - Not price or depreciable life / Need not be recorded to be effective between Grantor and Grantee.

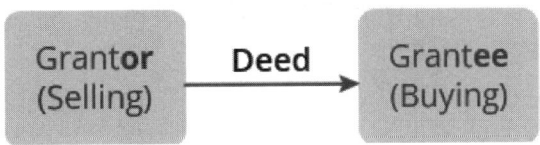

There are three types of deeds:

- **Quitclaim deed** – ("As is") The transferor makes no warranties whatsoever. Such deeds are rarely used in sales but are the primary means for transferring property by gift or inheritance.
- **Grant deed** – The transferor warrants that they have done nothing to create any impairments of title during their period of ownership. This warranty does not, however, protect the transferee against defects in title that arose prior to the transferor's period of ownership. This deed is sometimes known as a **bargain and sale** deed or **special warranty** deed.
- **Warranty deed** – The transferee is guaranteed full rights of use and enjoyment of the property, including a promise that there are no undisclosed claims against the property by any other party from the time the property was first used to the date of transfer. This deed is sometimes known as a **general warranty** deed.

 For example, assume a house is built during 20X1 and the original owner lives there until 3/18/X5 before selling it, then the second owner lives there until 8/13/X7. If, in the 20X7 sale, the buyer (third owner) receives a warranty deed, the seller (second owner) is promising the buyer that there are no defects in title from any events prior to 8/13/X7.

If the buyer receives a grant deed, the promise is only that no defects in title resulted from events between 3/18/X5 and 8/13/X7. If the buyer receives a quitclaim deed, the seller is making no promises about title, but is only transferring the title they possess.

Interests in Real Property: Any claim in, to or on real property, including title, security or lease. Types of present interest:

- *Fee simple absolute* – highest estate in law (has most rights). May be transferred *inter vivos* (while living), or upon death. May be subject to mortgage or other lien.
- *Fee simple defeasible* – subject to a condition or subsequent event.
- *Life interest* – an interest whose term is usually the life of the holder, but may be measured by the life of others.
- *Leaseholds* – Lessor-Lessee, pursuant to a lease agreement.

A transferee may obtain **title insurance** to protect their deed. Such a policy compensates the insured if a defect existed at the date the transferee acquired the property. The insurance company will perform a title search prior to issuing such a policy, and any defects (eg, an **easement**) they identify will be listed as **exceptions** (to the policy, meaning the company is not liable for these defects.

The policy is personal to the insured and cannot be transferred to another party. Also, it does not cover defects that arise after the date of acquisition by the insured.

For a deed to be valid against third parties, it must be recorded at the appropriate government office. If a deed is recorded prior to any other claims being made against the property, the recorder will have priority over all later parties.

Marketable title means that the title to real estate is free from encumbrances, such as mortgages, easements, liens and defects. It does not mean free from recorded zoning restrictions, public rights-of-way, or recorded easements.

If, however, a later claimant arises before the deed is recorded, the priority of the two claims will depend on the jurisdiction in which the real estate is located and the circumstances surrounding the two claims. The overwhelming number of states are **notice-race** jurisdictions, and in such cases the earlier claim will win if either of the following circumstances applies:

- The later claimant knew about the earlier claim when they obtained theirs.
- The earlier claimant eventually records the deed before the later claimant.

As a result, the only time the later claim prevails in a notice-race jurisdiction is when the later claimant records first **and** did not know about the earlier claim when they acquired their rights.

For example, assume that Roger originally sells his home to Frieda First, giving her a valid deed, which Frieda does not immediately record. Roger then sells the same home to Sidney Second, providing an identical deed. Both Frieda and Sidney later record their deeds. The party with priority in a notice-race jurisdiction depends on (1) Sidney's knowledge of Frieda's earlier claim at the time of his purchase and (2) who recorded first.

PRIORITY IF:	Sidney knew	Sidney didn't know
Frieda recorded first	Frieda	Frieda
Sidney recorded first	Frieda	Sidney

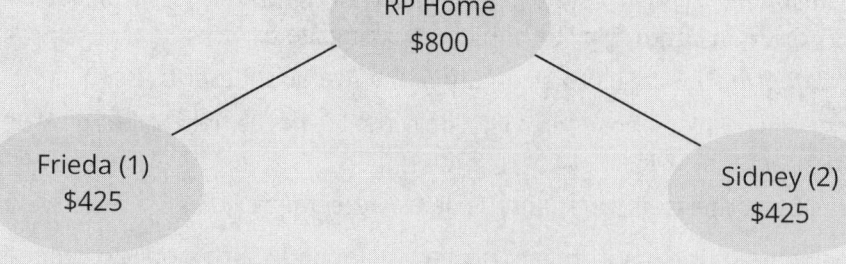

13.02 Different Forms of Concurrent Ownership

Property can be concurrently owned by more than one person. **Different forms of concurrent ownership** available in all states are:

- **Tenancy in common** (no "right of survivorship")
- **Joint tenancy** ("right of survivorship")
- **Tenancy by the entirety**

Tenancy in common refers to two or more persons with separate interests in the same property. This is the simplest form of concurrent ownership, and the following principles apply:

- The interests can be of different percentages of the property.
- Upon death of one of the co-owners, their interest will be distributed to their beneficiaries based on their will (or state intestate succession laws if they died without a will).
- Each person may transfer their interest without the consent of the others and with no impact on the rights of the others.

A joint tenancy is a more restrictive arrangement that includes a **right of survivorship**, and the following principles apply:

- The interests must be equal as to **T**ime, **T**itle, **I**nterest, and **P**ossession. **(TTIP)**
- Upon death of one of the co-owners, their interest will be automatically transferred to the other joint tenants in equal shares, regardless of the provisions of any will of the decedent.
- Each person may transfer their interest without the consent of the others, but the right of survivorship will no longer apply between the transferee and other joint owners.

Tenancy by the entirety

- Joint interest held by a married couple
- Each spouse has a right of survivorship
- Divorce, death, or mutual agreement severs right of survivorship

For example, if A, B, and C are each 1/3 joint tenants in property, and A sells their interest to X, X will now have a 1/3 tenancy in common, and not share right of survivorship. If B subsequently dies, C will become a 2/3 owner (and a tenant in common, since there is no remaining party with whom C shares the right of survivorship). If X subsequently dies, X's heirs will receive X's 1/3 tenancy in common.

Mortgages – A Security Interest in Real Property

Mortgages are security interests in real estate. The UCC rules on secured transactions do not apply to mortgages, but many of the principles are similar.

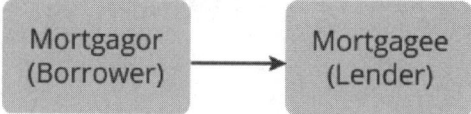

There must be a written mortgage signed by the debtor in order to attach the mortgage to the property and make it effective between the debtor (mortgagor) and creditor (mortgagee). To make the mortgage effective against later parties that may obtain mortgages or deeds on the property, the creditor must perfect the mortgage by recording it. If they fail to record the mortgage quickly, they may lose priority to a later party in a notice-race jurisdiction as long as the later party records first and doesn't know about the earlier claim at time of recording.

Mortgage – A security interest in Real Property (to be **effective**):

- Written
- Description
- Signed by mortgagor and delivered to mortgagee
    - Same rule as for deeds...**Notice-race**
    - Upon default by the mortgagor, the mortgagee may **Foreclose** on the property.

> Assume that Denny Debtor purchases a home in January, financing 75% of it through First Bank, and giving First a mortgage on the home, which the bank immediately records. In February, Denny takes out a home improvement loan with Second Bank, giving them a mortgage on the same property. Second fails to record the mortgage until April. In March, Denny borrows money from Third Bank to consolidate personal debts, and gives Third a mortgage, which Third records immediately.
>
> First has highest priority by having the earliest mortgage and recording before the others. Second failed to record in a timely fashion, so Third will have the next priority in a notice-race jurisdiction as long as Third Bank didn't know about the mortgage given to Second Bank at the time Third recorded. Second's claim will be the last of the three. If Third knew about Second's earlier claim, then Second will have priority over Third.

If the debtor defaults on a loan secured by a mortgage, the court may **foreclose** on the property and sell it at auction on behalf of the secured creditor or creditors.

The proceeds are paid in the exact order of priority established for the creditors, and the debtor receives any remaining available funds once all secured claims are repaid. If there is not a sufficient amount to pay all secured creditors, the debtor remains personally liable for the unpaid amounts. Prior to the court-ordered sale, the buyer may redeem the property by paying all amounts owed, but cannot do so after the sale.

If property is sold at a time a recorded mortgage is still outstanding, the mortgagee will retain the right to foreclose on the property and have priority over the buyer with respect to the proceeds from foreclosure. If, however, the proceeds are not sufficient to satisfy the unpaid debt, a question arises as to the liabilities of the seller and buyer for the deficiency.

There are three possible situations, depending on the buyer's actions at the time of purchase:

1. If the buyer **assumes** the mortgage, then the buyer is accepting personal liability for the deficiency. The seller remains liable as well, since they borrowed from the mortgagee originally.
2. If the buyer takes the property **subject to** the mortgage, without assuming it, then the buyer is merely acknowledging the priority of the mortgagee on the property for the unpaid balance of the loan, but is not accepting personal liability for the debt itself. The seller remains liable to the mortgagee for the entire unpaid debt.
3. If the buyer and mortgagee agree to a **novation** on the debt, then the buyer is accepting personal liability on it in exchange for the mortgagee's agreement to completely release the seller from liability.

Mortgage lenders are regulated by the Real Estate Settlement Procedures Act (RESPA) of 1974, whereby home buyers must be provided with adequate disclosures and explanations of the closing procedures followed and fees charged.

Leases

When property is leased by the owner to another party, the lessee (tenant) obtains the rights identified in the contract to use the property for a certain time period. Unless these are **specifically** and **individually** prohibited in the agreement, the lessee also has the right to:

- **Assign** – This is a transfer of the balance of the lease to another person, giving the assignee both the right to use the premises and the obligation to pay the owner. The assignor loses the right to the use the premises (since they've been assigned to another) but retains the obligation to the owner as a guarantee of performance by the assignee.
- **Sublet** – This is a separate contract made by the lessee to transfer a portion of the rights under the contract to a sub-lessee for a payment to the lessee. The sub-lessee has the rights under the sub-lease and the obligation to pay the lessee, but no obligation to the owner. The lessee retains the obligations to the owner and must honor whatever promises they've made to the sub-lessee as far as transferred rights.
  - If lease expires and person will not move, it is called "tenancy at sufferance."
  - If it is ok for the tenant to stay, called "tenancy from period to period."
  - A landlord implies 3 different Warranties:
    - The right of Possession
    - The warranty of Quiet Enjoyment
    - The warranty of Habitability (up to code)

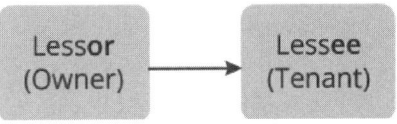

A residential lease agreement must contain the following:

- The parties involved
- Lease payment amount
- Lease term
- Description of the leased property

If receive money to cancel a lease (money to move out early), this is considered a capital gain and is L/T or S/T based on the length of the lease.

 Assume a lessee signs a rental agreement on a house, giving them the right to live there for the entire 20X1 year, with payments of $1,000 per month. In June, the lessee rents the property out to another family for a month for $800, to live there while the lessee is on vacation. This is a sublet: the sub-lessee is obligated to pay the lessee $800, and the lessee is responsible to pay the owner the regular $1,000.

At the beginning of September, the lessee buys their own home, and transfers the remaining 4 months of the lease to another family that agrees to move in and take over the $1,000 monthly payments to the owner. This is an assignment: the assignee is obligated to pay the owner $1,000 per month, and the assignor is liable for the $1,000 as well in the event the assignee doesn't honor the promise.

13.03 Intellectual Property & Computer Technology Rights

Overview

Entities and individuals use a wide variety of means by which to protect intellectual property. Various laws have been enacted to take into account the unique characteristics of intellectual property. Some of the means of protection are:

- Copyright
- Patent
- Trademark

Copyrights (©)

Copyrights are designed to protect the creators of original works by giving them the exclusive rights to it. Prior to the application of electronic media, most original works were in written form and a copyright is, literally, **an exclusive right to reproduce and distribute a creative work**. The copyright holder also has the exclusive right to:

- Create work that is derived from the original work, referred to as derivative work
- Perform, display, or otherwise transmit the work
- Sell, assign, license, or otherwise transfer the legal rights to the work

A copyright is valid for the life of the creator plus 70 years. Once the creator has been deceased for 70 years, the work is considered part of the public domain. Copyrights of works by corporations or businesses expire at the earlier of 100 years from the date of creation or 75 years from the date of publication.

A copyright may be registered with the U.S. Copyright office, but the rights also may be obtained by indicating that the item is copyrighted on its face with the date, generally using the copyright symbol, such as © 2018 by John Johnson, CPA. Copyright of a sound recording protected under the copyright laws is denoted with a similar symbol that has a letter "p" in a circle ℗ instead of the letter "c."

The creator of an original work is presumably entitled to the rights afforded by copyright protection. When the identity of the creator is in question, however, the first party to obtain a copyright will generally prevail.

One of the limitations on the rights of a copyright holder is referred to as the **fair use doctrine**, which allows the reproduction of a work that has been copyrighted if it is for a purpose that is considered fair, such as for criticism or comment, news reporting, or teaching or research.

The Computer Software Copyright Act of 1989 was enacted to extend copyright protection to computer programs, which are defined as sets of instructions, whether written or in machine-readable form, used directly or indirectly by a computer to achieve a particular objective. It does allow an owner of a copy to make copies or adaptations in order to be able to use the software for its intended purpose.

The **No Electronic Theft (NET) Act** was enacted in 1997 to make it a crime to infringe a copyright over the Internet. Infringement is punishable by up to 3 years in prison and a fine of up to $250,000.

The **Digital Millennium Copyright Act of 1998** is an attempt to protect copyright holders against infringement (pirating) and, at the same time, protect internet service providers (ISPs) from liability from the actions of their users. It prohibits unauthorized access to copyrighted digital works and the circumvention of access controls, whether access is obtained or not. It also protects ISPs from liability if they take reasonable steps to prevent or properly react to infringements.

Patents

Patents are designed to protect inventors similarly to how copyrights protect creators of original works. *They prevent someone other than the patent holder from making, using, or offering the patented item for sale.* The three types of patents are:

- **Utility** (usefulness) patents are granted to one who invents or discovers a "new and useful" process, machine, or item to be manufactured or an improvement to one.
- **Design** patents are granted to one who invents a "new, original, and ornamental design" for an item to be manufactured.
- **Plant** patents are granted to one who discovers and reproduces a distinct new plant variety.
    - Utility and plant patents are valid for 20 years and design patents are valid for 14 years from the date of filing.

Trademarks (® and TM)

Trademark protection is given to a *distinctive sign*, which may be a *word, name, symbol, shape, or other format that will be recognizable.* It is used to distinguish goods as being identified with a particular entity, such as a merchant or manufacturer. Companies may use a symbol, like Nike's "Swoosh," which makes a garment or other sports-related product immediately recognizable as a Nike product, even if the name is not displayed.

- Trademark protection is generally provided for 10 years.
- During the 6th year of a 10-year term, the holder is required to indicate that the trademark is still in use.
- Trademarks that remain in use can be renewed in 10 year incremental periods indefinitely.
- Trademarks for which an affidavit of use is not filed expire.

Trade Secrets

The **Uniform Trade Secrets Act** was enacted to provide entities with enhanced protection for their trade secrets, which are *formulae, patterns, processes, and other techniques* that have actual or potential economic value and are the subject to reasonable efforts to maintain their secrecy. Protection is for an indefinite period of time and remains in effect as long as the trade secret is relevant.

Semiconductor Chip Protection Act

The Semiconductor Chip Protection Act of 1984 provides layouts of printed circuits with protections similar to copyrights or patents. It also protects "mask works," which are "a series of related images, however fixed or encoded (1) having or representing the predetermined three-dimensional pattern of metallic, insulating, or semiconductor material present or removed from the layers of a semiconductor chip product...." This protects the creator of a semiconductor chip from another party "reverse engineering" the chip by taking it apart and copying it. Protection is given for 10 years, expiring at the end of the 10th calendar year after the protection began.

Money Laundering Control Act (MLCA)

The Money Laundering Control Act of 1986 makes money laundering a federal crime. Money laundering is the process of changing large sums of money that have been gained through illegitimate means to make it appear as if it came from a legitimate source. Under the law, transactions involving transfers of money in excess of $10,000 must be disclosed.

13.04 Regulation of Employment, Environment & Antitrust

Federal Unemployment Tax Act (FUTA)

The Federal Unemployment Tax Act (FUTA) imposes a tax *paid entirely by employers* on applicable wages of employees. There are a few categories of employment exempt from FUTA, and an employer is not required to pay these taxes unless at least one person is employed in each of 20 different weeks of the year (or total wages in a calendar quarter exceed $1,500). The law permits a credit against the federal tax for employers that are subject to state unemployment taxes for an amount equal to the standard tax rate imposed by the state.

Unemployment benefits are fully taxable to former employees. Benefits are **not paid** if the person:

- Left employment voluntarily (business reversals – ok)
- Refuses to accept equivalent work that has been offered
- Was dismissed by the employer for illegal activity

Federal Insurance Contributions Act (FICA)

The Federal Insurance Contributions Act (FICA) (7.65%) imposes a tax *paid equally by employer and employee* based on the gross wages of the employee (self-employed persons pay a combined employer-employee rate of 15.3% on net self-employment income).

- The employer withholds the employee's share from gross pay and remits it along with the employer's share. An employer who fails to withhold is liable for both shares, and the employee is considered to have received additional compensation if they do not reimburse the employer. The employer may be assessed penalties for failing to make timely deposits of amounts owed to the IRS or for failing to provide the tax identification number of the employee.
- All compensation for services is subject to FICA taxes, including awards for productivity and fees paid to directors.
- **Benefits** are paid by the Social Security Administration for old age, survivors, spouses (including divorced spouses), disability, and Medicare (1.45%). Benefits for old age may be reduced or eliminated prior to a certain age (typically 70) if the person continues to receive compensation for services, but investment income will not affect the amount of benefits. Cash benefits may be non-taxable or partially taxable, depending on the overall adjusted gross income of the recipient.
    - Old age or retirement benefits
    - Benefits to survivors and divorced spouses
    - Payments for disability and to disabled children
    - Medicare benefits

Regulation of Employee Benefits & Compensation

Several laws regulate benefits provided to employees by their employer. The **Employment Retirement Income Security Act (ERISA)** applies to employers who have chosen to provide private *pension benefits* to employees (the law doesn't require such benefits). There are requirements related to:

- **Participation** – The plan must cover all employees that fall within the same class.
- **Vesting** – Amounts paid into plans by employees (these are known as contributory plans) must be vested immediately. Amounts paid into plans by employers must vest within a reasonable period of time (usually within 5 years).
- **Funding** – The employer must remit amounts collected from employees and amounts owed by the employer to an independent trustee within a reasonable period of time.

The **Comprehensive Omnibus Budget Reconciliation Act (COBRA)** allows employees to continue medical, dental, and optical coverage provided by their employer after termination of employment for up to *18 months* (longer in the case of disability) by remitting to the employer the cost of such coverage. Coverage may be continued for the employee and other family members who were included under the plan during employment.

The **Family Medical Leave Act (FMLA)** requires companies with 50 or more employees to permit them up to 12 weeks in any 12-month period of unpaid leave for family or medical reasons. The employer must continue health coverage during this time and offer the employee a return to their previous position or comparable work.

With regard to hiring and pay arrangements, employers are subject to several laws under the **Fair Labor Standards Act (FLSA)**.

- It requires a **minimum wage** (the amount is periodically revised) that must be paid to all employees without exception, including hourly and salaried employees. Payment on the basis of piecework is allowed, provided workers receive at least the equivalent of the minimum hourly wage.
- It prohibits **child labor** in certain occupations or for more than a certain number of hours.
- It also establishes a workweek of 40 hours, and requires **overtime compensation** at the rate of 1 ½ times normal pay for any work exceeding 40 hours in any calendar week, but this provision doesn't apply to executives, professional employees, and outside salespersons.

Telephone Consumer Protection Act - TCPA (Do Not Call List)

The Telephone Consumer Protection Act (TCPA) was enacted to restrict telephone solicitations and the use of automated telephone equipment. The Act:

- Prohibits solicitors from calling residences before 8 am or after 9 pm
- Requires them to maintain and honor a "do not call" (DNC) list
- Requires solicitors to identify themselves
- Prohibits solicitors from using an artificial voice or recording

- Prohibits the use of automated calling equipment to call emergency numbers, hospitals, doctors' offices, and any recipient required to pay for the call
- Prohibits the sending of unsolicited faxes

Violations of the act are punishable by a fine or up to one year of imprisonment, or both. A second conviction is punishable by a fine and imprisonment of up to 2 years. Alternatively, violators may be subject to a criminal fine for each violation or 3 times that amount for a continuing violation.

In addition, a violator may be subject to a forfeiture penalty for each violation or 3 times that for each day in the case of a continuing violation, with a maximum penalty of $1,000,000 for a single continuing violation.

A call is exempt from the TCPA if the call:

- Is made on behalf of a tax-exempt nonprofit organization.
- Is not made for a commercial purpose.
- Does not include an unsolicited advertisement, even if it is made for a commercial purpose.
- Is made to a consumer with whom the calling company has an established business relationship.

Prior express written consent is required for all autodialed and/or pre-recorded calls/texts sent/made to cell phone and pre-recorded calls made to residential land lines for marketing purposes.

Other Employment Regulations

The **National Labor Relations Act (NLRA)** guarantees employees the right to **form unions** and demands good faith collective bargaining by both sides in disputes. The law applies to bargaining involving wages as well as vacation and sick pay.

The Labor-Management Relations Act, also known as the **Taft-Hartley Act,** prohibits an employer from requiring union membership of all employees.

The **Occupational Safety and Health Act (OSHA)** was enacted to provide safe and healthful workplaces for employees. The Department of Labor has responsibility for setting standards, making inspections, and enforcing the provisions of the act. When employees are injured:

- The company must maintain records of injury and illness for each employee if 11 or more are employed.
- Each record must be available for inspection by an OSHA inspector.

Employers are subject to a large number of federal and state laws governing their relations with employees. Perhaps the earliest involvement of legislation on the relationship was in the area of **workers' compensation laws**.

- These statutes guarantee an employee compensation for a job-related injury or illness (or an existing injury/illness exacerbated by the job). At the same time, they prohibit the employee from suing their employer in an attempt to collect additional sums; however, they can still sue third parties other than the employer that are responsible for their injury/illness.

- Workers' compensation laws apply to employees (whose time and performance of work are controlled by their employer); they do not apply to independent contractors.
- The effect of workers' compensation laws was to eliminate many of the defenses against payment available to an employer under common law (a form of **Strict Liability**). A worker is entitled to collect benefits under these laws, even if one or more of the following conditions is applicable:
  - **Contributory negligence** – The employee's own carelessness (or even recklessness) in violating workplace rules was a contributing factor in causing the injury or illness.
  - **Assumption of risk** – The employee was aware of the dangers of the occupation and signed a waiver of liability.
  - **Negligence of fellow employee** – The injury or illness resulted from the careless or reckless violation of employer rules by another employee.
- On the other hand, there are still some **defenses available** against payment. A worker will not be able to collect under workers' compensation if one of the following conditions is applicable (**BIND**):
  - **Brawling** – The employee is injured while fighting on the job.
  - **Intoxication** – The injury or illness resulted from the employee's intoxication from alcohol or other drugs.
  - **Not job-related** – The employee is injured while commuting to or from work or at some other time when they weren't on the job.
  - **Deliberate self-infliction** – The employee intentionally attempts to become injured or ill.
- **Benefits** may include:
  - Burial expenses
  - The cost of prosthetic devices
  - Monthly payments to surviving dependent(s)

There are several laws dealing with **discrimination in employment** and in treatment of customers:

- Title VII of the Civil Rights Act (CRA) of 1964 prohibits discrimination on the basis of **race, color, national origin, religion, or gender.**
- The Age Discrimination in Employment Act (**ADEA**) prohibits discrimination against workers who are at least 40 years old and generally prohibits mandatory retirement under age 70.
- The **Equal Pay Act** prohibits unequal pay on the basis of gender.
  - Differences may be based on merit, quality of work, or seniority.
- The Americans with Disabilities Act (**ADA**) prohibits discrimination against disabled employees and requires that reasonable accommodation be made to the needs of disabled workers and customers.
- The **Pregnancy Discrimination Act** requires that pregnant workers be categorized as disabled, and receive the same protections.
- **Whistleblower Protection Act** protects employees from retaliation by employers for blowing the whistle on employers.

- **Federal Employee Polygraph Protection Act** says that private employers may not require employees or prospective employees to take lie detector test or make adverse employment decisions based on such tests or refusal to take them.
    - Government employees are exempted.
    - Private employer may use the test as part of investigation of economic loss when employer has reason to suspect individual.

An employer is liable for actions that are intended to discriminate, as well as actions that have the unintended effect of discriminating against a protected group.

All discrimination laws allow an employer to dismiss an employee for misconduct, and to engage in discrimination that has a business necessity, is a clear occupational qualification, or results from a fair seniority system. For example, a studio can limit the auditions for the part of *Queen Victoria* in a movie to women.

Antitrust Laws

To prevent large corporations from taking actions that may be in restraint of trade, several antitrust laws have been passed to promote fair competition. The most significant of these are the Sherman Antitrust Act, the Clayton Antitrust Act, the Federal Trade Commission Act, the Robinson-Patman Act, and the Celler-Kefauver Act.

The **Sherman Antitrust Act**, enacted in 1890, the purpose of which was, according to Senator John Sherman of Ohio, "To protect the consumers by preventing arrangements designed, or which tend, to advance the cost of goods to the consumer." One of the two main provisions of the act makes contracts, combinations, or conspiracies that are in restraint of trade illegal. The other makes it a felony to monopolize, *attempt to monopolize*, or combine or conspire to monopolize any part of trade or commerce.

The **Clayton Antitrust Act**, enacted in 1914, was intended to enhance the Sherman Antitrust Act by prohibiting specific types of conduct that are not considered to be in the best interests of a competitive market. These include:

- Price discrimination between different purchasers;
- Tying products by making the purchase of a product a requirement in order to be able to purchase the desired product;
- Mergers and acquisitions that will lessen competition; and
- A director serving on the boards of competing entities.

The **Federal Trade Commission Act**, also enacted in 1914, created the Federal Trade Commission, which issues "cease and desist" orders to large corporations that are involved in *unfair trade practices*.

The **Robinson-Patman Act** (also referred to as the Anti-Price Discrimination Act) was enacted in 1936 as an amendment to the Clayton Act; it prohibits price discrimination when selling goods to different distributors such that it causes a decrease in competition, such as by selling goods at a lower price to a chain store than to a locally owned store that is in competition with the chain store.

The **Celler-Kefauver Act**, enacted in 1950, enhanced the Clayton Antitrust Act by making acquisitions of assets and of entities *that are not direct competitors* subject to comparable scrutiny, restrictions, and sanctions as provided for in the Clayton Antitrust Act.

Environmental Regulation

Businesses are affected by several laws designed to **protect the environment**. Among these are:

- **Environmental Protection Act** – This law created the Environmental Protection Agency (**EPA**), empowering it to establish regulations and pursue civil and criminal actions against companies and responsible corporate officers for damage to the environment. Suits may also be filed by private citizens and the various states against polluters or the EPA.

- **Comprehensive Environmental Response, Compensation, and Liability Act (CERCLA)** – Also known as the **Superfund law,** it authorizes the government to clean up dangerous toxic sites and attempt to recover the costs from current or former owners and operators of the site and persons transporting wastes to the site. All parties are jointly and severally liable for the costs of cleanup, allowing the government to recover the entire cost from a party who is responsible for only a small part of the pollution.

- Various federal laws **governing the use of toxic substances** exist, including the Toxic Substances Control Act, the Federal Insecticide, Fungicide, and Rodenticide Act, the Nuclear Waste Policy Act, and the Federal Environmental Pesticide Control Act.

- **Federal Water Pollution Control Act** – Also known as the Clean Water Act, it allows the EPA to regulate any actions that may harm public waters.

- **Clean Air and Noise Pollution Acts** –Requires use of the best available technology by companies to reduce harmful emissions and excessive noise. Emissions from nuclear power plants are governed by this act, and not the Nuclear Waste Policy Act.

- **National Environmental Policy Act (NEPA)** - This 1969 act established the Council on Environmental Quality (CEQ), which helps ensure that various environmental laws are followed. NEPA also requires an environmental impact statement before any federal laws can be adopted or activities undertaken that might affect the environment.

REG 14
Agency

REG 14: Agency

14.01 Agency Law Overview — 1
- Agency Relationship Defined — 1
- Employees vs. Independent Contractors — 2

14.02 Types of Authority — 3
- Power of Attorney — 4

14.03 Types of Agency Relationships, Termination & Responsibilities — 5
- Types of Principals — 5
- Types of Agents — 5
- Termination of an Agency — 5
- Principal & Agent Responsibilities — 7

14.01 Agency Law Overview

Agency Relationship Defined

An **agency relationship** exists when one party acts on behalf of another for contractual obligations. The **principal needs capacity**, but the agent does not. An agent must have authority from the principal in order to act on the principal's behalf. The agent must merely have sufficient mental and physical ability to carry out the instructions of their principal.

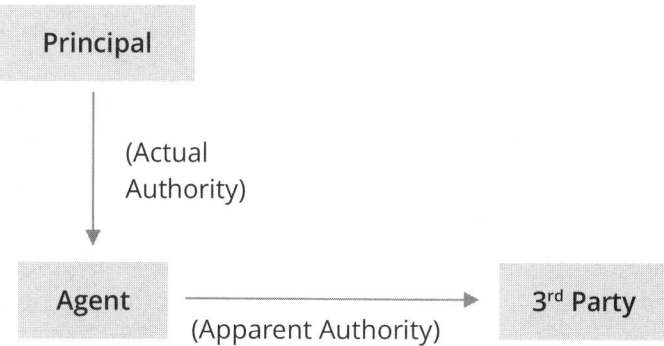

Agency Agreement

An agency does not require a contract and no consideration need be offered, but there must be consent ("a meeting of the minds"). The agency agreement itself **need not be in writing**, except under circumstances when the **Statute of Frauds** (GROSS) applies. Examples where the statute applies include:

- An agency to sell real estate (**Real estate**).
- An agency to run for a period exceeding one year (**Over 1 year**).

Fiduciary Duty

An agent has a fiduciary duty to act loyally on behalf of the principal. The agent must always act in the best interest of the principal. This includes a duty to account for any property of the principal the agent handles, and a prohibition against commingling the funds of the principal with other funds held or owned by the agent. Also, an agent is liable to the principal if the agent binds the principal to a contract based on apparent authority when the agent knew they did not have the actual authority to enter the contract. The principal, however, does not owe a fiduciary duty to the agent.

Employees vs. Independent Contractors

Businesses may engage in relationships with **two special types of agents**: employees and independent contractors. In determining whether one is an employee or an independent contractor, the most significant factors to consider are who controls the behavior of the individual, who controls the financial aspects of the individual's efforts, and how the parties perceive their relationship.

Employees

An employee is under the control of the employer. The employer (a type of principal) determines what behavior on the part of the employee (the agent) is appropriate or inappropriate. The employer not only determines the objective of the relationship, but also the means by which the objective is met as well as when the employee will perform the functions necessary to achieve it (ie, employer controls the *time and manner* of performance).

The employer is also responsible for the financial risks associated with the relationship. The employee may be paid on a piecemeal basis or by the hour, week, month, or some other basis and is entitled to payment for hours worked, regardless of effectiveness. The employee will receive a **W-2** from the employer, indicating amounts earned and taxes withheld.

Since an employer has control over the actions of the employee while engaged in employment-related activities, the employer will be liable for the employee's *torts* committed during the *course* of employment and within the parameters (*scope*) of the employment relationship.

Independent Contractors

An independent contractor is not subject to the control of the principal. Although the principal will determine what constitutes acceptable results, the independent contractor is responsible for determining the means by which objectives will be achieved, as well as when and how the functions necessary to achieve it will be performed. The independent contractor bears financial risk in that efficiencies and inefficiencies are their own responsibility.

The independent contractor is normally paid an agreed-upon amount, is responsible for paying their own taxes without having taxes withheld, and receives a **1099**, indicating the gross amount received, against which expenses may be deducted.

Since the principal is not in control of the actions of the independent contractors, the principal is *generally not responsible for their torts*; however, there are always exceptions to the general rule.

14.02 Types of Authority

There are three ways an agent may obtain this authority.

Actual Authority

The principal intends to give the agent the authority. This includes **express authority**, in which the principal explicitly states that the agent has authority, and **implied authority**, in which the principal assigns the agent a task which cannot be carried out without having certain authority to act on the principal's behalf.

For example, hiring someone as a bartender gives them the actual authority to sell drinks at the bar.

Apparent Authority

The principal takes an action that creates the appearance to third parties that the agent has certain authority. This could result from hiring someone to a position that normally has great authority, or where the customs of the profession provide certain authority. (Note that the principal must take an action that creates the appearance the agent has authority. This doctrine doesn't bind a person simply because another person is claiming to be their agent).

For example, giving someone a title of vice-president in the company gives them apparent authority for a broad range of contracts on the company's behalf, even if the private agreement among the principal and agent is that the new title is simply for prestige.

Ratification (Unauthorized)

The agent acts without authority, but the principal decides after the contract is made to honor it anyway. To ratify, the principal must have been *fully or partially disclosed, understand the contract made on their behalf by the agent, and act to ratify before the third party discovers that the agent acted without authority.* The principal can ratify by explicitly stating their intention to honor the contract, or by accepting the benefits of the contract.

For example, if the friend of someone trying to sell their car finds out about an interested party and contracts on behalf of the owner to sell the car without their knowledge or consent, the contract is without authority. If, however, the friend gives the owner a check from that party, indicating that it is the agreed payment for the car, the deposit of the check by the owner is a ratification of the deal and makes it valid and binding on all parties.

One important point to note is that a principal who has accepted contracts made by the agent in the past creates the appearance that the agent has the authority to make similar contracts in the future.

> **Summary – Types of Authority**
>
> - **Actual** – Principal intends to give agent power to contract.
>   - **Express** – Principal explicitly states agent has authority.
>   - **Implied** – Principal assigns task, which requires authority to carry out duties. Reasonable and necessary to get job done.
> - **Apparent** – Principal creates impression that agent has authority.
>   - **Good faith 3rd party** reasonably assumes you have.
>   - Hires agent to position that customarily has authority.
>   - Has acquiesced to contracts made in past by agent on principal's behalf.
> - **Unauthorized action** – not liable unless ratify.
>   - **Ratification** – Principal gives agent authority after contract is made.
>   - Principal must be fully or partially disclosed.
>   - Must know details of contract made by agent on behalf.
>   - Must ratify before 3rd party withdraws.

Power of Attorney

A common form of agency is a **power of attorney**, which is a written authorization for the agent to act on behalf of the principal for a specific or indefinite period of time. It may be *a limited power of attorney* that only grants the authority to act in certain matters, or *a general power of attorney* allowing the agent to act on behalf of the principal on all matters affecting them.

A power of attorney is often written with a specific provision keeping it enforceable in the event of the insanity or incapacity of the principal, since it may be created in anticipation of possible mental deterioration of the principal. A power of attorney always terminates upon the death of the principal, however.

14.03 Types of Agency Relationships, Termination & Responsibilities

Types of Principals

- Fully disclosed
    - 3rd party knows identity of principal.
    - Principal liable – Agent not liable to 3rd party.
- Partially disclosed
    - 3rd party knows agent is acting for another, but not identity.
    - Principal and agent jointly and severally liable.
- Undisclosed
    - 3rd party believes agent is acting for themselves only.
    - 3rd party may hold either principal or agent liable.
    - Agent required to perform under the contract.
    - When principal is undisclosed, the agent *cannot have apparent authority*.
    - 3rd party not entitled to disclosure of principal.

Types of Agents

- **General Agent** – Has broad authority to act for the principal in a variety of transactions.
- **Special Agent** – Has authority that is limited to a single transaction or series of transactions.
- **Sub-Agent** – An agent appointed by another agent who is authorized to appoint sub-agents in connection with his performance of the principal's business. A sub-agent has a fiduciary duty and a duty of loyalty to both the principal and agent.

Termination of an Agency

Once an agent has authority, it can be terminated in the following ways:

- **Agreement** – The parties originally contracted for the agency to last a period of time that has elapsed, or the parties mutually agree to terminate an agency of indefinite duration.
- **Unilateral** – The principal dismisses the agent, or the agent resigns. Normally, either party has the power to terminate the agency at any time, even in breach of contract.
- **Operation of law** – The agency terminates due to a provision of the law. These include death, insanity, illegality and destruction of the subject matter. The death or insanity of a party will not affect the enforceability of contracts made before such an event. An illegal contract, however, will be unenforceable, even if the provisions were agreed to before the law declared them illegal.
    - **Authority terminates without notice.**

- Death of principal or agent (contracts already made, stand).
- Insanity of principal
- The subject of the agreement becomes Illegal or impossible (destroyed).
- Principal bankrupt

Occasionally, the agent will obtain an **agency coupled with an interest**. This results from an arrangement in which the agent has some legal rights to the subject matter of the agency, and such an agency **cannot be terminated unilaterally by the principal**.

> For example, a secured creditor who has seized the debtor's collateral as a result of default is an agent with the right to sell the debtor's property. Since the creditor is entitled to some of the sales proceeds, their agency is coupled with an interest in the property, and cannot be terminated by the debtor unilaterally (it can still be terminated by the creditor unilaterally or by mutual agreement of the creditor and debtor).

The termination of an agency by operation of law applies to both actual and apparent authority. Other terminations, however, only apply to actual authority, and it is necessary to give **notice to third parties** to terminate apparent authority. Two kinds of notice are needed:

- **Actual notice** – Third parties are directly informed that the agency has terminated (Personal Notice).
- **Constructive notice** – An announcement of the termination is made in publications that third parties are likely to read (Public Notice).

Actual notice must be given to each third party that dealt with the agent in the past. Constructive notice must be given so as to eliminate apparent authority with third parties who haven't dealt with the agent, but who might have been aware of the agency relationship.

> For example, assume Sal Salesperson has been working for Western Widgets for 5 years. If Western fires Sal, that terminates Sal's actual authority to make contracts, but if none of the customers know about this, apparent authority remains. Western must notify the customers that previously made purchases of Western products through Sal of the termination.
>
> Nevertheless, there is a danger that Sal will go to a person who hasn't made previous purchases, but who is aware that Sal worked for Western as a salesperson through various business contacts. Western, to protect itself, must place ads indicating that Sal is no longer an employee of Western.

Principal & Agent Responsibilities

A principal and agent have responsibilities toward one another.

- If an agent has acted without actual authority, binding the principal due to the agent's apparent authority, the **agent** is **liable** to the principal **for losses** or damages incurred.
- Similarly, if an agent acts with actual authority, the **principal** is **obligated to reimburse** or indemnify the agent for payments made that were either expressly authorized or necessary in promoting the principal's business.

In the case of a **breach by the principal**, the courts are reluctant to require parties to interact and specific performance would not be available. The agent may, however, be entitled to:

- Recovery for past services
- Recovery for future damages
- The authority to withhold further performance for the principal

A **tort** is an action that causes injury to another person or their property, whether intentional or caused by negligence, which may result in a *civil trial*. Generally, when there is criminal intent and a criminal act, the action may also constitute a **crime**, which would result in a *criminal trial*; however, not all crimes require criminal intent (eg, selling alcohol to a minor without knowing he or she is, in fact, a minor). An individual is always responsible for their own torts and crimes.

A **principal is responsible for torts** committed by an agent when committed in the course and scope of the agency relationship. A principal, however, is **not** responsible for **crimes** committed by an agent, although some states are expanding a principal's liability for actions of their agents.

REG 15
Debtor-Creditor Relationships

REG 15: Debtor-Creditor Relationships

15.01 Secured Transactions: Overview — 1
- Secured Transaction Defined — 1
- Types of Collateral — 1
- Purchase Money Security Interest (PMSI) — 1

15.02 Secured Transactions: Attachment & Perfection — 3
- Attachment — 3
- Perfection — 5

15.03 Secured Transactions: Other — 8
- Inventory Rule — 8
- Priority among Creditors — 8
- Creditor Responsibilities — 9
- Procedures on Default of Debtor — 10

15.04 Bankruptcy: Overview & Chapter 7 — 11
- Overview — 11
- Petitions to Enter Bankruptcy — 11
- Chapter 7 Bankruptcy — 13

15.05 Bankruptcy: Avoiding Powers of Trustee — 15
- Overview — 15
- Fraudulent Transfers — 15
- Liens — 16
- Transfers Made After Filing — 16
- Preferential Transfers — 16

15.06 Bankruptcy: Order of Distribution — 17
- Exceptions versus Denial of Discharge — 19

15.07 Bankruptcy: Other — 21
- Chapter 11 – Reorganization Plan — 21
- Chapter 13 – Debt Adjustment Plan — 21
- Chapter 9 – Municipalities — 22
- Chapter 12 – Family Farmers and Fishermen — 22
- Chapter 15 – Cross-Border Insolvency Cases — 22
- Bankruptcy Abuse Prevention & Consumer Protection Act of 2005 — 22

15.08 Suretyship — 24
- Types of Suretyship Agreements — 24
- Surety's Liability — 24
- Surety's Rights — 25
- Cosureties — 26
- Creditors' Rights — 27

15.01 Secured Transactions: Overview

Secured Transaction Defined

A transaction where a Creditor either lends money or extends credit to the Debtor and, in exchange, obtains a security interest in the Debtor's property, called Collateral (**UCC Article 9**). The property is usually either Personal property or Fixtures, not Real property.

Types of Collateral

- Tangibles
    - *Inventory* – goods held for sale or lease in the normal course of business, raw materials used in manufacturing (TV a store will sell)
    - *Equipment* – goods that will be used in a trade or business (TV located in a Gym)
    - *Consumer goods* – goods used for personal or household purposes (TV in your home)
    - *Chattel paper* – Writings that evidence both a monetary obligation (buy equipment on credit, the loan agreement then becomes the collateral for another loan by the previous creditor) and security interest in specific goods or equipment
- Intangibles
    - *Accounts* – Any right to payment for goods or services that is not evidenced by an instrument
    - *Negotiable instruments*, warehouse receipts, bills of lading

Note: Items may change from one category to another, depending on who has possession.

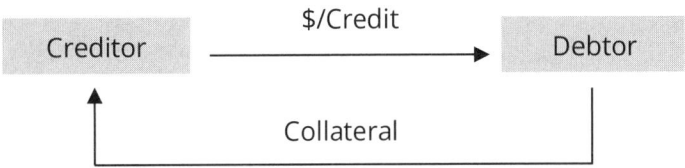

The character of the collateral depends on the debtor's intended use. A personal computer is inventory to a computer store, consumer goods to a family that is using it to play video games, and equipment to a business that is using it to maintain accounting records.

Purchase Money Security Interest (PMSI)

When the Creditor gives the Debtor the purchase money or the credit to acquire the collateral. This gives the creditor priority over all other types of security interests in the same collateral.

- **PMSI** – an interest in personal property or fixtures that secures payment of an obligation that is:
    - Taken by the seller of the collateral to secure all or part of its price, OR
    - Taken by a person who loans money or extends credit to enable the debtor to acquire the collateral.

The Creditor would like to protect their interest from several different parties: (**DOTS**)

- **D**ebtor – (Only needs Attachment)
- **O**ther creditor claiming an interest in the same collateral
- **T**rustee in Bankruptcy
- **S**ubsequent purchaser from the debtor without knowledge of perfection

} Attach & Perfect

For the creditor to protect themselves from the debtor (D), they must only attach; to protect themselves from the other parties (OTS), they must first Attach and then Perfect.

15.02 Secured Transactions: Attachment & Perfection

Attachment

If the debtor does not pay the debt as promised, the creditor will be able to enforce the security agreement, seizing the asset and selling it to raise funds, then returning to the debtor any value exceeding the debt owed, as long as the security interest has attached to the collateral.

Attachment gives a secured party the right to repossess collateral, when the debtor doesn't pay the secured debt. This gives the creditor legally enforceable rights against only the debtor. To attach, **all three** must occur. When the last of the 3 occurs, the interest is considered to have attached.

- **Property owned** by the debtor ("**rights**") (this may involve ownership of the collateral or other claims, such as royalty rights).
- **Interest is created** (one of two ways).
    - Signed security agreement
        - A reasonable description of the collateral
        - Signed by the debtor
    - *Take possession* (pledge as collateral)
- **Give value** to the debtor (a promise to give value in the future is not sufficient).
    - Line of credit is value when given authority, not when money is distributed.

Attachment also covers the following:

- Can attach to the **proceeds** from the sale of the collateral, if debtor sells the property.
- A security agreement also may apply to **after-acquired property**. If the debtor were to purchase inventory or equipment after the attachment occurred, the creditor may attach to these items.

Once all three conditions are satisfied, the creditor has a security interest that can be enforced against the debtor. In some cases, the creditor was the one who provided the debtor with the financing that allowed the debtor to purchase the collateral. In such cases, the creditor has a **purchase money security interest (PMSI)**. In certain cases, a PMSI has advantages over other security interests.

Assume that D purchases a television for personal use (consumer goods) for cash on November 1. On December 10, D arranges to borrow $300 from C, signing and delivering to C a security agreement giving C the right to use the television as collateral for the loan. On December 15, C lends D the money. Attachment takes place on December 15, based on the application of the rules of attachment:

- November 1 – The debtor obtained rights in the collateral.
- December 10 – The debtor provided the creditor with a signed security agreement.
- December 15 – The creditor gave value to the debtor.

As of December 15, all three events required for attachment have occurred, and C obtains a security interest. It is not a purchase money security interest, since C did not provide D with the financing to purchase the television.

As a second example, assume D goes to C on April 24 and asks to borrow $1,000 to purchase a video surveillance camera for D's business (equipment). D signs a security agreement and C loans the money. On May 12, D purchases the camera from a video supplier for $1,500, using the funds obtained from C earlier and an additional $500 of D's own money. Attachment takes place on May 12, based on the application of the rules:

- April 24 – The creditor gave value, and the debtor provided a signed security agreement.
- May 12 – The debtor obtained rights in the collateral.

As of May 12, all three events have occurred, and C obtains a security interest. It is a purchase money security interest, since C did provide D with the financing to purchase the camera.

Once attachment has occurred, the creditor has a nonpossessory right in the debtor's collateral. This means the creditor has rights but not ownership. In the event the debtor defaults on the debt, the creditor may demand the asset, and then may sell it in either a public or private sale. The creditor may even retain the asset in some cases to satisfy the debt, but may not do so if the collateral is consumer goods and the debtor has paid at least 60% of the purchase price of the collateral before default. The creditor is entitled to keep only the amount owed to them, and the remaining value must be returned to the debtor.

Furthermore, the debtor may redeem the property (demand its return) after the creditor has seized it, but prior to sale to a third party by paying the amount owed to the creditor and any reasonable expenses incurred by the creditor. Once a sale has taken place to a third party, though, the debtor will no longer be able to redeem it. The third party is not liable for any of the claims against the property by the creditors of the debtor as long as they purchased it without knowledge of any defects in title.

The law provides creditors with rights *similar to attachment* in various circumstances:

- **Judicial lien** – A court orders certain property to be made available to the plaintiff to satisfy a claim against the defendant in a case. Under Article 9 of the UCC, security interests in tort claims already assessed by a court of law are available to satisfy plaintiff's judgments.
- **Statutory lien** – A service person who repairs *personal property* is given rights by legal statute in the property in the form of an **artisan's lien** until the owner pays for the repairs (this is called a **mechanic's lien** when work is done in connection with *real property*).
- **Garnishment** – A creditor obtains a judicial order allowing them to be paid a portion of the debtor's wages out of each paycheck directly from the debtor's employer.

In general, these types of claims have priority over creditors who have attached the same property, unless the creditors perfected their interests before these claims arose. A statutory lien has priority over all other claims, including prior perfected claims, unless the statute expressly denies this.

Perfection

Perfection gives the creditor legally enforceable rights against the debtor (D) and all other parties (OTS) claiming an interest in the same collateral. To perfect, must satisfy **any 1** of the following:

- **File a financing statement** in the appropriate public office
    - A listing or description of the types of collateral
    - Signature and address of debtor (jurisdiction for filing)
    - Name and address of creditor
        - Must be done for accounts (A/R, copyrights, trademarks, goodwill)
        - The filing lasts for 5 years and can be continued indefinitely if refiled within 6 months of expiring for another 5 years.
- Automatic Perfection
    - A PMSI in **consumer goods** is automatically perfected without filing or taking possession as soon as it attaches.
        - *Loophole* – if the debtor sells the consumer goods to another good faith consumer, the new purchaser takes the property free of the automatic perfection ("garage sale" rule).
        - To close the loophole, the creditor must file a financing statement within **20 days of attachment.** (Retroactive to date of attachment if within 20 days)
            - The 20-day rule also applies to equipment, but not to inventory.
- **Take possession** of the collateral
    - Must be done for negotiable and nonnegotiable instruments, investment securities (stock certificates or promissory notes) and money. Example: a pawnbroker lending money.

Of course, a security interest can be perfected only if it has been attached. If a creditor files a financing statement prior to the 3 requirements of attachment being satisfied, the perfection will occur once attachment occurs.

Filing a financing statement is a way of informing other potential claimants against the property of the creditor's claim. The statement is filed in the jurisdiction of the debtor. If the property was acquired by the debtor for personal use (consumer goods), the jurisdiction is based on the debtor's principal residence. If the property was acquired by the debtor for resale (inventory) or use in their trade or business (equipment), the jurisdiction is based on the debtor's principal place of business. If the jurisdiction of the debtor changes, the financing statement remains valid for **120 days** before the creditor must refile in the new jurisdiction. To summarize, the jurisdiction for almost all Filings is determined by the *Debtor's location*, rather than the collateral's location.

Normally, perfection occurs at the time the financing statement is filed. If, however, a creditor with a **PMSI files within 20 days** of the debtor's acquisition of the collateral, the perfection will become effective retroactively to the date of attachment, unless the collateral is inventory.

If a creditor lends money and obtains a security agreement in previously purchased equipment of a debtor on February 1, and files a financing statement on February 11, perfection occurs on February 11. If, on the other hand, the creditor lends the debtor the money to buy the equipment currently on February 1, and files a financing statement on February 11, perfection occurs on February 1, because the creditor has a PMSI. If the PMSI creditor doesn't file until February 22, the perfection occurs on February 22, since it doesn't satisfy the 20-day rule.

Perfections against **inventory** are not as complete as those against other types of property (**Inventory Rule**). Since inventory is acquired by the debtor for the specific purpose of being sold, a perfection against inventory will not protect the creditor after the debtor sells the inventory in the ordinary course of business, even if the buyer knows of the security interest and even if the buyer is not a consumer. However, the creditor will have rights against the proceeds from sale, and the perfection against inventory will give the creditor priority over other creditors and the trustee-in-bankruptcy.

There is one method of perfection that requires no further action by the creditor beyond the requirements of attachment. The creditor's claim is perfected automatically when they attach a purchase money security interest **in consumer goods** acquired from a dealer.

For example, if a consumer purchases goods from a store and the transaction is financed by the store directly, the store will obtain an automatic perfection at the time of the sale. Similarly, if the consumer purchases goods from a store and finances the transaction with a loan from the bank, the bank will obtain an automatic perfection at the time of the sale. The automatic perfection does not apply to goods the debtor is buying for business purposes, nor to purchases of consumer goods from other consumers, but to regular dealers in the goods. In other words, the goods must have been inventory to the seller and must be consumer goods to the buyer (debtor).

Although the creditor obtains a perfection in these consumer goods without having to file a financing statement, there is a **loophole** in the perfection which may cause the creditor to decide to file anyway. This loophole allows another consumer who purchases the goods from the consumer-debtor to be free of the perfection as long as they didn't know about it.

If a consumer purchases a home exercise machine from a department store on credit from the store, the store obtains an automatic perfection since they financed the purchase of the collateral. If the debtor sells the machine to a friend without telling them the store has a claim against it, the friend will acquire the machine free of the store's security interest if the store relied on the automatic perfection. If the store filed a financing statement before the sale, however, they will have an enforceable perfection against the friend.

In rare cases, the creditor will perfect their interest by **taking possession** of the collateral. This is usually impractical because it prevents the debtor from using the property. In the case of automobiles, however, the creditor may take possession of the document of title (pink slip) to the vehicle. There are no loopholes to a perfection by possession (assuming there are no creditors who have already perfected their security interest by filing a financing statement).

Summary – Perfection		
Method	Loophole	Comment
Filing a financing statement	Sale of inventory	Filing of PMSI within 20 days retroactive to attachment.
Attaching PMSI in consumer good purchase from dealer	Sale by debtor to another good faith consumer	Loophole can be closed if the creditor files a financing statement.
Take possession of collateral	No loophole	May take possession of document of title.

Special Rules for Perfection

When collateral is taken from one state to another, the creditor must perfect in the new state within **4 months**, or lose their priority.

A security interest in instruments and negotiable documents of title is automatically perfected upon attachment without filing or possession for a period of **20 days,** to allow the creditor to gain possession of the collateral. (For example, if you loan me money in exchange for my bank CD, you will have 20 days to take possession of the CD.)

15.03 Secured Transactions: Other

Inventory Rule

If acquiring goods in the ordinary course of business (inventory to seller), buyer's claim is superior to all other claims. So, if the goods are purchased from a retailer, the inventory is acquired free of all other claims, even if the purchaser is aware of the claims (I – Inventory, C – Consumer Goods, E- Equipment).

Inventory Rule

Manufacturer-I → Wholesaler-I → Retailer-I

From Retailer-I:
- Retailer-I — No 20-Day Window — X
- Consumer-C — 20-Day Window — X
- Health Club-E — 20-Day Window — X

Filings – The jurisdiction for almost all Filings is determined by the **debtor's location**, rather than the collateral's location.

Priority among Creditors

1. Inventory rule – buyer in the ordinary course of business.
2. Holder of a statutory lien (mechanic's lien), depending on state statute.
3. PMSI when attached and perfected simultaneously.
4. Among other perfections by filing, order of filing (even if not yet perfected).
5. Other Perfected interests or judicial liens (court order/garnish wages) in order of perfection.
6. Order of attachment, if no one perfected.

If more than one creditor has perfected their interest in the same collateral, the **priority** among the creditors is as follows:

- A PMSI has priority over all other interests if the creditor perfected at the same time as attachment. This is always the case for consumer goods bought from a dealer.
    - Would apply to perfection by filing within 20 days for other consumer goods and equipment.
    - Would not usually apply to inventory, unless filing took place before the debtor acquired the inventory.
- Among other perfections by filing, priority is based on the **order of filing.**

If one creditor has a perfection by filing, and another has perfection by possession, the one who has **perfected first** in their own way has priority over the other.

For example, assume that 3 different creditors have perfected interests by filing against a debtor's equipment. Creditor A financed the purchase of the equipment by the debtor on April 1, and filed a financing statement on April 10. Creditor B made a loan to the debtor on April 3, and filed on April 6. Creditor C made a loan to the debtor on April 7, but filed against the equipment on April 2 during the negotiations over the loan.

The highest priority goes to A, since they have a PMSI and filed within 20 days of the debtor's purchase of the collateral, so perfection occurred at the same time as attachment. Creditor C is second in line, since they filed on April 2, earlier than the April 6 filing of Creditor B. Notice that C has priority over B, even though C's perfection didn't occur until April 7; priority among filers is based on the order of filing and not the order of perfection.

If the facts in the example are changed so that the collateral in question is inventory, C is first, B is second, and A is last, because there is no 20-day rule for inventory, and A's perfection did not occur as of the date of attachment. In this case, the order of filing is used for all. Similarly, even if the collateral is equipment, if A filed on April 22, they would be last, since they filed more than 20 days after the debtor acquired the collateral.

Creditor Responsibilities

A secured creditor has certain responsibilities to the debtor in connection with the security agreement. They must:

- Use reasonable care to preserve any collateral in their possession.
- Confirm the unpaid amount of the debt when requested by the debtor.
- File or send the debtor a termination statement, releasing the collateral once the debt has been repaid.

Procedures on Default of Debtor

When a debtor fails to meet its obligations, it is in default and the secured creditor has a claim to the property that was used as security for the obligation. The creditor may obtain a general judgment against the debtor without foreclosing upon the property. Otherwise, the creditor will foreclose on the property, which is a legal means by which the lender attempts to recover amounts owed. The debtor's **right of redemption** is terminated, and the creditor repossesses the property and forces a sale.

Before the creditor may repossess and sell property pledged as collateral, the debtor's right of redemption must be terminated. The debtor's right of redemption allows the debtor to repay the loan, along with any penalties that may have arisen due to missed payments, and any costs incurred by the creditor.

If the debtor fails to redeem the property, the creditor will take possession of the property and force its sale in either a public or a private sale. When there is more than one creditor, the creditor with the highest priority has the right to repossess the property.

Upon sale, the proceeds will first be used to *pay any reasonable expenses* associated with the sale. Excess proceeds will be applied against the claim of the secured creditor with the highest priority.

If the proceeds are not sufficient:

- If the loan is "without recourse," the lender has no further claim against the debtor.
- If the loan is "with recourse," the debtor will be personally responsible for any unpaid portion, referred to as a **deficiency judgment**.

If the proceeds exceed the claims of the secured creditor with the highest priority:

- Any excess is first applied to the claims of other secured creditors, beginning with the secured creditor with the highest priority, followed by those with lower priorities.
- The debtor will be entitled to any remaining proceeds.

Some jurisdictions allow for "strict foreclosure." In a strict foreclosure, the creditor brings a suit against the debtor and, upon being successful, a court order is issued to the debtor to satisfy the obligation within a specific period of time. If the obligation is not paid off, the creditor obtains title to the property and has no obligation to sell it. If a court order is not obtained and the creditor decides to keep the property:

- The creditor must provide notice to the debtor and all other secured creditors.
- An objection within 21 days will require the creditor to sell the property.

In the case of consumer goods, a creditor may not retain the property and is required to dispose of it within **90 days** if the debtor has paid **at least 60%** of the obligation.

15.04 Bankruptcy: Overview & Chapter 7

Overview

Bankruptcy is the legal process whereby the debtor is relieved of his debts, and the debtor's creditors are given satisfaction in the fairest way possible. In general, any debts that are forgiven, in bankruptcy or otherwise, result in taxable income to the debtor. This is not the case, however, when the debtor is insolvent, which would be the case when the debtor's liabilities exceed the fair value of the debtor's assets, including retirement assets.

Chapters of Federal Bankruptcy Code

- **Chapter 7 – Liquidation** – The assets of the debtor are turned over to a trustee, who sells them and tries to satisfy creditor claims, with remaining claims discharged.
- **Chapter 11 – Business Reorganization** – The debtor continues to operate the business while the creditors meet to restructure the debts. No trustee is usually involved.
- **Chapter 13 – Debt Adjustment Plan** – The debtor and a trustee work out a plan to restructure the debts without the involvement of the creditors. This is only available to individual debtors and small businesses.

Petitions to Enter Bankruptcy

Voluntary – (7,11,13)

- The debtor files the petition for relief and the court enters immediate "order for relief" to stop individual collection efforts by creditors. Need **not be insolvent** in the "equity sense" (unable to pay debts as they come due) and spouses may file jointly to avoid duplicative fees.
- Any person, partnership or corporation may file a voluntary bankruptcy petition. However, certain entities may **not** file a voluntary petition, such as insurance companies, savings and loans, banks, credit unions and railroads.

Involuntary – (7,11)

- The creditors are not being paid so they force the debtor into involuntary bankruptcy. A hearing is scheduled to determine if conditions have been satisfied. The courts appoint a temporary trustee. Within 20 – 40 days after the *order for relief*, a creditors' meeting is held (Section 341 meeting) so the creditors can question the debtor about related issues, and the creditors can also vote to replace the trustee selected by the courts. The creditors have about 6 months to prove their claims by filing a "proof of claim" form.

- Certain entities may **not** be petitioned involuntarily into bankruptcy, such as farmers and nonprofit or charitable organizations.

- For **Involuntary Bankruptcy**:

    o **12 or more creditors** – Need 3 or more signatures from unsecured creditors with claims of at least $18,600[1] in the aggregate.

    o **Fewer than 12 creditors** – Need 1 (or more) signature(s) from unsecured creditors with claims of at least $18,600 in the aggregate.

Note: If debtor contests the petition, just show debtor is not paying debts as they become due (cash flow approach to insolvency), and courts will approve the petition.

In both cases, an **"Automatic Stay"** becomes effective against most creditors of the debtor. This freezes the debtor's assets so the courts can take an accounting. Certain actions are exempt, like criminal proceedings, eviction proceedings, alimony and child support. Secured creditors' interests must be protected, or the courts will grant a relief from the automatic stay.

Assume a debtor has 4 debts outstanding, all unsecured, which they are unable to pay as they come due. Creditors A, B, and C are each owed $3,000, while Creditor D is owed $20,500. In this case, Creditor D can satisfy all of the requirements for filing without any cooperation from the others, since D is owed more than the required amount and there are fewer than 12 unsecured creditors. A joint filing by A, B, and C, on the other hand, would be dismissed since the claims total only $9,000.

If, in addition to these claims, the debtor owed $100 each to 8 other unsecured creditors, then D couldn't file alone, since the 12 unsecured creditors in total require 3 signatures on the petition. D may, however, file jointly if any two other creditors join the petition (the sizes of their claims are irrelevant since the minimum required claims of the filing creditors is satisfied by D's claim alone). Notice, though, that a joint filing by all 11 of the creditors other than D would still fail since their claims total only $9,800.

Creditors who file against a debtor **without meeting the requirements** will have their petition dismissed by the court and may be liable to the debtor for **damages**, including:

- Court costs
- Compensatory damages
- Punitive damages

When a petition is filed voluntarily by a debtor, the court automatically enters an **order of relief**, which stops all creditors from pursuing claims directly and begins the orderly procedures of the bankruptcy. When a petition is filed involuntarily by the creditors, a court hearing date must be set before the petition is effective, so the order of relief occurs later. The time between the filing

---

[1] *Amounts are cost adjusted every 3 years; last changed 4/22.*

off the petition and the order of relief is called the **involuntary gap** since it only arises in an involuntary bankruptcy.

The acceptance of a bankruptcy petition and order of relief does not terminate security interests that were perfected before the petition date, nor judicial or statutory liens created earlier. Nevertheless, the stay against collection efforts applies to all claims, including these. Creditors with perfected security interests or liens must prove these to the bankruptcy court to enforce their claims against the collateral.

After the bankruptcy petition is filed, the debtor must submit a list of creditors, a schedule of assets & liabilities, income & expenditures, copies of tax returns, payroll stubs, a list of amounts in a QTIP and educational IRA, and a certificate from the credit counseling agency.

Chapter 7 Bankruptcy

Once a Chapter 7 bankruptcy petition is approved by the court, a trustee is appointed to take control of the debtor's property. The trustee will obtain all the **nonexempt** interests of the debtor as of the **filing date** of the bankruptcy petition. The debtor's exemptions will depend on whether the debtor has elected to take the federal or the state exemptions applicable to their specific state. Testing has been extremely light on exemptions, but there are a few useful **Exemption Rules** to keep in mind:

- Limited equity in a home (Homestead exemption)
- Limited equity in a motor vehicle
- The right to reasonable alimony and child support payments
- Household goods, furnishings, clothing, appliances, books not to exceed a specified amount per item
- Jewelry (within limits)
- Books and Tools of trade
- Social security, veteran's, and disability benefits and unemployment compensation
- Payments from pension, profit-sharing and annuity plans, up to specified limits in tax-exempt retirement accounts (IRAs).
- Educational IRAs (529 plans) exempt, unless deposited between 120 and 365 days prior to filing, then exempt only up to specified limits.

The trustee will also maintain control over the earnings generated from non-exempt property, and the proceeds from sale. In general, the trustee does not have a claim on property the debtor becomes entitled to receive after the date of filing of the petition, but exceptions are made if the debtor gains the right to receive property **within 180 days** from:

- Inheritances
- Life insurance proceeds
- Divorce property settlements

The calculation is based on the date the debtor gains the right, not the date the property is received.

For example, if a debtor files for bankruptcy on January 1, the debtor's father dies on June 1, and the debtor receives the proceeds from a life insurance policy on the father's life on August 1, these proceeds will be added to the bankruptcy estate. The right to receive the life insurance arose on the June 1 date of death, within 180 days of the petition date.

A trustee must determine how to deal with the **outstanding contracts** of the debtor at the time of the petition. The trustee has **three options** with respect to each contract:

- **Assume** the contract and perform the duties on behalf of the bankruptcy estate.
- **Assume** the contract and assign the benefits to a third party in exchange for a payment to the estate.
- **Reject (breach)** the contract.

The trustee should select the approach that is most beneficial to the estate. If the trustee does not assume the contract within *60 days* of the order of relief, it will be automatically rejected.

A trustee may employ court-approved professionals, such as accountants and attorneys, to handle estate matters which require professional expertise.

15.05 Bankruptcy: Avoiding Powers of Trustee

Overview

The trustee is given the power to maximize the property included in the debtor's estate. There are certain transfers the trustee can avoid or set aside to maximize the corpus available to the creditors. (**FLAP**)

- **F**raudulent transfers by the debtor within *2 years* of the filing of the petition.
- **L**iens by statute (not liens that were effective before the bankruptcy petition was filed).
- **A**fter filing the petition, a transfer was made by the debtor.
- **P**referential transfer of property: (**I-WAIT**)
    - Debtor was **I**nsolvent when the transfer was made.
    - **W**ithin 90 days of the filing of the petition.
    - For an **A**ntecedent debt (pre-existing debt); new value is ok.
    - **I**mproves the creditors position (creditor gets more money than would have gotten in bankruptcy).
    - **T**ime is increased from 90 days to 1 year for an insider (officer or close relative of Debtor.)
        - Not preferential transfers (C-CONAC)
            - Charity
            - Consumer debt
            - Ordinary course of business (current utility bill, lease payment)
            - New Value
            - Alimony and child support
            - Continuation of installment payments

Fraudulent Transfers

Fraudulent transfers refer to transfers made **within 2 years** before the filing of the petition that were made with the intent to hinder, delay, or defraud creditors; or a transfer made to prevent creditors from gaining access to property that would have been included in the bankruptcy estate, when the transfer was secret, or the debtor retained possession or beneficial rights in the property after its conveyance to a third party.

Liens

Statutory **liens** include claims by repair services against property that would allow them to keep the asset under normal circumstances, but which would deny other creditors a fair share of the property's value for bankruptcy distribution purposes. A trustee may set aside statutory liens that become effective when the bankruptcy petition is filed, but may not set aside those that were effective before the bankruptcy petition was filed.

Transfers Made After Filing

Transfers made **after the filing** of the petition can be avoided because the ownership of the debtor's property was supposed to transfer to the trustee-in-bankruptcy as of the filing date.

Preferential Transfers

Preferential transfers are the most common that may be avoided by a trustee. These refer to excessive payments made to one creditor at the expense of the others.

An **insider** refers to a creditor with a special relationship to the debtor that would enable them to know about the debtor's insolvency before others found out about it.

An **antecedent debt** refers to a debt created previously, and excludes from preferential transfers payments in exchange for value received at the same time and charitable contributions.

An **insolvent** debtor, according to federal bankruptcy law, is one whose liabilities exceed their assets (balance sheet approach to insolvency). The debtor is presumed to be insolvent in the 90 days prior to the date of the petition.

Payments on perfected secured debts are not preferential transfers, since the creditor is only receiving amounts that would have been paid in the bankruptcy from the collateral. Also, there are other priority claims that are paid before ordinary claims, and payments to these priority creditors are not preferential if there were enough assets in the bankruptcy estate to pay these claims. Priority claims are discussed in another module.

While making a payment on a secured loan is not a voidable preference, it **is** deemed a preferential transfer if a debtor gives a creditor a security interest on a debt that was previously unsecured. A PMSI is not a voidable preference if it is perfected within 30 days after the debtor receives possession of the collateral.

> For example, if the debtor takes out a loan in 20X1, giving the creditor a mortgage on the debtor's personal residence at the same time, subsequent payments on the loan are not preferential. If, however, a loan is taken out in 20X1, but the debtor does not give the creditor a mortgage on their home until 20X3, the granting of the mortgage may be considered a preferential transfer. In the former case, an exchange of value occurred at the same time. In the latter case, the debtor is providing the creditor with collateral they didn't previously have on an antecedent debt (since the loan was made two years before the collateral was offered).

15.06 Bankruptcy: Order of Distribution

Amounts get paid out one level at a time. If run out of money, give that one level a proportionate share of the cash available.

Order of Distribution of Assets Among Creditors

- **Secured creditors**
    - **Fully** secured – The collateral is worth the amount of the debt or more. Any excess is returned to the trustee.
    - **Partially** secured – The collateral is worth less than the debt. The creditor gets the collateral, but is a general/unsecured creditor for the remainder.
- **Priority claims (STOP-IT – Drunk driver)**
    - **S**upport and Alimony payments.
    - **T**rustee, attorney, accountant, and administrative expenses.
    - **O**wed after petition date in involuntary gap between filing and approval date (involuntary gap creditor).
    - **P**ayroll (90 days) and Employee benefit plans (180 days) up to $13,650 per employee. Farmers and Fishermen up to $6,725.
    - **I**ndividual Consumer deposits up to $3,025.
    - **T**ax claims arising within 3 years of the petition.
    - **Drunk Driver** injury claims.
- **General/unsecured creditors**
    - This includes all remaining non-priority timely filed claims or claims exceeding amounts above (employees/consumers). If any assets are remaining after paying the general creditors, they go to the debtor.

Creditors submit their claims to the court in a Chapter 7 bankruptcy, and available assets are used to satisfy these claims as best as possible. Payments are **not**, however, equal to each creditor. Certain creditors have special priority over the others.

The highest priority for distribution is secured creditors up to the value of their collateral, as long as their interests were perfected prior to the filing of the bankruptcy petition. Secured creditors with claims that can be **fully satisfied** out of the value of the collateral are paid in full. **Partially secured creditors** with claims that exceed the value of their collateral will be paid the collateral amount, with the remaining amounts treated as non-priority claims.

The distribution of free assets (those not subject to security interests) follows a strict order of priority (**Priority Claims**). The major categories are paid in the following order:

1. **S**upport and Alimony payments
2. **T**rustee expenses – Administrative costs incurred by the trustee, Attorneys, Accountants (including their own compensation).
3. **O**wed after filing date – In an involuntary bankruptcy, creditors with claims arising after the petition date but prior to the order of relief are given special priority to make it possible for a debtor to do business while challenging an involuntary petition.
4. **P**ayroll costs up to $15,150 – Claims by employees for payroll and related benefits costs within 180 days have priority up to a dollar limit. Remaining amounts are non-priority claims. Grain *Farmers and Fishermen* up to $6,725 against a debtor who operates a grain storage facility.
5. **I**ndividual consumer deposits up to $3,350 – Claims by customers of the debtor on consumer goods not delivered. Business deposits are not entitled to priority, and consumer deposits exceeding the limit are non-priority claims.
6. **T**ax claims – Within 3 years. Taxes on which the statute of limitations has expired are not included.
7. **Drunk Driver** injury claims - Claims for death or personal injury arising from the operation of a motor vehicle or vessel by the debtor while he was legally intoxicated.

The order of priority must be memorized for the exam. Notice that the first letter of each claim spells **STOP-IT Drunk Driver**, and this mnemonic may be helpful in remembering the list.

After all priority claims have been paid, *non-priority claims* are considered. These will include:

- Secured claims to the extent they exceeded the value of collateral.
- Payroll and benefits exceeding $15,150.
- Consumer deposits exceeding $3,350.
- All other **General Unsecured** claims filed on a timely basis.

Creditors who fail to notify the bankruptcy court on a timely basis of their claims will be paid after all other creditors.

At some point in the distribution process, it is likely that the estate will not have sufficient funds to pay remaining claims. At the level where this occurs, all claims will be paid an equal percentage of the amount owed. Claims at lower levels will receive nothing in such cases.

Assume that $14,000 was available to pay the following claims outstanding in a bankruptcy:

Trustee expenses	$10,000
Wages owed to Pat Day	$3,000
Wages owed to Nat Night	$2,000
Tax claims	$5,000
Electric bill owed to power company	$1,000

After paying the highest priority trustee expenses of $10,000, only $4,000 remains to pay the next applicable priority, payroll owed to Pat and Nat totaling $5,000. There is enough to pay $4,000 / $5,000 = 80% of these claims, so Pat Day receives $3,000 × 80% = $2,400 and Nat Night receives $2,000 × 80% = $1,600. The lower priority claim for taxes and the nonpriority electric bill are not paid.

Exceptions versus Denial of Discharge

Exceptions (Debtor doesn't owe anyone EXCEPT these people)

Assuming a general discharge is granted, a debtor may still not be discharged from certain specific types of debts, including:

- **A**limony or child support (maintenance)
- *Credit Card* purchases for luxury goods of $800 or more within 90 days of filing and *cash advances* of $1,100 or more within 70 days of filing. *Auto loans* within 3 years of filing.
- **L**oans obtained by fraud or false representations.
- **U**nscheduled/unlisted debt- Amounts owed which the debtor fails to list on the schedule of debts they must submit to the court.
- **S**tudent loans - During the period that payments are not yet owed.
- **T**ax claims within 3 years of the filing of the petition - The same debts qualifying as priority claims in distribution of assets.
  - Other items (**STD**)
    - Any debt from a securities law violation under the **S**arbanes-Oxley Act
    - Debts incurred to pay **T**axes
    - **D**runk Driver injuries or death judgments

Denial (Debtor is denied and owes everyone)

In general, unpaid claims in a Chapter 7 liquidation are discharged by the bankruptcy court at the end of the case. There are certain cases in which discharge is denied, however:

- Inadequate books and records / Intentionally destroys records
- Refusing to explain a loss of assets (why missing)
- Bankruptcy offense
    - Withholding records
    - Refusing to obey a court order
- Being discharged **within 8 years**. 8 years must elapse before another discharge can be granted.
- Fraudulent transfer of property within 1 year of filing with the intent to hinder, delay or defraud creditors (concealing property).
- Debtor must be an individual. A Corporation or Partnership doesn't receive a discharge under Chapter 7; instead, the entity is dissolved. Once all assets have been fully used, the case is closed.

Generally, court judgments against the debtor resulting from breach of contract and torts (negligence) may be discharged, but judgments resulting from criminal action are not.

Once discharge has occurred, a debt generally cannot be reinstated. The discharge on a debt may be revoked within one year of discharge, however, if a creditor can prove that the debtor committed fraud to conceal assets or otherwise reduce payments in the bankruptcy case.

A debtor's attempt to **reaffirm a discharged debt** after it has been discharged will not be valid. A debtor may reaffirm a debt prior to discharge, but:

- Reaffirmation must take place before the discharge is granted and be approved by the bankruptcy court.
- The debtor must be informed by the court of the consequences of reaffirming the debt.
- The debtor has 60 days to rescind the reaffirmation.

Even in these circumstances, the court may prevent the action if it feels it imposes an undue hardship on the debtor.

15.07 Bankruptcy: Other

Chapter 11 – Reorganization Plan

The debtor and creditors formulate a plan under which the debtor repays a portion of the debts owed and the remainder is discharged. Not available to banks, savings and loans, insurance companies, and stockbrokers. Chapter 11 is typically for corporations or partnerships. Individuals, especially those whose debts exceed the limits of Chapter 13, may file Chapter 11.

- Voluntary or Involuntary (if involuntary, must meet the same requirements as Chapter 7).
- Creditors committee of unsecured creditors.
- Usually no trustee, but the debtor remains in control of the company and submits a plan for reorganization to each class of creditors.
    - Requires approval by 2/3 of the dollar ($) amount of all claims and ½ the number of claims in that class.
- Courts need to confirm the plan, but will not unless it provides payment for:
    - Trustee expenses
    - Owed to Involuntary Gap creditors
    - Payroll and employee benefits
    - Consumer advances

Under Chapter 11 (Business Reorganizations), a committee of creditors is formed. Only unsecured creditors may be included. The debtor will continue to operate the business and be advised by the committee.

Creditors (and shareholders for a corporate debtor) with similar types of claims will then form smaller committees to develop a plan of reorganization. In each creditor committee, creditors making up a majority of the total number of creditors and 2/3 of the total amount owed must approve the plan. In the shareholder committee, shareholders owning at least 2/3 of the stock must approve the plan.

After approval by the creditors and shareholders, the plan is submitted to the court, but the court may confirm a plan it deems fair, **even if some committees do not approve it**. Once the court has confirmed it, the plan is approved and requires no confirmation from the committees. The purpose of Chapter 11 is to restructure a business's finances so that it may continue to operate.

Chapter 13 – Debt Adjustment Plan

Enables a debtor who is an individual with regular income to formulate and perform a plan for the repayment of creditors over an extended period. The benefit is that the debtor gets to retain non-exempt property.

- Voluntary only.
- A trustee is appointed by the courts.
- The courts confirm or deny the plan without approval of unsecured creditors.

In a Chapter 13 (Debt Adjustment Plan) bankruptcy case, the debtor submits a repayment plan to a trustee appointed by the court. The plan must involve repayment of at least as much of the debts as would have been repaid under Chapter 7 liquidation, and may or may not involve discharge of some of the unpaid debts. The trustee may approve extensions of the due dates for loan payments for up to 3 years without court permission, or 5 years with it. The benefit of Chapter 13 is that it allows the debtor to retain their property, even that which is nonexempt.

Creditors do not participate in the administration of the case and, as mentioned earlier, cannot even file the petition to begin Chapter 13 proceedings. Chapter 13 is typically for individuals who have regular income, owe less than $465,275 of unsecured debts and less than $1,395,875 of secured debts.

Chapter 9 – Municipalities

Chapter 9 provides a procedure so that a municipality that has encountered financial difficulty and is insolvent may work with its creditors to adjust its debts. This provision is reserved for municipalities only.

Chapter 12 – Family Farmers and Fishermen

Family Farmers and Fishermen may qualify for a specialized form of bankruptcy. Family farmers can take advantage of this simplified reorganization. Modeled after Chapter 13, Chapter 12 allows the debtor to retain all property and pay creditors out of future income. However, farmers can still file using Chapters 7, 11 or 13 as well.

Chapter 15 – Cross-Border Insolvency Cases

Created by the Bankruptcy Abuse Prevention and Consumer Protection Act of 2005, Chapter 15 deals with *cross-border insolvency cases*.

- Meant to make bankruptcy proceedings across international borders more functional.
  - Favors and promotes cooperation and communication with both foreign courts and foreign representatives.

Bankruptcy Abuse Prevention & Consumer Protection Act of 2005

This act contains many provisions that make it more difficult for an individual or a business to file for bankruptcy. When debtors consist of individuals or married couples with debt that is primarily consumer debt, the court could convert a Chapter 7 case to a Chapter 11 or Chapter 13 case, or could dismiss the petition entirely, if the courts feel that granting relief under Chapter 7 would constitute abuse. A "means test" has been established to determine whether *abuse* has occurred.

A debtor will first complete a median income test in which the debtor's current monthly income, excluding Social Security benefits, is compared to the median income in the debtor's state. If the debtor's income is lower than the median amount, there is no presumption of abuse and the debtor is not required to complete the means test.

The financial **means test** that reduces or completely eliminates the debts that would be discharged under Chapter 7 for high-income bankruptcy petitioners, is the most significant provision of the rules. If **income minus allowable living expenses exceeds** certain levels, a Chapter 7 filing will be **dismissed** or, with the debtor's permission, **converted** to a Chapter 13 filing.

Monthly Income – Living Expenses = **Net Disposable Monthly Income**

- Living Expenses include food, clothing, housing, utilities, transportation, personal care, entertainment, health and disability insurance, primary and secondary education costs, child support & alimony, for example.
    - Adjusted income under this formula is multiplied by 60 (months) to give what is called disposable income (DI) for the next 5 years. If DI is less than $9,075, the Chapter 7 filing will be allowed, as no presumption of abuse.
    - If DI is less than $15,150, a determination will be made as to whether DI is sufficient to pay at least 25% of the debtor's unsecured debt. If not, the Chapter 7 filing will be allowed, as there is no assumption of abuse. In other words, if DI is sufficient to pay at least 25% of the debtor's unsecured debt, or if the amount exceeds $15,150, the Chapter 7 filing will be disallowed as abuse is assumed (cannot go bankrupt).

For example, net monthly income = $150 × 60 months = $9,000. If total debt was less than or equal to $36,000, the Chapter 7 petition would be disallowed because the means test was surpassed (ie, $36,000 debt × .25 = $9,000 that could be paid with $9,000 DI). If the debt was greater than $36,000, the Chapter 7 filing would be allowed because there would not be enough DI to cover 25% of the debtor's unsecured debt.

The debtor may **rebut the presumption of** *abuse* by showing special circumstances (eg, serious illness or call to active military duty) that create additional expenses or a need to adjust current monthly income. To rebut the presumption, the additional expenses and/or income adjustments must place the current monthly income after expenses below the dollar amounts that trigger the presumption.

The time allowed between Chapter 7 or 11 discharges is **eight years**. Furthermore, a Chapter 13 discharge is given to any debtor who received a discharge in a Chapter 7, 11, or 12 case within the preceding four years, or in another Chapter 13 case within the preceding two years.

An individual debtor is prohibited from filing a bankruptcy petition under Chapter 7 or 11 until the debtor receives a briefing from an approved nonprofit budget and credit counseling service. The briefing must be within 180 days of filing the bankruptcy petition.

Under the federal fair debt collection practices act, it is illegal for a debt collector to attempt to communicate with a debtor who is currently being represented by an attorney. This is to help minimize the harassment that was occurring by debt collectors.

15.08 Suretyship

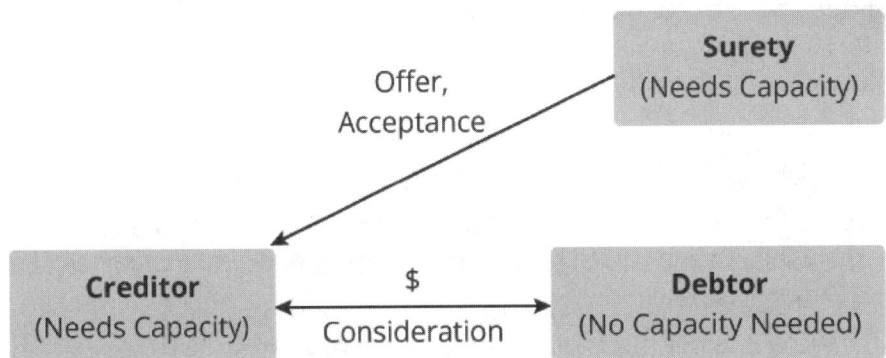

Defined

A suretyship is an arrangement in which a person agrees to be answerable to a creditor for a claim against another person.

Types of Suretyship Agreements

There are several possible varieties of agreements:

- **Primary** – When a person agrees to be a **surety accommodation party** or **cosigner**, the creditor is permitted to treat them as the debtor and demand payment without any proof of default by the principal debtor.

- **Secondary** – When a person agrees to be a **guarantor** or **endorser** of a check or negotiable instrument, the creditor may only demand payment if the principal debtor defaults on the agreement.
  - In order to transfer a check or note, transferor may be required to obtain a surety (accommodation endorser) to guarantee payment.
  - Official bonds, whereby a surety insures the performance of the issuer in compliance with laws and regulations.

- **Last Resort** – When a person agrees to be a **conditional surety** or **guarantor of collection**, the creditor may not demand payment from them until all available means of collection from the principal debtor are exhausted, including seizing collateral, obtaining court judgments, and filing a bankruptcy petition, as appropriate. This is a special form of secondary liability.

Surety's Liability

The behavior of the debtor is irrelevant in determining the liability of a surety (or equivalent). A **surety is obligated to pay** once the creditor has met the requirements for demanding payment, even if the debtor:

- Lacks the capacity to make contracts.
- Is discharged in bankruptcy from all debts.
- Used fraud to induce the surety to make their promise to the creditor.

The surety may assert defenses of incapacity or bankruptcy to limit liability but may not assume the debtor's personal defenses.

Requirements

- Suretyships fall within the **statute of frauds** and require that the promise be in writing and signed by the surety.
- The creditor must provide consideration to bind the surety. Usually, this is done by obtaining the surety's promise at the time the debt is created, so that the loan itself is the consideration. If the surety is obtained later, the loan is **past consideration and cannot be used to bind**. In that case, the creditor may pay the surety for their promise, and the compensation to the surety serves as consideration.

A compensated surety (bonding company) is generally liable on the debt, unless the surety's risk of loss is increased due to a material change in the contract. An uncompensated surety (**Gratuitous Surety**) (eg, co-signing a loan for your child) is relieved anytime the creditor makes a change to the agreement.

Surety's Rights

A surety has certain rights that may be exercised **upon a demand for payment** from the creditor without the surety actually having to pay. These include:

- **Offset** – The surety may offset amounts the creditor owes the surety against the amount the creditor is demanding.
- **Exoneration** – The surety may sue the principal debtor to compel them to make payment to the creditor.

If the surety makes payment to the creditor, the surety gains certain additional rights. These include:

- **Indemnification** – The surety has the right to demand reimbursement from the principal debtor for amounts paid to the creditor.
- **Subrogation** – The surety obtains all creditor claims against the debtor, including the right to **collateral pledged** by the debtor to the creditor to secure the loan.

Because the obligation of the surety is to the creditor, the creditor owes the surety a fiduciary duty to act in their best interests. A surety is released from their obligation if the creditor:

- Fails to disclose negative information the creditor has about the principal debtor.
- Makes any agreement with the debtor that increases the surety's risk of loss.
- Releases collateral that had secured the debt (this releases the surety for the value of the collateral).
- Extends the due date for repayment by the principal debtor (a compensated surety is not released unless the extension materially increases their risk).

- Refuses a tender of payment from the principal debtor.
- Releases the principal debtor from the obligation.

A special exception allows the creditor to release the debtor but **reserve rights against the surety**. In such cases, the surety still has the right to pursue the debtor for reimbursement, and is not harmed by the release, so the creditor is still entitled to seek collection from the surety. The creditor can reserve rights against the surety in connection with other actions as well.

Cosureties

A creditor may obtain more than one surety on a debt. When there are two or more cosureties, each is *jointly and severally liable* to the creditor, but a cosurety who pays has a **right of contribution** from the others.

For example, if Daryl Debtor borrows $10,000 from Chris Creditor, and Chris obtains written promises from Gary Guarantor and Eve Endorser on the full debt, a later default by Daryl when the remaining balance on the loan is $6,000 allows Chris to recover the entire $6,000 from either Gary or Eve. If Gary pays the entire $6,000, he has the right to obtain a contribution of $6,000 × 1/2 = $3,000 from Eve (the cosureties have the right to obtain full reimbursement from Daryl for amounts they each pay).

If cosureties have unequal limits on liability, they are expected to contribute in proportion to their limits.

For example, if Gary agreed to be liable for the entire $10,000 debt, while Eve's agreement with Chris limited her obligation to $5,000, then Gary's relative responsibility is $10,000 / ($10,000 + $5,000) = 2/3 and Eve's is $5,000 / ($10,000 + $5,000) = 1/3. If Daryl defaults when the balance is $6,000, and Gary pays the entire amount to Chris, he can expect a contribution of $6,000 × 1/3 = $2,000 from Eve.

If the creditor releases a cosurety, that will release the other cosureties to the extent they lose the right of contribution from the released one.

In the last example, a release by Chris of Eve's liability will reduce the amount Chris can obtain from Gary after the default from $6,000 to only $4,000, since Gary can no longer obtain Eve's 1/3 contribution as a result of the release. Once again, though, if Chris releases Eve but **reserves rights** against Gary, then the full $6,000 can be recovered, since Gary will be permitted to pursue a contribution from Eve.

The bankruptcy of a cosurety doesn't release the others, and they will be liable as if the bankrupt party had never been involved.

Co-Sureties

```
    $1  →  $2
       ⤸ ⤹
Creditor ←——— Debtor
```

Creditors' Rights

When a debtor owes money, there are several options available to satisfy the debt.

- **Composition of creditors** – An agreement in which creditors accept a proportionate amount as full settlement for their debts.
- **Assignment for the benefit of creditors** – The Debtor voluntarily transfers assets to the trustee for the benefit of creditors, but the debtor still owes the debt.
- **Writ of Attachment** – Prejudicial remedy in which a creditor is allowed to take possession of personal property of the debtor prior to getting a judgment for the past-due debt.
- **Garnishment** – Permits the creditor to seize property of the debtor that is being held by a third party.
    - Could include wages or money held in a bank account.
    - Federal social security benefits are exempt from garnishment.
- **Lien** – A claim against a debtor's property that must be satisfied before the property is available to satisfy the claims of other creditors.
    - **Consensual** – Mortgages or secured transactions
    - **Nonconsensual** – Judicial proceeding, mechanics' liens (real property – home), tax liens, artisans' liens (personal property – auto)
        - Must give notice before you sell the debtor's property.
- **Credit Card Fraud Act (CCFA)** – A credit card holder is protected from losses in excess of $50 due to unauthorized use of the holder's credit card.
- **Homestead exemption** – When going bankrupt, one can claim a certain amount of equity in one's home as exempt property; however, this doesn't prevent one from being liable if there is an IRS tax lien or a valid home mortgage lien.
- **Debt collectors** – The Fair Debt Collection Practices Act prohibits a debt collector from harassing the debtor. They are permitted to take reasonable measures to ascertain the debtor's location and collect the debt and may commence a lawsuit to obtain collection. A debt collector may contact the debtor but may not do so at inconvenient times and places or at the debtor's workplace if the employer objects. They must provide written notice of the amount and payee of the debt within 5 days of their first communication with the debtor and must send verification of the validity of the debt if contested by the debtor. If the debtor is represented by an attorney, the debt collector may not communicate directly with the debtor but must do so only through the attorney.

# REG 16 Research Appendix

REG 16: Research Appendix

16.01 Research Task Format   1
    Internal Revenue Code (IRC)   1

16.01 Research Task Format

Research is tested in its own independent task-based simulation problem. Each REG exam will include at least 1 Research-type TBS. Candidates will be asked to search through the database to find the appropriate reference to the Internal Revenue Code (IRC) that addresses the issue presented in the research problem.

Using the Authoritative Literature, the candidate will search for keywords associated with the question using the search box, which will pull up all references to those keywords within the literature. From there, the candidate should use the "search within" function to find specific instances of keywords within each subsection. Keywords will be highlighted in the text, and the candidate can skim through them to find the relevant text that answers the research problem. Note: The candidate also has the option to drill down the table of contents of the relevant authoritative literature (in this case, the Internal Revenue Code), but this requires a bit more familiarity with the titles (see below).

Research questions will also alert the candidate if they have correctly formatted their answer by displaying "Your response is correctly formatted" in a box below the candidate response if the candidate has entered reference numbers correctly.

Don't forget that you can use the Authoritative Literature to look up answers to other TBSs in the exam!

Internal Revenue Code (IRC)

Officially Title 26 of the United States Code, the IRC is comprised of eleven subtitles, A through K. The subtitles are each divided into chapters as follows (some chapters omitted):

Subtitle A – Income Taxes

- 1 – Normal taxes and surtaxes
- 2 – Tax on self-employment income
- 2A – Unearned income Medicare contribution
- 3 – Withholding of tax on nonresident aliens and foreign corporations
- 4 – Taxes to enforce reporting on certain foreign accounts
- 6 – Consolidated returns

Subtitle B – Estate and Gift Taxes

- 11 – Estate tax
- 12 – Gift tax
- 13 – Tax on generation-skipping transfers

- 14 – Special valuation rules
- 15 – Gifts and bequests from expatriates

Subtitle C – Employment Taxes

- 21 – Federal Insurance Contributions Act
- 22 – Railroad Retirement Tax Act
- 23 – Federal Unemployment Tax Act
- 23A – Railroad Unemployment Repayment Tax
- 24 – Collection of income tax at source on wages
- 25 – General provisions relating to employment taxes

Subtitle D – Miscellaneous Excise Taxes

***

Subtitle E – Alcohol, Tobacco, and Certain Other Excise Taxes

***

Subtitle F – Procedure and Administration

- 61 – Information and returns
- 62 – Time and place for paying tax
- 63 – Assessment
- 64 – Collection
- 65 – Abatements, credits, and refunds
- 66 – Limitations
- 67 – Interest
- 68 – Additions to the tax, additional amounts, and assessable penalties
- 69 – General provisions relating to stamps
- 70 – Jeopardy, receiverships, etc.
- 71 – Transferees and fiduciaries
- 72 – Licensing and registration
- 73 – Bonds
- 74 – Closing agreements and compromises
- 75 – Crimes, other offenses, and forfeitures
- 76 – Judicial proceedings
- 77 – Miscellaneous provisions

- 78 – Discover of liability and enforcement of title
- 79 – Definitions
- 80 – General rules

Subtitle G – The Joint Committee on Taxation

***

Subtitle H – Financing of Presidential Election Campaigns

***

Subtitle K – Group Health Plan Requirements

- 100 – Group health plan requirements

Each chapter is further divided into subchapters. Some chapters are too specific to require subchapters, in which case the individual tax code sections are identified. Most research questions are derived from Subtitle A, *Income Taxes*, and Subtitle B, *Estate and Gift Taxes*. The subchapters for these are as follows:

Subtitle A – Income Taxes

- CHAPTER 1 - NORMAL TAXES AND SURTAXES
  - Subchapter A - Determination of Tax Liability (Sections 1-59)
  - Subchapter B - Computation of Taxable Income (Sections 61-291)
  - Subchapter C - Corporate Distributions and Adjustments (Sections 301-385)
  - Subchapter D - Deferred Compensation, Etc. (Sections 401-436)
  - Subchapter E - Accounting Periods and Methods of Accounting (Sections 441-483)
  - Subchapter F - Exempt Organizations (Sections 501-530)
  - Subchapter G - Corporations Used to Avoid Income Tax on Shareholders (Sections 531-565)
  - Subchapter H - Banking Institutions (Sections 581-601)
  - Subchapter I - Natural Resources (Sections 611-638)
  - Subchapter J - Estates, Trusts, Beneficiaries, and Decedents (Sections 641-692)
  - Subchapter K - Partners and Partnerships (Sections 701-777)
  - Subchapter L - Insurance Companies (Sections 801-848)
  - Subchapter M - Regulated Investment Companies and Real Estate Investment Trusts (Sections 851-860)
  - Subchapter N - Tax Based on Income From Sources Within or Without the United States (Sections 861-1000)
  - Subchapter O - Gain or Loss on Disposition of Property (Sections 1001-1111)
  - Subchapter P - Capital Gains and Losses (Sections 1201-1298)

- Subchapter Q - Readjustment of Tax Between Years and Special Limitations (Sections 1301-1351)
- Subchapter R - Election to Determine Corporate Tax on Certain International Shipping Activities Using Per Ton Rate (Sections 1352-1359)
- Subchapter S - Tax Treatment of S Corporations and Their Shareholders (Sections 1361-1379)
- Subchapter T - Cooperatives and Their Patrons (Section 1381-1388)
- Subchapter U - Designation and Treatment of Empowerment Zones, Enterprise Communities, and Rural Development Investment Areas (Sections 1391-1397)
- Subchapter V - Title 11 Cases (Sections 1398-1399)
- Subchapter W - District of Columbia Enterprise Zone (Sections 1400-1400C)
- Subchapter X - Renewal Communities (Sections 1400E-1400J)
- Subchapter Y - Short-Term Regional Benefits (Sections 1400L-1400U3)

- CHAPTER 2 - TAX ON SELF-EMPLOYMENT INCOME (Sections 1401-1403)
  - Section 1401 – Rate of tax
  - Section 1402 – Definitions
  - Section 1403 – Miscellaneous provisions
- CHAPTER 2A – UNEARNED INCOME MEDICARE CONTRIBUTION (Section 1411)
  - Section 1411 – Imposition of tax
- CHAPTER 3 - WITHHOLDING OF TAX ON NONRESIDENT ALIENS AND FOREIGN CORPORATIONS (Sections 1441-1465)
  - Subchapter A – Nonresident Aliens and Foreign Corporations (Sections 1441-1446)
  - Subchapter B – Application of Withholding Provisions (Sections 1451-1465)
- CHAPTER 4 - TAXES TO ENFORCE REPORTING ON CERTAIN FOREIGN ACCOUNTS (Sections 1471-1474)
  - Section 1471 – Withholdable payments to foreign financial institutions
  - Section 1472 – Withholdable payments to other foreign entities
  - Section 1473 – Definitions
  - Section 1474 – Special rules
- CHAPTER 5 - REPEALED
- CHAPTER 6 - CONSOLIDATED RETURNS (Sections 1501-1564)
  - Subchapter A – Returns and Payment of Tax (Sections 1501-1505)
  - Subchapter B – Related Rules (Sections 1551-1564)

Subtitle B – Estate and Gift Taxes

- CHAPTER 11 - ESTATE TAX (Sections 2001-2210)
  - Subchapter A – Estates of Citizens or Residents (Sections 2001-2058)
  - Subchapter B – Estates of Nonresidents Not Citizens (Sections 2101-2108)

Research Appendix   REG 16

-○ Subchapter C – Miscellaneous (Sections 2201-2210)
- CHAPTER 12 - GIFT TAX (Sections 2501-2524)
    - ○ Subchapter A – Determination of Tax Liability (Sections 2501-2505)
    - ○ Subchapter B – Transfers (Sections 2511-2519)
    - ○ Subchapter C – Deductions (Sections 2521-2524)
- CHAPTER 13 - TAX ON GENERATION-SKIPPING TRANSFERS (Sections 2601-2664)
    - ○ Subchapter A – Tax Imposed (Sections 2601-2604)
    - ○ Subchapter B – Generation-Skipping Transfers (Sections 2611-2614)
    - ○ Subchapter C – Taxable Amount (Sections 2621-2624)
    - ○ Subchapter D – GST Exemption (Sections 2631-2632)
    - ○ Subchapter E – Applicable Rate; Inclusion Ratio (Sections 2641-2642)
    - ○ Subchapter F – Other Definitions and Special Rules (Sections 2651-2654)
    - ○ Subchapter G – Administration (Sections 2661-2664)
- CHAPTER 14 - SPECIAL VALUATION RULES (Sections 2701-2704)
    - ○ Section 2701 – Special valuation rules in case of transfers of certain interests in corporations or partnerships
    - ○ Section 2702 – Special valuation rules in case of transfers of interests in trusts
    - ○ Section 2703 – Certain rights and restrictions disregarded
    - ○ Section 2704 – Treatment of certain lapsing rights and restrictions
- CHAPTER 15 – GIFTS AND BEQUESTS FROM EXPATRIATES (Section 2801)
    - ○ Section 2801 – Imposition of tax

Sample research question

Mr. Philipp received a distribution from a qualified tuition program that was not used to pay qualified higher education expenses and is trying to determine what portion, if any, should be included in gross income. To what section of the Internal Revenue Code will Mr. Philipp refer to determine the amount?

Solution: Since a qualified tuition program is considered an exempt organization, the information will be found in Subchapter F, Exempt Organizations, of Chapter 1, Normal Taxes and Surtaxes, from Subtitle A, Income Taxes.

Section	Subsection
§ 529	(c)

REG 17
Final Review

REG 17 Final Review

17.01 REG Final Review   1
   YOU FINISHED YOUR REG COURSE...NOW WHAT?   1

17.01 REG Final Review

You finished your REG Course...now what?

A quick guide to the final days leading up to, and following, the exam

I. FINAL REVIEW

Now is the time to make connections and solidify your understanding of the topics you found most challenging, and to review the most heavily tested topics on the exam.

- ❏ Review your SmartPath data to ensure you have hit all targets. Revisit any areas marked "Needs Improvement."
- ❏ Reread your course notes and review your digital flash cards.
- ❏ If it is included in your program package, use the Cram Course to do a final review of the most heavily tested topics.
- ❏ Take at least one Full CPA Practice Exam in your QBank to hone your test-taking skills in an environment that follows the same 5-testlet, 4-hour structure of the exam.
- ❏ Checkout an AICPA Sample Test at www.cpa-exam.org to familiarize yourself with the exam format and welcome (instruction) screens.

II. DAY OF THE EXAM

- ❏ Get a good night's rest before heading into your exam.
- ❏ Arrive to the Prometric testing center at least 60 minutes before your appointment so you have time to park, check-in, and use the restroom before your exam begins.
- ❏ Bring your Notice to Schedule (NTS) and two forms of acceptable identification (see Intro for more details).
- ❏ Proceed through check-in: store belongings, get fingerprinted, have photo taken, sign log book, get seated, write your Launch Code (from your NTS) on your noteboard.
- ❏ Don't stress. You've prepared for this; now, just breathe and power through!

III. DURING THE EXAM

- ❏ Remember your AUD Exam time strategy, and jot down the times at which you want to be at your benchmarks:
    - o Use 75 seconds per multiple choice question as a benchmark
    - o Allocate 15-25 minutes per task-based simulation, depending on complexity
    - o Plan to use no more than 10 minutes per research question

- Take the standard 15-minute break after the 3rd testlet – it does not count against your time
- (Remember that any other break will count against your time)
- ❑ You will be given 10 minutes to review the welcome screens and exam instructions. You should already be familiar with these screens after taking the AICPA Sample Test and can bypass them during your exam.
- ❑ Once you begin testing, make sure to read each question carefully, paying close attention to the keywords that dictate the question's intention (eg *except, is greater than, always, never*).
- ❑ Take note if your questions are getting more difficult. That's a good sign! A progressively harder exam indicates that you are performing well.

IV. AFTER THE EXAM

- ❑ Remember, it is normal to not feel great afterwards. It's a tough exam and designed to challenge your confidence and competencies.
- ❑ Relax and celebrate! You've earned it.
- ❑ Your scores will be released within a couple of weeks.
- ❑ GOOD LUCK!!!